SISTERS
IN
ARMS

SISTERS
IN
ARMS

Helena Schrader

Pen & Sword
AVIATION

First published in Great Britain in 2006 by
Pen & Sword Aviation
an imprint of
Pen & Sword Books Ltd
47 Church Street
Barnsley
South Yorkshire
S70 2AS

ISBN 1 84415 388 6

Typeset in Palatino by
Phoenix Typesetting, Auldgirth, Dumfriesshire

Printed and bound in England by
Biddles Ltd, King's Lynn

Pen & Sword Books Ltd incorporates the imprints of Pen & Sword Aviation,
Pen & Sword Maritime, Pen & Sword Military, Wharncliffe Local History,
Pen & Sword Select, Pen & Sword Military Classics and Leo Cooper.

For a complete list of Pen & Sword titles please contact
PEN & SWORD BOOKS LIMITED
47 Church Street, Barnsley, South Yorkshire, S70 2AS, England
E-mail: enquiries@pen-and-sword.co.uk
Website: www.pen-and-sword.co.uk

Contents

Introduction

During the Second World War, a few carefully selected women in the United States and the United Kingdom were briefly given the unprecedented opportunity to fly military aircraft. It was not until more than thirty years later – after radical social changes with regard to women's rights and roles – that women were again given the chance to fly the most challenging and innovative aircraft of their age. The story of these pioneer women pilots is made even more intriguing by the fact that, despite many notable similarities in the utilisation and organisation of the women in their respective countries, they experienced radically different fates.

In both the United States and the United Kingdom, the women pilots were organised in auxiliary, civilian organisations, the WASP (Women Airforce Service Pilots) in the United States and the ATA (Air Transport Auxiliary) in Britain. Initially, only very highly qualified and experienced women pilots were accepted into the respective programmes, but eventually training programmes were established in both countries to train women with limited or no previous flying experience. The women pilots often had to overcome scepticism about their capabilities, and sometimes faced outright hostility. Yet in both countries women pilots rapidly proved that they were capable of performing the tasks assigned to them. In fact, women on both sides of the Atlantic proved that in some ways and at some tasks they were more capable than their male colleagues.

During nearly six years of service, the women of the ATA steadily won nearly all the privileges and status enjoyed by their male colleagues. Women in the ATA could and did have command authority over men. Most exceptionally, the women of the ATA were, in 1943, awarded equal pay for equal work. The American women pilots, in contrast, were expressly denied the same status, rank, privileges, pay, and benefits as their male colleagues. They were not even entitled to disability, pension or death benefits so that WASP killed in crashes along with USAAF men were the only members of the flight crew *not* entitled to military honours and their families received no compensation for the return and interment of the remains.

Throughout the war, the contribution of the women of the ATA to the war effort was recognised and praised both from official quarters and in the press. By contrast, the WASP were first glamorised and made into Hollywood stars – and then subjected to a slander campaign, which both denigrated their accomplishments and insulted their competence and motives. At the end of the war, the women of the ATA were honourably discharged with the same dignity and recognition as their male colleagues. The WASP, in contrast, were sent home in haste and secrecy before either the war or the job for which they had trained – at great expense – was done.

What accounts for this dramatic difference in the treatment of women pilots doing essentially the same job in the same war in two nations with the same cultural heritage and military objectives? *Why* did the WASP arouse such violent opposition at a time when the women in the ATA were harvesting praise and royal recognition?

This book seeks to answer these questions. Part 1 provides a description of the historical context, the organisational objectives and development, recruitment, training, terms of service, daily life and the deactivation of the respective organisations. The second part attempts to analyse the impact of differing military traditions, male and public attitudes, organisational composition and ethos, press relations and key personalities on the fate of the respective organisations. To the extent possible, the women who participated in the ATA and WASP have been allowed to speak for themselves. From memoirs, diaries, interviews and other secondary sources, their experiences and opinions are drawn and quoted. In addition, a number of survivors were contacted and more than a dozen kindly responded.

The story these women have to tell is exciting and intriguing. The love of flying and desire to contribute to the war effort are a common theme, binding the women across the Atlantic. But the differences are telling too. Indeed, the entire study casts light on some still very relevant differences between two nations that have repeatedly found themselves fighting side-by-side on diverse battlefields across the globe.

CHAPTER ONE

The Wings of War

A BRIEF HISTORY OF THE WOMEN PILOTS OF THE ATA, WAFS, WFTD AND WASP

The Second World War did not explode unexpectedly upon an unsuspecting world. Rather, it arrived with the slow, clanking certainty of an advancing panzer. Practically from the time Hitler came to power until the German invasion of Poland, the world moved inexorably toward conflict. Yet, while the world marched consciously toward conflagration, it did so – at least in the West – with reluctance and foreboding. The Western Powers – the United Kingdom, France and the United States – resisted war to the last possible moment consistent with their role in the world and their national character.

The First World War had been won by the Western Powers at such immeasurable cost in both blood and money that it created in its wake a profound and widespread abhorrence of war. Even as Germany started down a path of militant Revisionism, breaking one after another of the 'bonds' imposed upon it by the Treaty of Versailles, Anglo-American public opinion remained firmly pacifist or isolationist respectively. In Britain, the policy of Appeasement was not only popular, it was arguably the only policy that a democratically elected government could pursue given the mood among voters. In the United States the mood was isolationist rather than pacifist; after the US Senate refused to ratify the League of Nations Treaty and President Wilson had departed from the political stage, the American public took little interest in what was happening in the rest of the world. With widespread industrial violence, Prohibition and soon the Great Depression, there was enough to entertain – and frighten – them at home without taking on the added burden of Europe's 'domestic squabbles'.

All this explains why, despite the evidence of massive German and Japanese aggression coupled with the expectation that aerial warfare would be decisive in any future conflict, both the United States and

Great Britain responded only slowly to the growing air threat posed by the militant dictatorships. In 1934, just one year after Hitler came to power, Germany was producing nearly 2,000 aircraft annually; by 1939 German aircraft production topped 8,000. By contrast, British aircraft production was still well under 1,000 aircraft in 1934, and in 1939 still did not exceed 5,000. The figures for the United States are even more striking: despite its industrial might and a large and growing domestic airline industry, the United States produced fewer than 500 aircraft annually in 1934, and expanded production erratically to just over 2,000 in 1939.[1]

The situation with regard to pilots was similar. By 1938, a total of 16,000 pilot's licences had been issued in Britain – but many of these were no longer valid. Furthermore, a great many of those holding valid licences were being absorbed into the expanding Royal Air Force (RAF), the Auxiliary Air Force and the RAF Volunteer Reserve.[2] Yet, despite this expansion, the RAF still only numbered 7,214 officers and 93,849 men in 1939.[3] Meanwhile, irrespective of the vastly larger manpower resources of the United States, there were only 21,000 civilian and 5,000 military pilots registered in 1938,[4] while the US Army Air Corps numbered just 1,650 officers and roughly 16,000 enlisted men.[5]

As the figures for aircraft production, Air Force strength and qualified pilots demonstrate, by the time the war broke out in 1939 the United Kingdom was notably better prepared to face a conflict entailing aerial warfare than was the United States. This was because, despite widespread hope that the Policy of Appeasement would succeed in averting war, there were enough realists in the Air Ministry willing to consider the 'worst case' scenario even before war became inevitable. The Air Ministry recognised the very real and growing threat to Britain posed by the *Luftwaffe*. Large parts of Britain were, after all, within range of German long-range bombers, and prevailing theories of aerial warfare suggested that massive air raids would immediately follow the outbreak of any war. It was estimated that as many as 40,000 civilians would be killed by aerial bombardment within the first week of war. Furthermore, massive bombing was expected to disrupt road and rail communications. Clearly, if it came to war, the RAF was going to be hard-pressed.

Among other measures initiated by Sir Kingsley Wood, the Air Minister, was the launch in October 1938 of the Civil Air Guard. The purpose of the Civil Air Guard was to increase the available pool of qualified pilots by subsidising pilot training of volunteers in a civilian context. Applicants had to be between the ages of eighteen and fifty and were to be trained at some sixty private and commercial flying schools around the country. The programme made no distinction between men and women, fixing neither minimum nor maximum quotas for either sex. By July 1939, between 3,000 and 4,000 pilots had received their licences via this programme, while a further 10,000 were in training. The Civil Air Guard by this time numbered close to 900 women, of which roughly 200 already held their licences.[6]

Also in response to the Munich Crisis, a Director of British Airways, Gerard d'Erlanger, devised and proposed to the Director General of Civil Aviation a scheme by which pilots ineligible for active service with the RAF could assist the nation in wartime. D'Erlanger foresaw that pilots – like himself – who were too old or otherwise unfit for operational service with the RAF, might nevertheless render valuable service in a support capacity. He envisaged such tasks as carrying mail, news and dispatches, the transport of medical and other vital but lightweight equipment as well as VIPs, ambulance services and co-operation work with police and fire brigades. The scheme won almost immediate approval, and d'Erlanger – as its originator – was put in charge. The tentative name Air Transport Auxiliary (ATA) was adopted, and the organisation was placed under the authority of British Airways/BOAC[7] for administrative and financial purposes.

After the German invasion of Czechoslovakia in March 1939 made war all but inevitable, plans for the ATA went ahead rapidly, with details of ranks, wages and uniforms all settled on paper. When the next international crisis came to a head in August 1939, d'Erlanger was in a position to write to over 1,000 pilots holding 'A' (private) or 'B' (commercial) licences, enquiring about interest in service with the embryonic organisation. Roughly 100 pilots responded positively.

At the outbreak of the war, it was decided to recruit thirty of these pilots, and invitations were sent out to the most suitable of the respondents. They were asked to report for a flight check at very short notice. By 11 September 1939, just one week after the start of the war, twenty-six pilots were under contract with the ATA – but the anticipated work for them had not materialised. The Germans had not yet bombed London. There were neither tens of thousands of casualties nor any disruption of ground transportation and communication. On the other hand, the RAF found itself rather short of pilots for ferrying aircraft about the country. It was, therefore, suggested that the ATA pilots might be helpful in this capacity. As this would entail piloting Service aircraft with which the civilian fliers were unfamiliar, the ATA pilots were sent to the RAF's Central Flying School at Upavon to check out on Service aircraft. The ATA had found its mission.

Throughout the remainder of 1939 and into early 1940, the RAF and the ATA shared the task of ferrying service aircraft, operating from the same airfields. The presence of civilians at RAF establishments created some friction and difficulties, however, and after earnest discussion about incorporating the ATA into the RAF, the decision was made in December 1939 to keep the organisation separate and civilian. D'Erlanger was authorised to establish his own headquarters in early 1940, and the new organisation proved so effective that by 1 May 1940 the entire responsibility for ferrying aircraft for the RAF and the Fleet Air Arm (FAA) was turned over to the ATA. All RAF pilots were withdrawn from ferrying duties – just in time.

On 10 May the Germans launched their long-expected offensive against the Western Powers. Within five days Holland had surrendered and the RAF in France was experiencing losses in excess of twenty Hurricanes a day. The situation was so perilous, that the Commander-in-Chief of Fighter Command, Air Chief Marshal Sir Hugh Dowding, felt compelled to speak personally before the Cabinet. Dowding warned that: 'if the Home Defence Force is drained away in desperate attempts to remedy the situation in France, the defeat of France will involve the final, complete and irremediable defeat of this country.'[8] Reluctantly, Churchill was persuaded to stop sending RAF fighter squadrons to France. Meanwhile, the British land forces of the British Expeditionary Force (BEF) found themselves cut off by the rapid advances of the German panzers. In the last days of May and the first days of June, the bulk of the BEF was evacuated from Dunkirk and the last RAF units were repatriated to the United Kingdom. On 22 June France signed an armistice with Germany, and Northern France became a German Occupied Territory. Not since the wars against Napoleon had an enemy been so close to Britain, nor the threat of invasion so tangible and acute.

For the next year, Britain stood alone against Nazi Germany, facing both an invasion threat and strategic and terror bombing from aircraft based just across the Channel. While the RAF bore the brunt of these air battles, withstanding substantial casualties in both personnel and aircraft, the ATA expanded as rapidly as possible in order to keep the RAF supplied with the aircraft it desperately needed. This was a period in which the RAF had literally no pilots to spare. Furthermore, the failure of the ATA to deliver replacement aircraft could have impaired the ability of the RAF to resist the threat posed by a very aggressive and still substantially larger *Luftwaffe*.

While the RAF stepped up its training of young recruits, the ATA appealed over the media for older, qualified pilots to volunteer. When no more of these could be found, the ATA instituted its own training scheme to train persons not fit for active service to be ferry pilots. In addition, pilots were recruited from abroad, particularly from the Commonwealth and the United States. Pilot and flight engineer strengths thus grew in fits and starts, peaking in August 1944 when aircrew flying with the ATA numbered almost 800.

This expansion in the air was accompanied by an even more dramatic increase in ground crews and staff, as the organisation grew from an improvised, informal operation with just seven non-flying support staff in February 1940, into a highly efficient and well-organised 'company' employing more than 3,000 people in early 1945. Likewise, the number of Ferry Pools, the bases from which the ATA operated, increased dramatically from one in early 1940 to twenty-two in 1944. In addition, the ATA operated two flying schools with an average of 143 aircraft in the peak year 1944. Last but not least, the ATA operated its own 'taxi service', starting with just one aircraft in early 1940 and building up to 218 'taxis' by February 1945.[9]

The Allied invasion of Europe temporarily increased the burden on the ATA, but just as inevitably heralded its imminent demise. The ATA had been created to meet a wartime emergency and its utility ended automatically with the end of hostilities. From early 1945 onwards, therefore, the ATA began preparing itself for deactivation. When, on 30 November 1945, the ATA's last flight ended, the improvised organisation had delivered 309,011 aircraft of 147 different types, flown a total of 742,614 hours, transported 3430 passengers and carried 883 tons of freight.[10] While the price had been far from negligible, 174 men and women gave their lives in service with the ATA, the record of accomplishment was outstanding. By the end of the war two CBEs, thirteen OBEs, thirty-six MBEs, six BEMs, one George Medal, six Commendations, six Commendations for Gallantry and eighteen King's Commendations for Valuable Service in the Air had been awarded to members of the ATA for their service with the organisation. Of these, 5 MBEs, 4 BEMs, 1 Commendation and 2 King's Commendations for Valuable Service in the ATA went to women.

Yet, real accomplishments of this remarkable organisation cannot be summarised in hours flown, decorations awarded or any other quantitative measure. The ATA's greatest achievement was not merely one of helping the Allies win the war by ensuring that vitally needed aircraft were delivered to the RAF and FAA, nor was it one of relieving healthy young men for combat duty. What makes the ATA a fascinating case study even to this day is the unprecedented, unorthodox and creative way in which the ATA mastered the problems it faced with human resources deemed 'sub-standard' by all conventional measures.

To fully appreciate the achievements of the ATA it is important to remember what extraordinary demands were made upon its pilots. First of all, the ATA required a previously unheard of versatility. ATA pilots were required to be able to fly aircraft they had never seen before simply on the basis of a few hours 'conversion' training in similar 'classes' of aircraft and on the basis of 'Pilot's Notes' printed on four by six-inch cards. ATA pilots flew without radios and so without the benefit of radio navigation aids, in-flight weather advisories or emergency communication. Furthermore, the ATA initially provided no, and later only very limited, training in the use of instruments for blind flying. Unlike the RAF flying in and out of their own stations, pilots of the ATA were expected to fly in and out of aerodromes they had never seen before all across the country. It expected its pilots to fly in airspace regularly invaded by enemy aircraft without any means of self defence. Most remarkable of all, the ATA expected all this of pilots who were deemed 'unfit' for military service. Flying for the ATA were men with one arm or one eye, men who were short-sighted, men who were over-weight, over-aged, several of these at once – and women.

The utilisation and integration of women pilots into the ATA is one of its most striking successes. Less than a month after the start of the war, on 25 September 1939, the Director General of Civil Aviation indicated in a letter to the Air Ministry that the use of women pilots was already under consideration. After some initial resistance from the RAF was overcome, one of the female Commissioners of the Civil Air Guard, Pauline Gower, was asked to recruit eight pilots for an all-woman ferry pool on 14 November 1939 – less than three months after the start of the war. These eight women pilots signed contracts with the ATA effective from 1 January 1940. From then on, the number of women pilots grew until by the end of the war a total of 162 women pilots and four women flight engineers had flown with the ATA.

By the time the ATA disbanded, women were receiving equal pay for equal work – a remarkable fact in 1945. Furthermore, women had served as instructors of both men and women, as Operations Officers and as Pool Commanders with the corresponding authority over men. Women had been qualified on virtually every kind of aircraft the ATA flew, with the exception of the large flying boats. Nor were these the accomplishments of a few select, token or 'experimental' women pilots. On the contrary, women represented a significant proportion of the ATA's total pilot strength (on average 16 per cent) and included women who had received their first flying training from the ATA.

In just six years the women pilots of the ATA had amply demonstrated that women could fly virtually any aircraft in service with the

RAF or FAA from the lightest training aircraft to the heaviest bomber, including the first jets. They had demonstrated the same versatility as their male colleagues in flying a wide variety of aircraft in and out of unfamiliar airfields without radio. They had faced the same hazards from enemy aircraft, friendly fire, mechanical failure and – above all – the weather. They had flown in the same theatres of operation, including all the way to Occupied Germany. They had delivered aircraft with lower accident and casualty rates than the men. They had in every sense earned the equality of opportunity and remuneration granted to them, and they enjoyed – without discrimination – the accolades, praise and thanks awarded the ATA as a whole. In short, the story of the women of the ATA is an exemplary case study in eliminating sex discrimination and integrating women into an – already extraordinary – organisation to the benefit of all concerned.

On the other side of the Atlantic, American women pilots were also given the exceptional opportunity to prove their capabilities during the Second World War. They proved equally successful – as pilots. Unfortunately, their progress was neither so smooth nor the result, in terms of compensation and recognition, so satisfactory as in the ATA.

In 1938 the United States faced an even more dramatic shortage of pilots proportional to population than did Great Britain. Furthermore, the United States did not yet possess an independent Air Force comparable to the RAF and *Luftwaffe*. Instead, all military flying was still the preserve of the traditional services, the Army and the Navy. The flying arm of the US Army, the Air Corps, numbered fewer than 18,000 officers and men and possessed fewer than 2,000 aircraft, the vast majority of which were obsolete. Furthermore, the US Army was training on average just 300 pilots a year.

It was not until Europe was at war that the US government recognised the need for a civilian flying training programme to create a pilot reserve from which the Army Air Corps could draw in time of war, and the Civilian Pilot Training (CPT) Program was launched. The goal of this programme was to increase the pool of civilian pilots by offering subsidised flying training at universities and colleges around the nation, while relying on local aviation companies to provide flying instruction. CPT training cost applicants only a nominal fee, and it therefore made flying training affordable to people with limited financial means for the first time in US history – provided they had been accepted by and could afford to attend an institution of higher education. The programme was correspondingly popular.

Notably, unlike the British Civil Air Guard scheme, the CPT discriminated against women from its inception. It put a limit on the number of women who could be accepted in the programme; female participation was capped at just 10 per cent.[11] Furthermore, women were initially confined to 'elementary' flying training, leading to a private licence, but excluded from training in aerobatics, cross-country navigation and blind flying. Only after a woman flier won a competition, whose prize was advanced aerobatics training, was more advanced flight training grudgingly opened up to women in late 1940. Less than a year later, on 1 July 1941, this decision was not only reversed, but now women were excluded from the programme completely.[12]

Despite its short duration and limitations, the CPT dramatically increased the pool of civilian pilots in the United States. By August 1941 more than 78,000 non-airline, male pilots – nearly four times the 1938 figure – were available to the nation. Including airline and military pilots, the United States had, in a very short time, built up its pilot reserve to roughly 90,000 – of which fewer than 3,000 were women.[13]

Under the circumstances, it is perhaps understandable that the Commander-in-Chief of the Army Air Corps, General Henry H. Arnold, felt he would have no need for women pilots, even in wartime. He stated unequivocally in a memo dated 25 August 1941 that: 'the use of women pilots serves no military purpose in a country, which has adequate manpower at this time.'[14]

The above memo from General Arnold was a direct response to proposals for the use of women pilots in the military that had reached his desk from two sources. On the one hand, the commander of the Ferrying Command, Lt-Col Olds, had approached him with regard to the use of women pilots in his command – a suggestion that clearly reflected knowledge of the successful use of women as ferry pilots in the United Kingdom. On the other hand, Arnold had been approached by the celebrity pilot Jacqueline Cochran. After flying in one of the Lend-Lease bombers across the Atlantic in a well-organised publicity stunt, Cochran claimed to have been tasked by President Roosevelt personally to research a plan for an organisation of women pilots to serve with the US Army Air Corps.[15] Cochran, the wife of a millionaire financier and Chief Executive Officer (CEO) of a successful cosmetics firm, had analysed the records of the Civil Aviation Administration and discovered that only 150 of the 2,733 American women pilots with licences had the minimum of 200 hours flying time required by Ferrying Command. Cochran therefore proposed training women pilots within the US Army Air Corps to bring them up to the standards required.

Arnold was if anything *less* interested in Cochran's proposal than that of Lt-Col Olds. It would have required him to divert scarce Army training resources, needed for the training of fully operational male pilots, to the training of women, whose utility would be limited to non-combatant functions. Furthermore, at the time Cochran approached him (July 1941), General Arnold had more pilots than aeroplanes in his fledgling Air Force.

Tragically, this was still the state of affairs when the United States finally entered the war in December 1941 – a situation aggravated by the fact that half the military aircraft on Hawaii and the bulk of those in the Philippines were destroyed in the Japanese raids of 7 December 1941. Thus the US Army Air Force (USAAF) entered 1942 with roughly 1,100 serviceable combat aircraft, of which many were obsolete, but roughly 22,000 officers and 270,000 men. Furthermore, incredible as it seems today, the USAAF seems to have completely underestimated its wartime requirements for both aircraft and pilots.

Yet, while the USAAF struggled to overcome its inadequate pre-paration, US aircraft production took off immediately. The US aviation industry, starting from an anaemic production of just 2,195 aircraft in the year Europe went to war, attained the phenomenal production level of 47,800 aircraft in America's first full year of war; it nearly doubled production again in 1943 to 86,000.[16] Many of these aircraft were destined for America's European Allies, others for the combat units of the USAAF itself, but many more were destined for the training schools of the USAAF, which now mushroomed across the country in a frantic effort to meet the hugely increased demand for pilots. All these aircraft had to be moved from the factories churning them out in such unpre-cedented numbers to their destinations both at home and abroad. The responsibility for delivering them fell to the Ferrying Command, which was already suffering from a shortage of pilots and had floated the idea of employing women six months earlier. Now, with the greatly expanded workload occasioned by the US entry into the war, this or-ganisation (re-organised as the Air Transport Command (ATC), of which the Ferrying Division (FERD) was just one very important component) 'alone needed more pilots than existed in the entire AAF'.[17]

The ATC at once began a programme of hiring civilian pilots to ferry planes. Within six months of Pearl Harbor 3,500 civilian pilots had been hired by the ATC, of which half would later be commissioned into the USAAF.[18] The half that retained their civilian status consisted pre-dominantly of men too old for, or otherwise unable, to meet the USAAF's medical standards.[19] In short, they came from exactly the same pool of pilots as the ATA successfully drew its initial recruits.

In light of this acute need for qualified pilots, FERD's interest in hiring women pilots also revived. The Commanding General of the Ferrying Command, General William Tunner, writes in his memoirs that he was unaware of the previous efforts to hire women or Arnold's opposition to the idea.[20] He and a professional woman pilot, Nancy Harkness Love, whose husband was a staff officer in the ATC, developed guidelines and policies for the employment of women pilots within FERD. Tunner was 'so sure the proposal would be accepted that the same day I went to Wilmington, Delaware, headquarters of my Second Ferrying Group, to make arrangements for housing the women we hoped to get'.[21] (Then) Colonel Tunner's proposal was submitted to Army Air Forces HQ in June 1942, but the initiative was not immediately acted upon. General Arnold still wanted to exhaust all possible male resources first. Three months later, however, Arnold capitulated in the face of sheer necessity and gave his approval to the scheme. The creation of a Women's Auxiliary Ferrying Squadron (WAFS) was announced in a press conference on 10 September 1942.

Meanwhile, possibly at General Arnold's suggestion, Cochran had undertaken to recruit American women pilots for the ATA. She selected twenty-five women, and in the spring and summer of 1942 helped organise their flight checks in Canada as well as their transport to England. Cochran herself went to England as a volunteer and was given an honorary position as Commander of the American women, but never flew for the ATA. Instead, she returned from England in September 1942 only to discover the USAAF had approved a women pilots programme without her knowledge, participation or appointment to command.

Cochran was outraged. She immediately confronted General Arnold, apparently reminding him of some real or imagined promise to make her head of any women pilots organisation within the USAAF. In a memorandum dated just two days after the announcement of the WAFS, Cochran revived her earlier proposal to train women pilots, stressing that ferrying was only one of many tasks for which women might be suitable. She furthermore explicitly demanded that an immediate announcement be made of the establishment of a larger organisation of women pilots with broader functions – under her command.[22]

Although initially irritated by the notion of having two separate women pilots organisations, Arnold – like any good military commander – was capable of rapidly responding to changing circumstances. While there was no legitimate reason for reversing the decision to establish the WAFS merely because Cochran was displeased not to have been appointed the commander, the idea of training women for other types of flying duties no longer looked so ridiculous. This being September 1942 (and hence a period when the Allies were not enjoying particular success on any front), the war's duration and cost in lives was incalculable. Arnold anticipated having to draw on 'sub-standard' male material in the near future. He therefore decided to give Cochran a chance, appointed her 'Director of Women's Flying Training' and tasked her to recruit and organise a Flying Training Detachment for women.

Meanwhile, cables had gone out to eighty-three American women pilots with commercial licences, 500 flying hours and 200-hp rating, asking if they were interested in serving with the USAAF as civilian ferry pilots. If they were, they were to report to New Castle Army Air Force Base near Wilmington, Delaware, immediately. On 21 September, less then two weeks after the WAFS had been announced, the first eleven women were sworn in as civilian pilots of FERD. On 21 October 1942, just one month after signing on, the first WAFS commenced their duties as ferry pilots. Altogether, twenty-eight women with an average of 1,000 hours flying experience would serve in this elite squadron during its short eleven-month existence.

Cochran's Women's Flying Training Detachment (WFTD) got off to a rockier start. Facilities were not available for training the first thirty recruits to the WFTD until mid-November 1942 (two months after launch), and despite the high requirements for the first class (over 200 flying hours), it was the following April, five full months later, before the first twenty-three women graduated. New classes, increasing in size, had meanwhile reported monthly. Starting in February 1943 an entire training facility, Avenger Field in Sweetwater, Texas, was put at the disposal of the WFTD. From November 1942 until December 1944, when the last class of women graduated from flying training, a total of roughly 25,000 American women had applied for flying training at the WFTD – 1,830 had been accepted and a total of 1,074 had graduated in eighteen classes.

While the graduates of the first five classes (April to September 1943) were assigned exclusively to FERD, starting in October 1943 the graduates of the WFTD at Avenger Field were increasingly assigned to duties other than ferrying. These duties included target towing for air and anti-aircraft gunners, searchlight and tracking missions, maintenance testing, weather flights, passenger transportation, instrument and flight instruction, and remote-controlled flying of drones. In order to perform these increasingly complex tasks, the women were required to undergo extensive additional training both in the aircraft they were expected to fly and in instrument flying, high-altitude flying and the like. Meanwhile, effective from 5 August 1943 the two separate organisations for women pilots, the WAFS and WFTD, were merged into a single organisation under Cochran's command and re-designated Women Airforce Service Pilots, or WASP.

Shortly after the creation of the WASP, Cochran began her campaign to attain militarisation for her new organisation. Her stated objective was to gain better 'control' over the women under her command and also to give them equal rights and status with officers of the USAAF, particularly with regard to pay, insurance and death benefits. WASP, regardless of qualifications or duty, were paid significantly less than even the most junior second lieutenant of the USAAF. Furthermore, the WASP lived in a no-man's land with regard to health care and were completely without compensation in the event of injury or death.

Efforts to militarise the WASP within the existing Women's Army Corps (WAC) had been repeatedly and vehemently opposed by Cochran, who insisted on a separate organisation, of which she was to be the commander. Suggestions for the direct commissioning of individuals, as with the male civilian pilots hired by FERD, were pursued only half-heartedly, apparently because the applicability of this procedure to WASP serving in other commands was uncertain. At Cochran's urging it was instead decided that the WASP should be militarised as an independent organisation. This, however, required an Act of Congress. Thus, in September 1943, roughly one year after the initiation of the women pilots programmes, legislation to militarise the WASP was introduced in the House of Representatives.

While the wheels of democracy ground slowly forward, the WASP training got into its stride. Month for month, roughly 100 young women reported to Avenger Field for training. By January 1944, there were a thousand American women either in flying training or on active duty with the USAAF. Meanwhile, USAAF Training Command as a whole had also geared up to a frenetic level of activity. By January 1944 it had trained nearly 200,000 male pilots since America's entry into the war. At the same time, an increasing number of combat pilots had completed their tours of duty abroad and were returning to the domestic establishment.[23] In short, the pilot shortage was already overcome, and the demand for women graduates started to decline.

As early as the autumn of 1943, FERD started to resist hiring any more graduates from the WFTD at Avenger Field. Resistance increased with each passing month. By March 1944, WASP also began to encounter difficulties finding employment in other Commands as well. In August 1944 the situation in Training Command was further aggravated by the return from FERD to Training Command of 125 WASP, who did not want to or could not fly fighters – now a requirement of FERD.

The opportunities for WASP continued to deteriorate as casualties among aircrew, particularly in the European Theatre, fell far below expectations, thereby reducing the overall need for pilots. With a declining need for replacement pilots, the need for training fell off sharply. In early 1944, the USAAF started to cut back pilot training and close down many, particularly elementary, training facilities for male cadets. This meant cancelling large numbers of contracts with the civilian aviation companies, which had until then provided the elementary flying training for future Air Force pilots. Thousands of civilian flying instructors, whose work had given them draft-exempt status, found themselves not only out of work but out of a draft exemption as well. They faced the possibility of being drafted into the 'walking army' at a time when the Invasion of Continental Europe and the Japanese mainland were both very imminent prospects.

It is hardly surprising that these pilots concluded that if there were no WASP, they would have access to the non-combat flying jobs being performed by the women pilots and so avoid being drafted into the 'walking army'. These men started agitating against the WASP and particularly the militarisation bill before Congress. It was particularly unfortunate that at this point in time another Congressional Committee, the House Civil Services Committee, also reported unfavourably on the WASP programme. Most particularly, the House Civil Services Committee drew attention to the fact that Congress had never explicitly approved the appropriation of funds for the training of women pilots. The Committee recommended discontinuing the training programme and retaining only those pilots who were already enrolled in training or already on active service with the USAAF.

Significantly, as the WASP militarisation bill moved through Congress, media and public sentiment became increasingly hostile to the WASP. Articles in the press often contained blatantly inaccurate information about the WASP, their qualifications, the cost and quality of their training, the cost of their uniforms, their casualty and accident rates and more. The tone of the public debate was highly emotional and often slanderous. It was implied that Cochran had only induced otherwise rational military leaders to approve her implicitly superfluous and luxurious programme by seducing them. It was suggested that many of the WASP also used their 'charms' to obtain privileges and duties to which they were not entitled and for which they were not qualified. On 22 June 1944 the House Bill granting the WASP military status was defeated.

This did not in itself end the WASP. In fact, even while the acrimonious debate on the militarisation of the WASP was raging, the House Appropriations Committee approved $6.4 million to fund the WASP programme in 1945.[24] Even the more hostile Civil Services Committee had explicitly recommended continuing to employ those WASP who were already in or had completed training. When the militarisation bill was defeated in Congress, General Arnold immediately took steps to comply with the recommendations of the Civil Services Committee. He stopped recruiting and ordered all WASP candidates due to report to Avenger Field in the near future to stay home. The WASP on active service and already enrolled in the training programme, however, were not in any way immediately affected by the defeat of the House bill on militarisation.

On 1 August 1944, however, in a curiously delayed response to the entire debate about militarisation, Cochran issued a lengthy (eleven-page, single-spaced) report on the WASP. The report undoubtedly contained many valuable facts and details about the success of the programme – e.g. the range of missions performed, the low accident rates, the costs of training etc. – but it unfortunately also reiterated the case for militarisation. Apparently unable to accept defeat, Cochran went so far as to question whether it wouldn't be better to disband the entire organisation than to continue on the civilian basis under which it had operated – according to her own account –so successfully for almost two years.

The press and many within the USAAF interpreted Cochran's report as an ultimatum. Whether Cochran intended it that way or not, her report certainly contained a lengthy and very heavy-handed polemic in favour of militarisation. The benefits of continued civilian status were not discussed as an alternative. On the contrary, the report stated that: 'the only effective means by which the AAF can obtain efficient and economical use of women pilots is through a militarised program which makes the WASP a part of the AAF'.[25] The report furthermore explicitly suggested that disbanding was better than the status quo, stating: 'serious consideration should be given to inactivation of the WASP program if militarisation is not soon authorised.'[26] It is unclear how General Arnold should 'soon authorise militarisation' since this required Congressional approval, and Congress had voted against this measure not six weeks earlier.

Thus, whether it was an ultimatum or not, Cochran's memo was certainly a tactical error. General Arnold was still fighting a war in two theatres and had already suffered two heart attacks. He did not need to reopen a battle with the public, the media and Congress over militarisation for a mere 1,000 women pilots, who were no longer urgently needed. Furthermore, General Arnold personally had been insulted during the debate on the House bill and the media campaign surrounding it by the ugly insinuations about his own relationship to Cochran.

The response was swift. Almost immediately, on 24 August 1944, plans were set in motion to disband the WASP. By 12 September, almost two years to the day after its inception, the recommendation for deactivation was official. On 1 October 1944 General Arnold informed both Cochran and the individual WASP members in a letter that the programme would be discontinued on 20 December.

The rapid demise of the WASP caught FERD off-guard. Although FERD had refused to absorb into its ranks all of the increasing number of graduates from Avenger Field and had even returned to Training Command a number of WASP it found unsuitable for ferrying duties, it still had a need for those WASP on active service with the Command. By the autumn of 1944, half of all FERD pilots qualified to fly fighter aircraft were women, and three fifths of all domestic deliveries of fighters was done by women.[27] The orders to disband the WASP were therefore received with alarm by FERD. In a memorandum dated 1 November 1944, FERD drew attention to the fact that the deactivation and dismissal of the WASP would require the replacement of the 117 women pilots, qualified to ferry fighter aircraft, by male pilots. FERD went on to quantify the costs of replacing the women at over $9,000 per pilot or over $1 million for all 117 women.[28] FERD specifically sought permission to hire these qualified women individually as civilians following the deactivation of the WASP programme. General Arnold – one suspects out of exasperation with the whole issue or out of fear of more negative press – said 'no'. In consequence, on 20 December, when the WASP were sent home '[n]early a hundred P-51s were stuck in Los Angeles and . . . 161 combat pilots [had to be loaned to Ferry Command] for a thirty-day tour of duty. Scuttlebutt indicated that this was an entire pursuit squadron that had been about to depart for overseas'.[29]

The WASP programme thus became 'the only non-training component of the military to be fully disbanded and its personnel sent home before the war was over'.[30] Furthermore, the deactivation of the programme cost the US government and taxpayer more than it would have cost to continue it. All the WASP on active service had to be replaced by male pilots not yet trained in the tasks the WASPs were fulfilling. If one assumes the costs would have been roughly the same in all commands as in FERD, the total cost for training WASP replacements would have amounted to roughly $8 million, compared with the approved budget for the WASP of just $6.4 million. Most tragically, however, the programme had cost thirty-eight young women their lives, and their sacrifice seemed to be denigrated by the manner in which their colleagues were sent home in such an indecent hurry as 'superfluous'.

This fate seems particularly unfair when one considers the

accomplishments of the young American women who had flown with the WASP. Women had proved capable of performing a wide variety of flying missions, in addition to making a significant contribution to ferrying aircraft domestically. WASP had flown forty-five different kinds of aircraft, including America's most modern heavy bomber, the B-29 Super Fortress. One WASP helped test-fly America's first jet. The WASP assigned to FERD flew 12,650 missions over more than 9 million miles.[31] For the WASP as a whole the miles flown is given by Cochran as 60 million.[32] They had done all this while earning a salary significantly below that of a USAAF second lieutenant, much less the male civilians flying with FERD.

Adding insult to injury, the recognition accorded the WASP seems paltry. Of the 916 women who actively served with the USAAF, only three received decorations for their services. Two of these medals went to the influential and politically well-connected initiators and commanders, Jacqueline Cochran and Nancy Love. Only one 'ordinary' WASP, Barbara Erickson, was awarded an Air Medal.

What had the WASP accomplished in its short existence? In his address to the last graduating class of WASP, General Arnold claimed that the 'entire operation has been a success. It is on record that women can fly as well as men. . . . We will not again look upon a woman's flying organisation as experimental'.[33] But the results of the 'experiment' were not only ignored, they were classified – hidden away from public view and duly buried in bureaucratic dust until they had been forgotten by institutional memory.

Actions, it is well known, speak louder than words. If the WASP was a successful experiment, then why were the women pilots sent home in a hurry at high cost to the taxpayer? Why did the WASP arouse so much media passion and public hostility? What was it about the WASP that induced the USAAF to seize upon a stupid – but completely gratuitous – report by the Director of Women's Pilots suggesting de-activation? If the WASP were doing such a good job and the costs of replacing them exceeded the costs of retaining them, why not just ignore the demands of a notoriously spoilt, self-seeking advisor and do what was right for the USAAF? In other words, what made the WASP so vulnerable to – even patently absurd – criticism?

The comparison with the success of the women in the ATA provides insight into the answers to these questions. In the following chapters, a closer look is taken at the objectives pursued by the respective organisations as reflected in their requirements, recruiting and terms of service. The quality of the organisations is compared, particularly with regard to training, organisation and operations. Last but not least, more light is thrown on the factors leading to the sudden and hasty deactivation of the WASP.

In the second part of the book, the differences between the British and American traditions and approaches to the employment of women pilots are highlighted and the impact of these differences scrutinised. Specifically, the effects of being in a 'war zone', the differing ethos of the two organisations, the issues of segregation and militarisation, the experimental nature of the WASP programme, and the role of both the press and key personalities are examined.

Notes:

1   Kennedy, Paul, *The Rise and Fall of the Great Powers: Economic Change and Military Conflict from 1500 to 2000*, 1987, 324.
2   Curtis, Lettice, *The Forgotten Pilots*, 1971, 10.
3   Armitage, Michael, *The Royal Air Force: An Illustrated History*, 1993, 278.
4   Keil, Sally Van Wagenen, *Those Wonderful Women in their Flying Machines: The Unknown Heroines of World War II*, 1979, 1990, 64.
5   Merryman, Molly, *Clipped Wings: The Rise and Fall of the Women Airforce Service Pilots (WASPs) of World War II*, 1998, 9.
6   Curtis, 12.
7   British Airways and Imperial Airways were merged to form BOAC on 1 April 1940.
8   Dowding, Sir Hugh (later Lord), Letter to the Undersecretary of State at the Air Ministry, dated 16 May 1940, quoted in full in Robert Wright, *Dowding and the Battle of Britain*, 1969, 112.
9   Cheeseman, E.C., Brief Glory: *The Story of the Air Transport Auxiliary*, 1946, 246.
10   Cheeseman, 246. Curtis, 257.
11   Keil, 64.
12   Keil, 67–8.
13   Granger, Byrd Howell, *On Final Approach: The Women Airforce Service Pilots of World War II*, 1991, 9, Keil, 107, and Merryman, 11.
14   Keil, 107. See also: Merryman, 11.
15   Although Cochran always claimed to have been tasked by President Roosevelt personally, to date no documentary evidence of this has been uncovered.
16   Merryman, 9.
17   Merryman, 9.
18   Merryman, 9.
19   Only in one case did the ATC manage to completely over-rule the Army Medical Corps, and commission a pilot who failed the Army medical. A pilot personally known to General Olds had a crippled arm. According to General Tunner, 'when he went for his physical examination, the Air Corps doctor took one look at him and turned

him down. Olds hated to be thwarted in anything. He was determined that Gimbel came in with us, and he carried the case all the way to the chief flight surgeon, Major General Grant . . . After some shouting, General Grant finally agreed to go up in a plane with Gimbel to see if he could fly it. It was a huge four-engine Liberator, but Gimbel handled it masterfully. Grant came down shaking his head, and Gimbel passed his physical examination' Tunner, William, *Over the Hump*, 1964, 24.

20   Tunner, William, *Over the Hump*, 1964, 35.
21   Tunner, 36.
22   Granger, 29–30.
23   Merryman, 62–3.
24   Merryman, 88.
25   Cochran quoted in Granger, 391 and Merryman, 111.
26   Granger, 391, Merryman, 112.
27   Tunner, 39.
28   Verges, Marianne, *On Silver Wings: The Women Airforce Service Pilots of World War II, 1942–1944*, 1991, 227
29   Verges, 229.
30   Merryman, 5.
31   Verges, 236.
32   Cochran, Jacqueline, *Final Report on Women Pilot Program*, 2.
33   Arnold, General Henry, quoted in Keil, 330.

CHAPTER TWO

Women at Arms

RECRUITMENT, REQUIREMENTS AND TERMS OF SERVICE

The perils confronting the women pilots who flew military aircraft in the Second World War were not always strictly a function of the job they were asked to do. When four American women ferry pilots arrived in a small town in the American South, weary from a day of flying, they found themselves besieged by frenzied American serviceman who mistook their profession altogether. The ardour of the soldier's attentions brought forth the Military Police – who promptly arrested the women rather than their assailants. It took a great deal of telephoning and the intervention of senior officers before the mistake was rectified.

This incident illustrates just how important Terms of Service – details like uniforms and rank – can really be. The women subjected to the humiliation cited above were victims of confusion largely because they were not wearing a recognised uniform at the time of the incident. Uniforms, rank, pay and benefits are all factors that have a very direct impact on the status and morale of personnel – no matter how important and enjoyable the job they are doing might otherwise be. Likewise, it is important to know just what an organisation's objectives are in order to understand recruiting requirements and the resulting composition of its staff.

OBJECTIVES, RECRUITMENT AND REQUIREMENTS

ATA

Even before the ATA was founded, its objectives had been clearly formulated by its subsequent Commander, Gerard d'Erlanger. The objective was simple: to put the skills of trained pilots, who would otherwise be grounded because they were not fit for service with the RAF or FAA, at the disposal of the nation in time of war. This objective shaped and defined the organisation that was subsequently created, and largely explains the evolution of the organisation as well as its character and ethos.

The primacy of serving the nation in wartime explains the flexibility of approach that characterised the ATA right from the start. It was expressed in the willingness of the organisation and its members to do *anything* from flying casualties and dispatches to carrying passengers and cargo. When the need for communication services did not material- ise as anticipated at the start of the war, the ATA without hesitation took on the unexpected task of ferrying service aircraft. Once it had been demonstrated beyond a shadow of a doubt that the civilian pilots could do the job of ferrying service aircraft to the satisfaction of the RAF and the FAA, the task was turned over to the ATA in its entirety. Henceforth, ferrying became the ATA's primary mission. From this point forward until almost the end of the war, the ATA held a monopoly on this key function and was *de facto* – with respect to ferrying – no longer a supplementary or auxiliary organisation but rather, despite its continued civilian status, *the* ferrying component of the British air forces.

In addition to holding this monopoly on ferrying, and in conformity with its flexible approach, the ATA also maintained an Air Movements Flight. This Flight was available on an *ad hoc* basis to perform various other tasks as necessary. Particularly important throughout the war was the flying of VIPs around the country and the transport of patients to the Fifth Royal Canadian Hospital at Taplow near Maidenhead. After D-Day, the transportation of stores and equipment to Continental Europe was added to the tasks assigned to this Flight, and the 'Overseas Freight Department' sprang up virtually overnight. Rather than return empty, the ATA aircraft often transported service personnel, casualties, refugees or released POWs home as well.

The key to all these activities was responsiveness to a need articu- lated by the RAF, FAA or Air Ministry. Typically, it was a need expressed spontaneously at the working level. It might be an un- expected but acute shortage of pilots or aircraft that induced a Squadron Leader or Wing Commander to ask an individual ATA pilot or pool if they could help out. Alternatively, the ATA might receive the frantic request for transportation from a senior official whose aircraft had suddenly gone unserviceable in the middle of newly liberated Europe.

Whatever the case, in accordance with their objective of helping the war effort in whatever way they could, the ATA pilots consistently responded with alacrity and creativity to any requests for assistance that they could reasonably fulfil. An organisational ethos that encouraged initiative and responsibility and disdained excessive bureaucracy evolved. Thus, for example, the ATA had been flying to the Continent *de facto* for more than three months before such flights were officially recognised and sanctioned. Likewise, women ferried service aircraft, including fighters, prior to being 'officially' allowed to do so. Certain ATA trips to Berlin, Rome, Naples and Cairo were never officially approved; they were spontaneously undertaken – and completed – before anyone 'higher up' was informed or could object.

But just as important as flexibility was competence. The ATA was an organisation that did anything which its specially qualified personnel could do – and that was fly. It was a pilot's organisation formed by and for experienced pilots who were not otherwise suitable for service with the RAF or FAA. Clearly, qualified women pilots fitted into this category. Yet, initially it was an exclusive organisation reserved for those pilots – male or female – who could *already* fly to a very high standard.

At the start, therefore, the ATA invited only selected pilots to apply to the organisation on the basis of their flying qualifications and experience. Policy, as stated by the Director General of Civil Aviation, was that the requirements were to be 'identical' for men and women. Initially, in 1939, the minimum flying requirements consisted of an 'A' (private) licence and several hundred solo flying hours. Candidates had to be between twenty-eight and fifty years of age for men but could be as young as twenty-two for women. (The lower age limit for women was dictated by the fact that men under twenty-eight were still eligible for service with the Armed Forces.)

Because initially only thirty men and eight women were to be recruited, the Air Ministry correctly anticipated that there would be more applicants than vacancies. It was therefore decided that no selection would be made until all applicants had been tested, ensuring that the very best pilots would be recruited by the ATA. Those pilots who responded to the invitation went before a 'selection committee', in the case of the men headed by d'Erlanger and in the case of the women headed by Gower. The Chief Flying Instructor, formerly of British Airways, A.R.O. MacMillan, then tested the candidates – both men and women – with regard to their flying skills. Because of the limited number of women being sought at this time, Gower was able to select her original eight pilots (and two additional pilots a few months later) exclusively from women who had more than 500 hours flying experience.

In the course of 1940, the ATA not only assumed sole responsibility for the ferrying of aircraft to the RAF and the FAA, but the demand for and production of aircraft grew dramatically as Britain's Continental Allies were defeated and the full burden of war fell upon the United Kingdom. The workload for the ATA increased correspondingly and the ATA expanded, increasing the number of pilots from roughly forty to more than 240 by the end of 1940.

By then the reserves of known pilots – both male and female – with the very high qualifications initially required had been fully depleted. To the meet the rising demand for pilots during the course of the year, BOAC pilots had been loaned temporarily to the ATA for flying duties. But the BOAC pilots were generally airline captains with extensive experience on four-engined aircraft and even heavy, transcontinental flying boats. These pilots were urgently needed to ferry aircraft across the Atlantic and keep the lines of communication open to the Far and Middle East. It therefore became increasingly evident that pilots with more limited experience from private flying would have to be recruited for the ATA's domestic duties. In December 1940 Lord Londonderry, Chief Commissioner of the Civil Air Guard, made a wireless appeal for pilots with private licences to apply to the ATA.

The response was encouraging. It appeared there were still many pilots with limited flying experience eager to support the war effort. The lowered requirements of just fifty solo hours enabled the ATA to tap a wider pool of manpower resources than they had a year earlier. To make these men and women competent ferry pilots, however, they required additional training. Since all civilian flying instruction had been suspended at the start of the war and the RAF's training establishment was already overburdened with the task of training Service pilots to replace the losses incurred during the Battles of France and Britain, the ATA responded to the new situation with its characteristic flexibility by assuming responsibility for training its own pilots. Thus, roughly one year after its launch, the ATA designed and launched a training programme specifically targeted at fulfilling the needs of the ATA.

Although the entry requirements were officially lowered to fifty solo hours at this time, there were still a considerable number of women with several hundred hours flying experience from before the war. Since applicants were still checked out and hired on the basis of 'ability' (as assessed by the professional instructors seconded from BOAC) women with considerable flying experience were still favoured over the eager young candidates with just a few hours. The previous experience of women pilots therefore only sank gradually over time as more and more women were hired.

By the summer of 1942, the pool of trained pilots had, however, been exhausted, and women with as little as four hours solo were being checked out and admitted to the ATA. One of the women recruits at this time, Diana Barnato Walker, believes that the ATA 'thought that young girls who had started to learn to fly (which was very unusual in those days) had probably picked up a lot of extra knowledge while hanging around their various flying clubs. Anyway, they had at least some initiative, which was one of the things the ATA was looking for in their future ferry pilots'.[1]

There was furthermore an active effort to recruit women pilots from the United States. At this point in time neither the WAFS nor WFTD had been established, so there was still a large untapped pool of ex-perienced women pilots in the United States. While the British women hired in 1942 had almost no experience, Jacqueline Cochran was in the enviable position of being able to set high standards for the American women pilots she recruited for the ATA; she required some 300 hours flying experience.

Despite the influx of twenty-five American women, the ATA was at this time losing the American male pilots it had recruited earlier as their contracts expired throughout 1942 and 1943. By May 1943 the pilot shortage had again become so acute that the decision was made to start training pilots from scratch. Candidates for *ab initio* training were first drawn from 'non-flying members of the RAF and WAAF (Women's Auxiliary Air Force) . . . [and] those of the clerical staff of the ATA, mostly girls from the offices, who were now given the chance to learn to fly'.[2] It was believed that RAF and ATA ground staff and WAAF had already demonstrated an interest in flying and, particularly with regard to ATA ground staff, possessed an understanding of the task awaiting them. There was also a bias toward women who had demonstrated particular keenness by repeated applications.

Once the floodgates were opened to candidates with absolutely no flying experience, however, the ATA could again afford to be highly selective in other regards. Joy Gough, recruited at this time, reports that candidates were required to have a school-leaving certificate, to be at least 5ft 6in tall and have an aptitude for sport. Meanwhile, it was agreed with the RAF that thirty WAAF would be released for service with the ATA, but these women also had to meet several requirements that had not applied to women *with* flying experience. Namely, WAAF had to be aged between twenty and twenty-eight, be a minimum of 5ft 5in tall, be in possession of a school certificate or equivalent, be fully mobile and be single.

Despite these more restrictive criteria, the Air Ministry Order enabling WAAF to volunteer for flying with the ATA was barely published before nearly 2000 WAAF meeting the criteria applied. In order to get the number of applications down to a manageable level, it was arbitrarily decided to 'short list' only those between twenty-three and twenty-six years of age, who had matriculated or held degrees. This, however, cut the list down to just eighty-seven candidates. As this number was deemed too few, the lower age was reduced to twenty-two and roughly 150 candidates now could be 'short-listed' for interviews.[3]

Unlike the women recruited from other sources, who were interviewed at ATA Headquarters in White Waltham by ATA commanders, the WAAF were selected by the Ministry of Aircraft Production (MAP). The Ministry – unlike the ATA itself – did not seem to view the project of recruiting WAAF with particular urgency. Perhaps this attitude on the part of the MAP was attributable to the fact that the Ministry was aware of efforts to open another (deemed more valuable) pool of pilots to the ATA. Namely, in early 1944 the RAF finally agreed to second pilots no longer fit for operational flying to the ATA. Thus by the time the lengthy selection process was completed, the need for the WAAF (who had no flying experience whatsoever) had effectively been eliminated. Only nineteen WAAF joined ATA in the spring of 1944, up to nine months after the Air Ministry Order that had opened the ATA to them. They were the last women recruited for the ATA.

WAFS/WFTD/WASP

As was outlined in the previous chapter, women pilots were first hired by the USAAF for flying duties under two distinct programmes. Each programme pursued very distinct objectives, which – as we shall see – often resulted in open conflict and tension. The WAFS was a squadron of women pilots hired as civilians by the ATC's Ferrying Division to meet an acute shortage of qualified ferry pilots. The WFTD, under the administration of the USAAF's Training Command, was an experimental flying training detachment, which was to *test* whether women could be trained up to Army Air Force standards. The combined programme, later designated the WASP, tried to fulfil both objectives, providing pilots for FERD *and* demonstrating on a experimental basis the various other capacities in which women pilots could be employed by the USAAF. While ostensibly responsive to USAAF needs, the WASP was in fact much more focused on and concerned about the experimental aspects of the programme than meeting USAAF needs.

The original twenty-eight women who were taken into the WAFS programme in the autumn of 1942 were required to be US citizens between the ages of twenty-one and thirty-five years, at least 5ft 2in tall, who had earned a high school diploma, and who had at least 500 flying hours. Furthermore, they had to hold a 200-hp rating and have logged at least fifty hours of flying on heavier aircraft in the last six months. (Men at this time did not need a high school diploma or the 200-hp rating and were only required to have 200 hours flying.) The women had to pass the Army medical exam as well – something not required of civilian males flying for the ATC. Last but not least, they were required to have two character references 'from reputable citizens' attesting to character and flying ability. The unofficial, subjective requirements were, as one recruit put it: 'You had to be a nice girl from a nice family'.[4] Furthermore:

> On one side, they needed to be women about whom no potential scandal might swirl. And Nancy [Love] knew each woman must exhibit a special mix of flying skill, ability to adapt – take orders and let potential insults roll off their backs – and sheer determination.[5]

At the time the WAFS was formed, roughly one hundred American women could meet the official flying qualifications – twenty-five of them were already serving with the ATA in England. It speaks highly for the patriotism and love of flying of these American women pilots that the WAFS was able to attract twenty-eight of the remaining women in just three short months.

From the start, the flying requirements for the women accepted into the WFTD were lower than the WAFS and they sank very rapidly. From an initial 200 hours in November 1942, the requirement was cut in half just one month later, then reduced to seventy-five hours the following month, and finally stabilised six months after the programme was launched so that from April 1943 onwards the minimum requirement was thirty-five hours. The upper age limit was held steady at just thirty-five years of age, while the lower limit was dropped from twenty-two in November 1942, to twenty-one a month later and to eighteen-and-a-half in August 1943. Only the height requirement increased: from 5ft 2in in November 1942 to 5ft 4in in August 1943. Throughout the programme applicants were required to have completed high school, to provide two letters of reference and to be US citizens.

Cochran placed great emphasis on the fact that the women candidates had to pass the same physical examination as men accepted into the USAAF as flight cadets. There were weight as well as height requirements intended to eliminate the overweight or excessively frail. Although not an official criterion for acceptance, pilots in the WASP had to be white. There were a number of black applicants, and while most of these were not qualified, Cochran personally 'persuaded' a highly qualified and exemplary black woman pilot to withdraw her application rather than cause 'trouble' for the programme.[6] It is only fair to note that the USAAF also resisted admitting blacks to flight training and eventually employed blacks only in segregated squadrons.

Beyond these objective criteria, Cochran had the luxury of being extremely subjective. Pilot training was available across the United States throughout the war at countless private flying schools run by pilots exempt from the draft due to age or disability. Any woman who could raise the money for flying lessons could therefore obtain the relatively low entry requirement of thirty-five flying hours. Thus, in contrast to the ATA, Cochran could draw on an *expanding* pool of candidates with flying qualifications. As soon as the WAFS and WFTD were announced, patriotic and adventurous young women all across America eagerly rushed to *learn* to fly, at their own expenses, just in order to be able to qualify for the WASP. In the event, more than 25,000 women applied for acceptance into the WFTD/WASP.

At this distance in time, it is impossible to determine what subjective criteria Cochran applied in order to select from the 25,000 applicants the 1,830 women who were admitted into the programme. Cochran's guidelines to the selection boards were to look for 'clean-cut, stable appearing young girls'[7] – but this criteria must surely have applied to the bulk of the 25,000 applicants and not just the 1,830 women accepted. Allegedly, Cochran also was very concerned about the 'image' of her pilots, but this did not stop her from hiring a strip-tease performer and a professional gambler. In short, her selection appears to have been not only subjective but capricious – at all events no longer comprehensible.

TERMS OF SERVICE, RANKS, UNIFORM, PAY AND BENEFITS

ATA

Significantly, throughout the short history of the ATA, the women pilots were employees of the same organisation as the men – not segregated into a separate women's organisation such as the WAAF, ATS (Auxiliary Territorial Services) or WRNS (Women's Royal Naval Service). Furthermore, the Director General of Civil Aviation had declared shortly after the outbreak of the war that the 'terms and conditions of employment, apart from basic remuneration, will be identical with those of male pilots'.[8]

Women thus wore the same uniform with the same insignia and were entitled to hold the same ranks as their male colleagues, provided they had the same qualifications and duties. They were issued with fleece-lined flying boots, helmets, goggles and the so-called 'Sidcot suits' for flying; these were overalls with detachable linings, very warm and practical for flying. Unfortunately, they were far less practical for women once they were on the ground, since they were too warm and bulky for moving about in – and completely unacceptable attire in an Officers' Mess. The women preferred – and generally managed to acquire – the coveted Irvin flight jackets, made famous by the Fighter Boys in the Battle of Britain. Eventually, bowing to the facts as in so many other instances, officialdom gave up its lost battle of reserving this item of clothing for the 'fighting forces' and officially allowed the women to buy them at their own expense.

As for the ATA uniform proper, it was a mixture between the dark blue, double-breasted and gold-trimmed uniforms of the airlines and the single-breasted uniform of the RAF. With the dark blue, single-breasted tunic, the women wore dark skirts or trousers, light-blue shirts and black tie. With skirts, black stockings and shoes were required. This uniform had already been selected in 1939 and was introduced very rapidly (by wartime standards). It was soon familiar and respected at all RAF aerodromes. The women wore this uniform right from the start, and felt it was 'very smart'.[9]

As the ATA expanded, so did the rank structure. Instead of just two ranks, as initially conceived, there were eventually nine. The lowest rank, introduced at the same time that training was instituted in the ATA, was cadet, and this applied to pilots in the first stage of training. Immediately after qualifying on light, single-engined aircraft, ATA pilots were promoted to Third Officer. After qualifying on light twin-engined aircraft, ATA pilots were promoted to Second Officer. The rank of First Officer was granted after checking out on the heavy twins or four-engined aircraft. All ranks above these, e.g. Flight Captain, Captain, Commander etc. were designations for pilots who held command or administrative functions.

Significantly, the ATA ranks were fully independent of previous ranks and status. Thus an RAF Air Vice-Marshal and a Rear Admiral of the Royal Navy 'went through the routine as "cadets" with the rest'.[10] This egalitarian spirit greatly benefited the women as it put the emphasis squarely on what a pilot was doing in the ATA with no reference to extraneous factors such as past profession, wealth, title, age or sex.

All pilots benefited in equal degree from the excellent medical services provided. These were developed to a 'state of efficiency second to none. Where facilities were not provided by the RAF, the ferry pilots had their own doctors and nurses, sick quarters, crash and ambulance crews'.[11] Medical care was offered free of charge to ATA personnel, and was not only available in emergencies but also ensured that pilots employed in flying duties 'were fit in accordance with the Air Ministry and insurance requirements'.[12] Full medical records were kept, and the ATA medical staff visited pilots who were ill. Last but not least, from inception all pilots flying with the ATA were covered by insurance against death, blindness or the loss of limb to a sum of £2,000 (at that time roughly $10,000).[13]

In only one regard were women explicitly disadvantaged in the ATA, and this was with regard to pay. It had been determined at establishment that the lowest ranking pilots of the ATA should earn the same salary as junior officers with British Airways, or between £350 and £400 annually. Women, however, were discriminated against because the Director General of Civil Aviation argued that 'the Treasury invariably insisted on a percentage reduction in basic salaries paid to women for the same jobs as men . . . .'[14] The salary for women Third Officers was therefore set at £230 p. a. plus £8 per month flying pay for a total of £326 p. a. or roughly 20 per cent less than their male colleagues of equivalent rank.

In 1942, however, the contracts offered to the American women pilots gave them the identical pay to the *men* of equivalent rank. Perhaps this served as a catalyst to equal pay for all the women pilots, or perhaps it was the visit of Mrs Churchill and Mrs Roosevelt in October 1942. During this highly publicised visit, the first woman pilot training on four-engined bombers was introduced, which – inevitably – focused public attention on the outstanding job being done by the women pilots of the ATA. Shortly afterwards an article appeared in the British press reporting with implied criticism the pay discrepancy between men and women of the ATA. Gower appears to have raised the issue with d'Erlanger at about this time and then taken her case to Sir Stafford Cripps, the Minister of Aircraft Production. Cripps, like the Director General of Civil Aviation in 1939, put the blame for the pay discrepancy on the Treasury. Gower, however, 'warned' him that he might be asked in Parliament why women were not receiving equal pay for equal work. When, on 18 May 1943 MP Irene Ward raised the issue in the House of Commons, Cripps 'was able to respond by saying that as from June, their [women ATA pilot's] salaries would be brought into line with the men'.[15]

From June 1943 onwards the women pilots of the ATA enjoyed full equality with the male pilots of the organisation. Furthermore, as one historian of the ATA, former ATA pilot Lettice Curtis, points out: 'it seems highly probable that this was the first time that the government gave its blessing to equal pay for equal work within an organisation under its jurisdiction.'[16] As this was also the period in which the ATA women were qualifying on ever larger and heavier aircraft, entitling them to the higher salary of more senior rank, this was more than a symbolic victory. Pay for a First Officer (flying heavy twin or four-engine aircraft) was set at £700 p.a. or more than double that of a Third Officer.

It is noteworthy that apparently no one within the ATA itself questioned the principle of paying the women at the same rates as the men – or Gower would not have been given the go-ahead to talk to Sir Stafford Cripps. Equally interesting is the speed with which the MAP conceded the point, preferring to ward off a parliamentary query rather than wait it out. It is, after all, rather hard to imagine that Parliament would have been prepared to start a widespread campaign for equal pay for equal work at this point in time. Such a policy would have cost the government millions of pounds if applied to the nearly half-a-million women serving in the women's auxiliary services. This easy and exceptional victory for the women of the ATA is made even more dramatic when contrasted with the disastrous efforts of the WASP to gain equality of pay and treatment through legislation.

WAFS/WFTD/WASP

The women who went into training with the WFTD were hired at a rate of $150/month during training and then had their pay increased to $250/month on graduation. From this salary, the women pilots had to pay for food, clothing and transportation. Only flying kit and text books were provided at Army expense. A green Second Lieutenant of the USAAF received at this time a base pay of $150. Once the various supplements such as flight pay, monthly quarters and uniform allowance were added to the base pay, however, the actual monthly remuneration of a Second Lieutenant straight out of flight school came to $291, a differential of 14 per cent above that of the women graduates of flight training.[17]

While the comparison of civilian and military salaries is always muddied by the various non-monetary benefits allowed members of the armed forces, the FERD had a large number of male civilian pilots on its pay roll. They provide a better measure of comparative rates of pay. While the women flying for FERD in the WAFS received the same $250 per month as the graduates of the WFTD, the civilian male pilots flying for FERD earned $380 monthly. This is a differential to the men's advantage of roughly 35 per cent.[18] The Ferrying Command justified the pay difference at the time the programme was initiated with the then valid contention that the women were to be restricted to flying light, simple aircraft (trainers and liaison aircraft), while the men were expected to progress up to heavy bombers and transatlantic flying.

Unfortunately, as the women pilots transitioned onto ever heavier and more difficult aircraft, including the four-engined heavy bombers, their pay remained fixed. Equally, the women flying target-towing missions or performing other dangerous and highly skilled tasks, such as instructing or maintenance testing, were also given no increase in pay. While the men of the USAAF could expect their salary to increase steadily as they were promoted in accordance with their abilities, experience and duties, the women could not. As First Lieutenants, male pilots earned the monthly rate of $330 and as Captains $396. Yet, although the women increasingly found themselves performing the same duties as First Lieutenants and Captains, their salary was frozen at the comparatively low rate of $250. (This was, incidentally, almost identical to the salary of an RAF Squadron Leader at this time.) Even if one accepts the principle of lower pay for women generally, the fact that the WASP pay structure never took experience, duties or command function into account was clearly a point of weakness.

If pay had been the only differential, however, it is fair to assume that the American women pilots would never have felt any need for complaint. Almost all women who flew with the WASP stress the extent to which they felt privileged to be allowed to fly with the USAAF at all. When they were forced out of service, a large number of them volunteered to fly for the USAAF without remuneration. Pay was not the issue that proved fatal to the WASP. The terms of service, on the other hand, arguably were. It was, at least allegedly, the need to bring WASP terms of service in line with that of men that caused Cochran to seek militarisation for her organisation, and it was the failure to obtain that goal that induced her to demand the deactivation of the entire WASP programme.

Women applying to either the WAFS or WFTD were required to report at their own expense, and to pay for their food and lodgings. Only after passing out of a probationary period of ninety days (in the case of the WAFS) or graduating from flying training (in the case of the WFTD/WASP) were the women hired as civilian employees of the USAAF. As civilian employees, however, the WASP were not in any strict legal sense subject to military discipline. This fact was often obscured – even to the participants – by the fact that the women were sworn into office and generally accorded all the privileges of officers, including access to the Officer's Mess. Furthermore, the women serving with the USAAF were expected to take part in parades, salute superiors and be saluted by other ranks. However, the critical point from the Army point of view was that the women could literally quit any time they liked. They were under no obligation to serve until the Army saw fit to discharge them. This was undoubtedly a serious disadvantage since, except for the original twenty-eight WAFS, who went onto active service after only four weeks' orientation training, the USAAF invested many months of training into the women pilots. Yet not a few women took advantage of the freedom to resign for personal reasons long before the Army had come close to recouping its investment in them.

From the women's point of view, the most serious drawback of their ambiguous status was reflected in the fact that they were not strictly entitled to treatment at Army medical facilities. Only while at Avenger Field (the Army Air Base, which had been allocated to the WFTD) did the women have access to a dedicated medical staff. Once the women were assigned to active duty, they were dispersed about the country at various Commands and bases and their access to medical care was completely at the discretion – or whim – of their respective commanders. Some base commanders treated the women as if they were an integral part of their command – and some did not. While many WASP were treated at military hospitals, there were instances of seriously ill WASP being denied treatment at military hospitals. Furthermore, at no time were the WASP covered by death or disability insurance. The thirty-eight WASP killed while on active service left their families nothing. The Army did not even pay to ship the bodies home.

Yet perhaps the most difficult aspect for the women serving in the WASP was the confusion with regard to rank and uniform. After all, the WASP were healthy young women and they were rarely ill; they did not want to and probably did not spend a great deal of time thinking about being injured, maimed or killed. The issue of rank and identity, however, was a daily problem, one that plagued them throughout their service with the USAAF.

While the WASP were granted 'officer's privileges' they were not officers and they had no rank whatsoever – neither military ones nor ranks similar to those used by the airlines or merchant navy. Nor did they, until almost eighteen months after founding, have official uniforms.

The importance of uniforms can hardly be overstated. Kate Adie in her book, *Corsets to Camouflage*, points out that at the start of the 20th century British women had 'recognised that uniform has its own power, commands respect and endows the wearer with a status . . . .'[19] The American women who joined the WAFS very quickly felt the disadvantages of not being in uniform. The women were encountering enough prejudice without adding fuel to the fire by offending against military codes for neatness and uniformity. The WAFS founder, Nancy Love (tipped off by her husband on the staff of ATC), therefore moved rapidly to standardise the attire of the women serving in the WAFS. She selected a modest, practical 'uniform' that the WAFS could rapidly purchase or have made. It consisted of slacks or skirt, belted-jacket with padded shoulders and patch pockets and a fore-and-aft cap, all in a soft shade of grey-green, and a tan shirt worn with a black tie. The women were allowed to wear the wings of the ATC and the patch of the FERD – as did the male civilian pilots flying with the same unit.

In contrast, the women in training at the WFTD simply wore civilian clothes when they weren't flying. For flying, they were issued with flying overalls. It is a commentary on the indifference of the base Commanding Officer, the inexperience of the woman appointed 'Establishment Officer' and the incompetence or insensitivity of Jacqueline Cochran herself, that no one took any interest in providing any kind of uniform for the women of the WFTD. Indeed, fully seven months after the start of the WFTD programme, as the women approached graduation, it was the graduates themselves – not their commanders – who took things into their own hands. The graduating pilots jointly decided on a 'uniform' and purchased (at their own expense) open-necked white shirts, khaki overseas caps and khaki trousers from the PX.[20]

Even that highly coveted and prized symbol of graduation from flight school, pilot's wings, were an afterthought for the WFTD. As the time for graduation approached, the 'Establishment Officer' realised that a large contingent of senior officers and reporters was flying in to see wings pinned on the chests of the first women graduates of a USAAF flying training detachment – and there were no wings to pin. Unable to reach Jacqueline Cochran, the Establishment Officer improvised with the help of an Army Lieutenant working at the air base in another capacity. In the absence of any official design, however, WFTD and WASP wings varied from class to class depending on what could be purchased and adapted most readily at any specific time. It was not until 1944 that an official design was available for graduates.

Yet, the importance of the uniform can hardly be over-stated. Cornelia Fort, one of the original WAFS, wrote shortly before her death in a flying accident with the WASP:

> For all the gals in the WAFS, I think the most concrete moment of happiness came at our first review. Suddenly and for the first

time we were part of something larger. *Because of our uniforms,* which we had earned, we were marching with the men, marching with all the freedom-loving people in the world. [Italics added.][21]

However, because there were so very few WAFS and WASP and the US Army was so large, the improvised uniforms never became familiar even at the USAAF bases to which the women flew, much less to the general public.

Furthermore, while the WAFS looked 'neat and workmanlike in their gabardine grays', the recent graduates from the WFTD stood out 'like pumpkins in a strawberry patch. They report[ed] . . . in coats of many colors, and wearing shoes to make a cobbler weep'.[22] For example, when the first WASP reported for B-17 training, proud as they were to be part of the programme, they were 'embarrassed because they look[ed] so scraggly in this 'n' that clothing'.[23] Others complained of feeling 'depressingly non-regulation at the Officer's Club in field jackets'.[24]

Because of the absence of an official – and lack of recognition for the improvised – uniform, WASP were sometimes denied the priority seating they are entitled to on domestic airlines. WASP who had to stop for weather or technical difficulties often encountered discourtesy and scepticism at bases across the country where the USAAF personnel was unfamiliar with the women pilot's programme. Because they were 'out of uniform' WASP frequently had difficulty getting accommodation or access to the Officer's Mess or Club.

Worse still, the absence of a recognisable and official uniform resulted in WASP getting arrested for 'impersonating' officers on more than one occasion. In an incident described in detail later, they were put in jail for being in trousers in public after dark. In another instance the consequences were even more humiliating. Former WASP, Byrd Howell Granger, described the 'adventures' of four of her colleagues as follows:

WASPs, who still have no uniform of any kind . . . wear what they have . . . .[O]n a southern delivery, 4 land as evening is creeping over the nearby town of Lebanon, TN. The man in the airport office has a bad time trying to find quarters for them. Seems the Red and the Blue Army are holding manoeuvres, which means thousands and thousands of rambunctious GIs loose in the town . . .

GIs spot the young women entering the hotel and word roars through town, 'Come and get 'em!' Wolf whistles are whispers compared to the noise of men yelling and yowling. Men in the next room pound on the thin walls. Others rattle the door ceaselessly and with fervor. It's enough to bring out the Military Police and it does. The black armbanded soldiers deem the four young women undoubtedly members of the oldest profession in the world. Arrest is swift and not gentle. Off to the local hoosegow they go for mug shots and incarceration. One woman pilot . . . speaks up, demanding that the MPs telephone Col. D'Arcy at Romulus. It takes time to penetrate that she really means it. The ensuing call nearly melts the wires as the Romulus CO reads the riot act.[25]

The lack of official uniform was directly attributable to Jacqueline Cochran. Although the USAAF suggested that Nancy Love's unofficial WAFS uniform be adopted by all women pilots and made official, Cochran resisted vehemently. According to most sources, she considered the WAFS uniform too drab. Cochran had previously run a cosmetics firm, and she was determined that her WASP were going to look smart. When she finally got around to addressing the issue of uniform, almost a year after the WFTD had been formed, she hired a New York designer and selected a professional model to present the uniform thus designed to General Arnold. The alternative uniforms, an adaptation of the Nurse Corps uniform and a WAC-like uniform, were modelled by female Pentagon employees. Cochran's particular coup was selecting blue for the uniform, because she knew General Arnold wanted an independent Air Force and favoured blue for the uniform of his coveted future service.[26]

While the uniform Cochran presented was undoubtedly smart and had been approved by late summer 1943, it was not available to the WASP until the spring of 1944 – and then only in small quantities. The uniforms consequently only gradually trickled into service during the spring of 1944. By then, many of the women who had been proud to wear their improvised uniform deeply resented being asked to wear a new uniform – no matter how smart. One of the original WAFS, and the only 'ordinary' pilot to receive a decoration, Barbara Erickson, almost refused to wear the new uniform at the ceremony in which she was to be honoured by General Arnold. According to Granger, just a half hour before the ceremony:

Miss Erickson . . . was wearing a WAF uniform and asserting quite loudly that she [was] a WAF and proud of it and ha[d] no intention of putting on a blue WASP uniform to be awarded that medal.[27]

The new 'Santiago blue' designer uniform had no meaning for her. Nor did the expensive, designer uniform sit well with a cost-conscious Congress already hostile to the unauthorised training programme. While the costs imputed to the designer uniforms were undoubtedly exaggerated, the mere fact that they *were* designer uniforms, tended to underline the 'glamorous' nature of the WASP at a time when this was a negative – indeed poisonous – descriptive.

Last but not least, the distinctive, flashy blue uniforms were not integrative. While the improvised uniform had also been different from Army or WAC uniforms, it was similar and discrete. Cochran's uniform stood out because of its colour scheme and its beret. The USAAF officers wore khaki and brown, not blue, and they wore either fore-and-aft or peaked caps, not berets. Thus the uniform, when it finally arrived, served more than ever to emphasise that the women flying with the WASP were *not* part of the USAAF, but something separate and distinct. It drew attention to the differences between the men and the women rather than suggesting that the women were colleagues doing the same job for the same cause as the men with whom they served.

Notes:

1 Walker, Diana Barnato, *Spreading My Wings*, 2003, 45–6.
2 Cheeseman, 53.
3 Lucas, Y.M., *WAAF with Wings*, 1992, 21.
4 Simbeck, *Daughter of the Air: The Brief Soaring Life of Cornelia Fort*, 1999, 126.
5 Rickman, Sarah Byrn, *The Originals: The Women's Auxiliary Ferrying Squadron of World War II*, 2001, 55.
6 Merryman, 16.
7 Cochran, Final Report, 4.
8 Curtis, 14
9 Du Cros, Rosemary, *ATA Girl: Memoirs of a Wartime Ferry Pilot*, 1983, 39.
10 Cheeseman, 47.
11 Cheeseman, 95.
12 Curtis, 168.
13 Curtis, 91.
14 Fahie, Michael, *A Harvest of Memories: The Life of Pauline Gower MBE*, 1995, 141.
15 Fahie, 178.
16 Curtis, 200.
17 Granger provides a comprehensive table of comparative remuneration and benefits, A-101.
18 Keil, 114.
19 Adie, Kate, *Corsets to Camouflage: Women and War*, 2003, 46.

20   Verges, 86.
21   Fort, Cornelia, quoted in Simbeck, 152.
22   Granger, 124.
23   Granger, 200.
24   Granger, 280.
25   Granger, 191–2.
26   Granger, 92.
27   Granger, 359.

CHAPTER THREE

Winning
Their Wings

TRAINING WOMEN TO FLY MILITARY AIRCRAFT

From March 1943 to December 1944 the USAAF Base at Avenger Field near Sweetwater, Texas, became the first military installation in US history to be exclusively dedicated to training women. Over 1,500 women went through roughly seven months of flight training in this dusty, Texan town in the middle of nowhere, encountering rattlesnakes and enduring military discipline in Spartan surroundings for the privilege of 'learning to fly the Army way'. A look at the WASP websites or a quick thumbing through any of the books published about the WASP will provide dozens of photos of smiling girls in baggy 'zoot suits' (ridiculously ill-fitting men's flying overalls) and turbans. The friendships formed at Avenger often lasted a lifetime, but the results of the training itself were far more ambiguous. While Cochran bragged that her training programme had proved women could be subjected to exactly the same regime as the men and emerge equally competent, two Air Inspectors of the USAAF reported on appalling inadequacies at Avenger Field and the USAAF Ferry Command called the graduates 'airport pilots'.

Meanwhile, on the other side of the Atlantic, the ATA also faced the task of training pilots to meet military standards for ferrying. The ATA chose a different route from that of the WASP, evolving its own training programme rather than trying to replicate RAF training. The results were uniformly praised, not only by the pilots who went through the training, but by the RAF and FAA, which depended on the ATA's competence. What then were the differences?

ATA

The defining characteristic of ATA training was that it had been designed for the sole purpose of providing competent ferry pilots for the ATA. As outlined earlier, initially no training was undertaken by the ATA, because only highly qualified pilots were accepted and the task of familiarising these pilots with Service aircraft was the responsibility of the RAF. Admittedly, this so-called 'conversion' training tended to be somewhat perfunctory. The wartime demands made on the RAF training establishment were simply too great to allow for the more thorough training that might have been advisable. Furthermore, because the RAF did not want the trouble of accommodating women at its training facilities, women pilots received training at the women's Ferry Pool at Hatfield from the women already there. The level of informality there appears to have been comparable to that experienced by their male colleagues at the hands of the RAF.

This state of affairs continued throughout 1940. Tony Phelps, a former RAF pilot who joined the ATA in the winter of 1940/41, remembers having only one check flight in a Tiger Moth and then being put to work. Ann Welch, a woman pilot who joined the ATA at roughly the same time, recalls being told to fly around in a Tiger Moth for just one day 'to get her hand in again' before she started ferrying. The conversion to single-engine service type aircraft at this time likewise consisted of just one day doing dual and solo circuits on the Miles Magister.

Yet, while this rather haphazard process of 'converting' experienced pilots to operational aircraft continued in practice, the decision had already been made at the Ministry of Aircraft Production that a dedicated flying school for the ATA must be established. Namely, during the height of the Battle of Britain, Lord Beaverbrook demanded control of BOAC's training establishment. The school and staff were moved to White Waltham and BOAC's Chief Flying Instructor, MacMillan, was given responsibility for developing a comprehensive training programme for the ATA.

The challenge MacMillan faced was that he had to train pilots rapidly to fly a vast variety of different aircraft types *safely* in wartime conditions. The goals of ATA training were to create pilots with great versatility with regard to type of aircraft flown, and great circumspection with regard to style of flying. An almost equally important goal of ATA training was to teach pilots how to fly safely cross-country in wartime conditions, which included coping with barrage balloons, camouflaged airfields, trigger-happy anti-aircraft batteries and enemy action – along with the usual hazards such as unpredictable weather and mechanical failure.

The training programme that MacMillan devised was thus carefully designed to train ATA ferry pilots – not fighter, bomber, airline or any other kind of pilot. It was a highly efficient, streamlined training scheme that placed maximum emphasis on optimising pilot utilisation and 'learning by doing'. The key characteristics of ATA training were:

1) training by 'class' of aircraft,

2) gradual progression from light to heavy aircraft,

3) heavy emphasis on cross-country experience and navigation,

4) alternating periods of training and periods of ferrying,

5) progress at one's own, individual pace,

6) the absence of training in extraneous skills such as blind-flying, aerobatics, formation flying or R/T use.

Undoubtedly, the most difficult aspect of MacMillan's task was to train pilots rapidly to fly a vast variety of different aircraft types. To achieve this goal, MacMillan developed the concept of grouping aircraft into 'classes' with similar flying characteristics, and then providing the pilots with very succinct and practical written information on each specific type of aircraft. The idea was that a pilot trained on any one aircraft of a certain class must then be qualified and could be expected to fly *all* aircraft of that given class. This entailed the 'most careful and wise "classing" of aircraft', but also the development of Handling and Pilot's Notes to help pilots fly completely unfamiliar aircraft safely.

Remarkably, this system of training worked extremely well. All pilots flying with the ATA indeed proved capable of flying aircraft they had never seen – much less flown – before on the basis of the training they had received and some 'Pilot's Notes'. (The Pilot's and Handling Notes are described in detail in Chapter 5.) As an ATA Operations Officer worded it: 'This ability to fly any aircraft from a book, after the all-round technique had been mastered, surprised the pilots themselves at times.'[1]

The six classes of aircraft introduced were:

Class I: light single-engine aircraft, generally training and liaison aircraft such as the various de Havilland Moths, but also some obsolete operational aircraft such as Gladiators.

Class II: advanced single-engine aircraft, primarily fighter aircraft such as Hurricanes, Spitfires, Typhoons, Mustangs, and the infamous Airacobras, but also other 'tricky' aircraft such as Walruses.

Class III: light twin-engine aircraft, generally more advanced training aircraft such as Oxfords, and small passenger aircraft such as Ansons and Dominies.

Class IV: advanced twin-engine aircraft, predominantly light and medium bombers, such as Blenheims, Wellingtons, Hampdens, Beaufighters, and Mosquitos, but also transports like the Dakota and even the first operational jet, the Meteor.

Class V: four-engine aircraft, predominantly heavy bombers such as Halifaxes, Lancasters, Stirlings, Fortresses and Liberators, but also the large transports such as Skymasters.

Class VI: flying boats such as Catalinas and Sunderlands as well as the smaller seaplanes (Walruses and Sea Otters) if landed on water.

The ATA required its pilots to progress up through the various classes of aircraft from the lightest and simplest aircraft through the progressively more difficult types of aircraft (i.e. from Class I up through Class II, III etc.) up to the highest level suitable for an individual pilot. Pilots were not, however, specialists. A pilot holding qualifications in the highest classification of aircraft might still, if the need arose, be expected to ferry a Class I aircraft – or anything in between. The emphasis remained on flexibility and versatility, at the individual as well as the organisational level.

In line with this ethos, ATA training was tailored very closely to the individual needs and capabilities of its pilots. Beyond a certain limited, ground-training that was provided to all pilots, training was very individualistic. Pilots progressed as far and as fast as their skills and temperament allowed, without being under any compulsion to keep pace with other pilots or being subjected to the fear of 'wash-outing' if they failed to move up within arbitrary time limits.

Mary de Bunsen's experience in the ATA is a good example of this philosophy of individual progress. In her memoirs, she described the care taken to see that she progressed at her own pace – which could be very different from that of other pilots. She personally found the transition to the Hurricane 'a bit breathtaking for inexperienced pilots' and was happy to be sent to the newly formed training pool for experience. But she reports:

> Faith Bennett and Jean Bird, who had done their Class II conversions with me, had managed to keep their heads above water and were allowed to go on ferrying Hurricanes, thereby gaining well-deserved seniority which it took me months to catch up . . . I emerged at the end of March restored to health, with high morale and a good report.[2]

When later she had a series of minor accidents, the decision was made to take her off the faster types of aircraft (Class II) but to let her fly the lighter twins (Class III). Again, after a period of flying with a different pool and regaining her confidence, she was then allowed to convert on to the fast, operational twins (Class IV), and flew these very successfully right to the end of the war.

It was possible to allow pilots to progress at their own pace because training was confined to short periods of training at the training schools followed by 'on the job' training at the Ferry Pools. After qualifying on a new class of aircraft, pilots returned to their Ferry Pools and resumed ferrying – including now the new class of aircraft on which they had just qualified. They were thus rapidly given an opportunity to put their newly acquired skills to work. The result was that the skills obtained in training were quickly solidified in the working environment. Diana Barnato Walker puts it this way: 'I had progressed so gently up the flying ladder, through the well-organised schooling, into the "training pool", and had delivered countless Hurricanes plus other single-engined types, so another new type didn't bother me at all.'[3] Later, she describes being 'nursed a bit' in that she was only given 'easy' flights with new classes of aircraft until she was comfortable with them.

Many former ATA pilots stressed in interviews, letters and memoirs the extent to which this system helped to build confidence. Furthermore, the system enabled the experienced pilots and Flight Commanders at the Ferry Pools to coach and encourage the more junior pilots. All ATA pilots benefited from the fact that many of their colleagues were men and women with years of commercial or military flying experience. The older pilots were able to give newcomers advice and tips not in a formal schoolroom setting but informally while they were actively flying for the ATA.

Formal training on the various classes of aircraft was conducted at the ATA's flying schools. The first of these was opened at White Waltham in March of 1941 with twenty flying instructors – all highly experienced men drawn from BOAC – and twenty-nine aircraft. However, the need for training grew with the growing establishment and the declining experience of new recruits. Just one year later, the number of aircraft employed at the training establishment had increased to well over 100 and it soon became evident that it was no longer safe to conduct all training at a single airfield. The slower elementary and primary trainers were hazards to the faster and/or multi-engined service aeroplanes – and vice versa. The decision was therefore taken to move the Elementary Flying School to Luton, leaving only more advanced conversion training at White Waltham. When *ab initio* training was introduced at the ATA, 'an 'infants' school was opened as a satellite to Luton at a pleasantly secluded little airfield at Barton in the Clay'.[4] Last but not least, starting in December 1942, four-engine training was conducted by ATA instructors at a Bomber Command aerodrome in Yorkshire to ensure reasonable maintenance of the aircraft involved in training.

The types of aircraft employed for training corresponded to the aircraft used by the RAF itself for training. Thus elementary training was carried out primarily on Tiger Moths and Magisters, Class II training primarily on Masters and Harvards, and Class III and IV training mostly on Oxfords and Blenheims. The Halifax became the standard trainer for heavy bombers.

The original instructors at the ATA's training school were all experienced BOAC instructors. When these instructors were recalled to BOAC to start preparing post-war training for the Corporation in March 1943, the ATA drew instructors from its own ranks and, to a lesser extent, from the RAF. While the original BOAC instructors had been men of vast experience both as pilots and instructors, the ATA's own instructors had the advantage of having done for a number of years the very job for which they were training pupils. It is notable that from this point (1943) onwards, women instructors were employed to train both men and women. Particularly impressive was the employment of Joan Hughes, one of the original eight women pilots, as an instructor on the heavy bombers.

Once the training programme was up and running, the routine for all new pilots entering the ATA followed roughly the following pattern – regardless of previous rank, position or title. Cadets were given a medical, signed articles and swore not to pass on official secrets. They were then given a basic ground course in meteorology, map-reading, navigation, signals, engines and other technical subjects. As the number of types and the sophistication of aircraft increased, so too did the technical training. Nevertheless, the ground course lasted only a total of two weeks per course (i.e. per class of aircraft). The idea was to give pilots 'an appreciation of the principles involved, and not a complete understanding' of the topics covered.[5]

Following the two weeks in ground school, ATA cadets were allowed to start flying dual in an open cockpit training aircraft such as the Gypsy Moth or the Magister. When the flying instructor felt a pupil was ready, the cadet would be allowed to fly solo in the same machine. The cadet, once comfortable with this aircraft, would be assigned thirty cross-country flights to various destinations across the country. These flights honed navigation skills and helped cadets become familiar with the hazards of flying in wartime Britain: avoiding barrage balloons and anti-aircraft batteries, finding camouflaged airfields, navigating without radio etc. An ATA pilot was awarded his or her wings following successful completion of these cross-country flights, was promoted from cadet to Third Officer and then assigned to a Ferry Pool.

The next stage of training took place 'on the job'. In addition to ferrying light aircraft, the new Third Officer would also be given responsibility for flying the smaller taxi aircraft to airfields to collect ferry pilots. Class I pilots were not allowed to carry passengers, however, and the rule was that the most senior pilot flew the taxi aircraft when there was more than one person in it. Class I pilots were required to have some fifty hours of taxi work before going on to Class II conversion training, but – as mentioned above – the ATA placed emphasis on each pilot moving at his or her own pace. When the Pool CO felt a pilot was ready for conversion training, he or she would be sent back to flying school for Class II training.

Here, the routine was much the same as before. A couple weeks of technical training on the ground would be followed by dual and then solo instruction in a more advanced trainer such as the Miles Master or the North American Harvard. When a pilot satisfied the flying instructor, he/she would be given a chance to fly the school Hurricane. Following successful conclusion of Class II training, the pilot again returned to his/her Ferry Pool and was qualified to carry a significantly greater share of the ferrying load until, again at the discretion of the Pool Commander, a pilot would be sent for training on Class III aircraft. The same followed for Class IV and Class V.

In this way, a pilot not only progressed at his/her own pace, but was available for ferrying duties in the shortest possible time. The entire system enabled pilots to spend as little time as practical in training and as much time as possible doing actual ferry and/or taxi service with the

ATA. As a rule, pilots with even a little experience rarely needed more than one month of training to obtain their Class I qualification and could then start performing useful service. In just four to six months – most of that time spent ferrying trainers or flying light taxi aircraft – ATA pilots would be qualified on Class II aircraft and could start pulling their full weight.

The more experienced a pilot, the shorter was the time needed for conversion. The very experienced women pilots who later converted to medium bombers did so in just three days and to heavy bombers with just three-and-a-half hours dual and three-and-a-half hours solo. Pilots of heavier types of aircraft in practice often did more 'dual' flying while 'on the job'. Because these larger aircraft were often used to transport other pilots to the airfields where they were to collect their own ferry aircraft or to bring them back after a delivery, a pilot newly converted to heavier aircraft could often find an (informal) opportunity to fly co-pilot on such flights. Curtis says, furthermore, that it was customary to fly at least ten deliveries on a familiar heavy bomber – such as the Halifax, on which the pilots trained – before moving on to the next type of heavy bomber.

The American women pilots recruited by Cochran in 1942, despite having a minimum of 300 flying hours, were also put through the ATA training programme. The emphasis of this training was on navigation in Britain, where conditions were very different to those found in the US.

The training for *ab initio* pilots was, naturally, somewhat lengthier. The first two weeks of training were – as for experienced pilots – spent in ground school, covering such subjects as the theory of flight, aircraft and their engines, meteorology, navigation, ferrying procedure, parachute use, maps and signals and the like. There then followed basic training in the open-cockpit, low monoplane Magister to learn simple take-offs, landings and 'circuits'. As a rule, there was one instructor for every three to four pupils. Once the cadets had soloed, they were taught steep turns, forced landings, compass use, and cross-country navigation all while flying dual, interspersed with more practice flying solo. The next stage of training was roughly twenty cross-country trips solo, along with learning about emergency landings. An important aspect of training was being checked out in an aircraft, which the cadets had *not* previously flown, to see how they got on in a strange machine. Finally, they had a test flight with the Chief Flying Instructor in the form of a cross-country trip including a (simulated) forced landing along the way. Only then were pilots posted to No. 5 Training Ferry Pool, based on the same airfield as the Flying Training School.

Here, the new pilot would carry out ferry work of light aircraft until he/she was sufficiently proficient for the next stage of training, Class II, followed by another spell with the Training Pool. Only after conversion to light twins (Class III) was a pilot posted to a regular Ferry Pool, and promoted to Third Officer.

> This method of dealing with the new pilot meant that she was able to have more personal supervision than would be possible in the rough-and-tumble of an ordinary Ferry Pool, and at the same time she would still be earning more than her keep, by ferrying more and more of the types within her scope, and so gain quickly the experience to enable her to go on to more advanced aircraft.[6]

Noticeably absent from ATA training were any kind of aerobatics, formation flying, R/T (radio) use or blind (instrument) flying. The reason for the absence of aerobatics training was quite simply that ATA pilots not only had no need for such training, but also were positively prohibited from engaging in such activities. Their job was the safe delivery of the aircraft and any kind of 'mucking about' only endangered both aircraft and pilot unnecessarily. Formation flying was equally unnecessary. It was not usual for more than one aircraft to be flying in the same direction at the same time. Even if several aircraft were going the same way, the pilots often came from different Pools and were not familiar with each other's style of flying. Since formation flying was dangerous, particularly for pilots who did not practise together regularly, there was no reason for ATA pilots to take unnecessary risks by flying in close formation.

The reason there was no training in radio use was simply that up until almost the end of the war the aircraft the ATA flew had no operable radios. This was because deliveries from the factories to the Maintenance Unit (MU) occurred before any radio had been installed, and subsequent deliveries over short distances did not justify tuning the radio for the needs of ATA. Furthermore, it was essential throughout the war to keep radio communications to a minimum for security reasons.

The lack of instrument training is perhaps the most controversial aspect of ATA training. With the exception of the Air Movement's Flight after it started flying regularly to the Continent in 1944, ATA pilots were supposed to fly 'contact' – i.e. always in sight of the ground. Curtis suggests that providing training in instrument flying would have encouraged pilots to defy this rule. Another ATA pilot (who later became an airline Captain flying such long-distance routes as South

Africa and the Atlantic) also felt that given the lack of radio contact, instrument instruction would have encouraged pilots to take unnecessary risks. He cites the case of Amy Johnson, the record breaking long distance pilot, who got caught above cloud in January 1941 and ran out of fuel. Although she parachuted out, she landed in the freezing Thames Estuary and drowned before she could be rescued.

Without doubt, flying above cloud was extremely dangerous in the absence of radio contact to the ground. Unfortunately, however, it was not always possible to avoid getting caught in cloud given the unpredictable and very changeable English weather. All pilots were caught out in bad weather at one time or another and usually more than once in the course of their service. This led one American ATA pilot to claim: 'They should have been teaching it [instrument flying] to their pilots instead of forbidding them to do it; had they done so, many lives might have been saved.'[7]

While there is no question that many pilots were the victims of poor weather, it is impossible to draw a direct correlation between losses in poor weather to an absence of instrument training. After all, the most prominent victim of poor weather, Amy Johnson, in fact had training on instruments prior to joining the ATA. Many other ATA pilots who were lost in weather were equally experienced. Nevertheless, it is understandable that many of the less experienced pilots without instrument training felt a *need* for this kind of instruction and undertook efforts to gain it on their own initiative. Freydis Sharland relates: 'I soon discovered it was essential to learn some instrument flying. Thus whenever I was held up at an RAF Station I would go to the link instructor and have an hour's tuition.'[8] Diana Barnato Walker also relates a very close call when caught in a weather 'inversion' in which she landed – quite by mistake – at the RAF Navigation and Blind Flying Establishment at Windrush; she too immediately took advantage of the situation to get some immediate instruction in blind flying on the link trainer.[9] It is commendable how readily and formlessly the RAF was willing to help out ATA pilots with regard to instrument flying – another example of the spirit of mutual co-operation, which existed between the RAF and the ATA for most of the war. Later, the official training offered by the ATA included some simple blind manoeuvres such as procedure turns and stop-watch methods of executing circuits in poor visibility.

In accordance with the ATA's objective of training as many pilots as was humanly possible to perform the ferrying duties of the ATA in a safe and efficient manner, very few pilots failed to pass out of the ATA training programme. Only 11.6 per cent of all women and 2.5 per cent of all men accepted into the ATA were let go for lack of flying aptitude.[10]

This low failure rate, however, was not attained by passing out questionable candidates. On the contrary, the very low number of accidents for which ATA pilots were found responsible is evidence of the high quality of the candidates who passed out of ATA training. Accidents occurred in less than one third of one per cent of all deliveries and in less than one third of these incidents was the ATA found to be at fault.

Before turning to the training provided to the WAFS, WFTD and WASP, one last note: most ATA pilots felt very positive about the quality of the training they received. June Farquhar's remarks are typical:

> What a fantastic training and how confident it made us all. I still marvel at the fact one could climb into a totally unknown aircraft, thumb through our Pilot's Handling Notes, spend a little time familiarising oneself with the layout of the aircraft and . . . then away into the wild blue yonder!'[11]

Diana Barnato Walker writes in her book, *Spreading My Wings*: 'The ATA training was second to none. It was thorough and extremely well worked out. The flying training was the best ever provided anywhere for pilots, before or since.'[12]

WAFS

While the duties of and hence the training required by the WAFS most closely paralleled those of the ATA, it must be remembered that the WAFS was a relatively short-lived organisation that was soon absorbed into the wider women pilot's organisation in the United States, the WASP. WAFS training was thus not an on-going programme but rather a singular event.

The twenty-eight women hired directly into the WAFS at the end of 1942 and the start of 1943 were all highly qualified pilots, generally with much more flying experience than the minimum requirement of 500 hours. They were given a one-month conversion course onto service aircraft at 2nd Ferry Group HQ at New Castle Army Air Force Base near Wilmington, Delaware, where they were also to be stationed. This training was *not* pilot training, but rather an initiation for the civilian women into flying 'the Army way'. This entailed not only familiarisation with the aircraft the women were expected to fly – light trainers and liaison aircraft – but Army regulations, forms, procedures, and security requirements. Altogether, it consisted of twenty-five hours of flying training and seventy hours of ground school.

The rigorous flying qualifications that had been required of the applicants to the WAFS almost proved a disadvantage during the early stages of training. While requiring the women to have recent experience in aircraft of 200 hp or more, the aircraft they were flying at New Castle (and would initially be expected to ferry) were very light aircraft, mostly Piper Cubs and PT-19s (175 hp, open-cockpit). For women used to larger, heavier machines, flying such light aircraft proved to be a challenge at first.

Another key component of the training provided was cross-country navigation in aircraft that were not equipped with radios. This training was undoubtedly essential despite the flying experience of the WAFS, since most were used to flying fully equipped aircraft.

Equally challenging for these women coming from a variety of civilian professions was mastering the Army bureaucracy and procedures. 'Each aircraft delivery would require forms and more forms, all with proper signatures.'[13] The women had to learn about the forms necessary to 'buy' (collect) and 'sell' (deliver) the aircraft they were tasked to ferry, to fill out the forms to Remain Over Night (RON) *en route*, to fill out transportation requests and much more. In addition came the – for the women pilots – new areas of military law and military drill. 'To the dismay of the [women] part of learning to fly the army way included learning to march the army way.'[14] Other ground school subjects were a review of navigation, communications, meteorology, and aircraft engines. Cornelia Fort's biographer points out that:

It galled some of [the WAFS] that the men would go through as little as nine days of training while they would be studying for a month. Cornelia was especially incensed. She and many of the other women had taught the ground school subjects they were now taking . . . .[15]

Nor did the WAFS fully understand why they were taught to stand guard, although they would never do so, or why they were given firearms instruction on .45s they were not issued nor permitted to fire. Evelyn Sharp wrote of being taught to handle rifles and 'dismantle and assemble a .45 caliber pistol blindfolded' as well.[16]

Yet for all its drawbacks, this one-month initiation course was the only kind of dedicated training most of the WAFS received for at least a year. Once the women pilots were out of this initial training, they went right to work ferrying the small primary trainers from nearby factories to air cadet training installations across the Southern United States. Thereafter, the WAFS, like all other pilots of FERD, were expected to continue their own training at their own pace, inclination, and convenience by regularly making use of link trainers or attending courses when not actually ferrying. There was considerable freedom left to the individual with regard to what kind of instruction one wanted to take. Evelyn Sharp, for example, wrote to her parents that she was learning about the armaments of fighters and bombers just because it was interesting; 'I am doing this on my own. I don't have to but I get credit for it.'[17]

In April 1943, the Commanding General of the FERD, General William Tunner, reorganised training within his command along the lines of the British ATA. In Tunner's words:

> I set up a program of on-the-job training in which the pilots actually performed the mission of the Command at the same time they bettered their flying. Thus those at the bottom of the ladder would deliver the simplest forms of aircraft, such as artillery spotting planes and primary trainers. As they built up their flying time in these basic types, they would be going to ground school and instrument flying school, preparing themselves for the next step up. Gradually, step-by-step, they worked their way from the short hops in trainers on clear days to delivering aircraft all over the world.[18]

Tunner also divided the aircraft into Classes just as the ATA did, but he grouped the aircraft somewhat differently from the ATA.* The most significant difference was that fighters (called 'pursuits' in USAAF jargon) were defined as a separate class of aircraft. This was in part because they were considered particularly difficult to fly; Tunner himself called them 'the most difficult of all ships'[19] and in Ferrying Command pursuits had three times the accident rate of heavy bombers.[20] Another consideration was that the skills required for flying

---

* Class I   low powered, single-engine aircraft such as PT-17, PT-19, PT-26 and Cubs.

  Class II   twin-engine trainers and utility planes such as UC-78, AT-19.

  Class III   twin-engine cargo/medium transport planes such as the C-47 and C-60.

  Class IV   medium bombers and heavy transports such as the B-25, A-20 and A-25.

  Class V   heavy bombers and transports such as the B-17 and B-24; pilots of this category were expected to make deliveries overseas.

  Class III P single-engine, high-performance aircraft such as P-39, P-40, P-47 and P-51

  Class IV P   twin-engine, high performance aircraft such as P-38 and P-61.

pursuits were not particularly useful in preparing pilots to perform long-distance, heavy transport duties on the transatlantic or India-China routes – something FERD Class V pilots were expected to do. 'Pursuits' were thus the only classification of aircraft in which pilots were allowed to specialise, once they had qualified on them.

It was usual for pilots to log at least 500 hours in Class I before moving up to Class II and then fifty hours in Class II before being eligible for Class III. The usual method of qualifying on higher classes of aircraft throughout 1943 was *ad hoc* and informal. That is, a pilot was expected to get training on higher Classes of aircraft from experienced pilots and/or instructors at his/her own Ferry Group whenever time allowed. While this system was highly flexible, it also left training to a combination of initiative on the part of the pilot and willingness on the part of the Base or Group Commanders or even individual instructors. Inevitably, some women proved more adept at getting what they wanted, while others were more easily intimidated or discouraged. Likewise some Base Commanders were helpful and supportive, while others proved reluctant to transition women pilots upwards. The system also meant that there could be considerable discrepancies in methodology, content and professionalism in the training provided at the different Ferry Groups and bases.

In late 1943, Ferrying Command recognised the need to set up centralised, specialist training schools for transitioning pilots to higher Classes of aircraft. The first 'Pursuit School' was established at Palm Springs, California, in December 1943 and fourteen WASP were among the first two graduating classes. This specialised pursuit training course lasted a total of four weeks.

In summary, after their initiation into the USAAF via an introductory one-month course in New Castle, WAFS – like the women of the ATA – were trained in the same manner as their male colleagues. However, unlike the ATA, where a training scheme was developed by a single, experienced instructor and instituted on a command-wide basis, training in the FERD evolved over time, showing a high degree of de-decentralisation and improvisation until early 1944.

WFTD/WASP

WASP training, in contrast to the dedicated ATA and FERD training, which were both designed to create versatile and safe ferry pilots in the shortest possible time, was intended to demonstrate that women could be subjected to the same training as male cadets, and be as successful as pilots. As was described earlier, the initial programme, the Women's

Flying Training Detachment (WFTD), was approved by General Arnold in response to an angry protest by Jacqueline Cochran about the creation of the WAFS. Cochran persuaded General Arnold that there were potentially more uses for women pilots in the USAAF than 'merely' ferrying, and that an experiment should be launched to test this thesis. 'Jacqueline Cochran's ultimate goal was to prove that any healthy, stable young American woman could learn to fly the army way as well as her brothers.'[21] In a memorandum to the Commanding General of Training Command, General Barton Yount, General Arnold stated cogently: 'The Air Forces objective is to provide at the earliest possible date a sufficient number of women pilots to replace men in every non-combatant flying duty in which it is feasible to employ women.'[22] Cochran's aim was to prove a point about women pilots while the USAAF's aim was to get women quickly onto the job. Although no one seemed to notice at the time, these two aims were not entirely compatible, and with time the first would increasingly interfere with the second.

Jacqueline Cochran, in accordance with her explicit demand, was named commanding officer (Director of Enlistment and Training) of the WFTD. Cochran confidently promised that she would have her WFTD up and running in just thirty days, i.e. by mid-October 1942. Unlike the founder of ATA training, A.R.O. MacMillan, Cochran had never qualified or worked as an instructor let alone run any kind of aviation school. She had never commanded a military organisation, although as CEO of her own cosmetics company she undoubtedly had managerial experience. After Cochran had singularly failed to make any progress toward finding facilities, equipment or staff for her new unit, General Arnold ordered the General Yount to give her every assistance.

As a result of General Yount's intervention, an improvised arrangement was made available to train the first class of women pilots, whom Cochran had diligently recruited. The WFTD programme started a month behind schedule in mid-November 1942 at Howard Hughes Airport, Houston, Texas, near Ellington Air Force Base. (Ellington was a huge USAAF training establishment where as many as 5,000 aviation cadets were in training at any one time.) Training itself was in the hands of a civilian company, Aviation Enterprises, whose government contract to train CPT pilots had just expired. The equipment put at the disposal of the WFTD was an assortment of bits-and-pieces that Yount scraped together from other training establishments, and consisted of over twenty different kinds of aircraft in various states of disrepair.

While Cochran took a very active and direct role in recruiting the first women from her lists of *already* experienced pilots, she apparently took no interest in the curriculum or the running of the WFTD. The Army appointed a Commanding Officer and Adjutant, while Cochran recruited Mrs L. Deaton to act as 'Establishment Officer.' Mrs Deaton's qualifications were that she had been a housewife, mother and Red Cross swimming instructor. She had no flying or military experience. Her only instructions from Cochran were to 'look after the girls'.[23] Although utterly lacking in experience and qualifications, Mrs Deaton was at least keen to perform her job. The attitude of the CO of the WFTD, Captain Paul Garrett, is summarised by his response to Mrs Deaton's plea for help: 'Just keep the girls happy and out of my hair.'[24]

The curriculum was apparently left entirely in the hands of the civilian contractors. Although the use of civilian contractors to provide USAAF cadets with the first stages of training (elementary, basic and advanced training on training – not service – aircraft) was standard practice at this time, in fact, Aviation Enterprises had up to this point been training pilots under the Civilian Pilot Training Programme. They had never trained pilots to USAAF standards. The Army, however, checked out all pilots passed by the civilian instructors, and so had the final say on whether trainees passed from stage to stage and graduated from the programme.

Aviation Enterprises presumably received some kind of guidance on what the Army expected, and according to all accounts the training was essentially the same as that provided to Army Air Force cadets. Although the first class of women to report to Houston had an average of 350 flying hours each – significantly more than the 200 hours required, there does not appear to have been any modification to the training programme to accommodate this. On the contrary, rather than training for just sixteen weeks as Cochran predicted and the trainees expected, the first class to graduate from the WFTD was in training for twenty-three weeks. During this time, the trainees were given 115 hours of flying instruction and 180 hours of ground school.

Over the next two years the training programme was repeatedly revised and altered at the Army's instigation. Subsequent commanders took greater interest and pride in the women's pilot programme, and feedback from the Commands of the USAAF employing the WFTD graduates provided a basis for changes as well. By the end, the course had been lengthened to thirty weeks and provided 210 hours of flying training, and 393 hours of ground school.

Initially, the programme was divided into three stages (primary, basic and advanced), but in the end it was organised into two principal phases (primary and advanced) with a concentrated period of instrument training, including thirty hours of link trainer instruction, as an additional phase. Twin-engine training was eliminated from the programme during one of the many modifications, so that when the programme closed down the USAAF was spending seven and a half month's training pilots up to FERD's Class I proficiency, albeit with considerable instrument flying experience.

As mentioned above, flying training was initially grouped into three phases. Primary training was in light, open-cockpit aircraft of roughly 175 hp. Initially, a variety of civilian aircraft were used for training, but as soon as standardised equipment was available to the WFTD, the basic trainer became the Fairchild PT-19. Again, after standardised equipment was introduced and for as long as the three-stage training programme was in effect, the trainees did their 'basic training' on Vultee BT-13s or BT-15s (closed cockpit, radio-equipped, 450 hp). The last stage of training, advanced training, was conducted on the North American AT-6 (650 hp, retractable undercarriage) and – so long as twin-engine training was included – the twin-engine Cessna AT-17 (245 hp). When training was reorganised into two phases, primary instruction was still carried out on the PT-19, but then trainees moved directly onto the AT-6. Although the middle phase of training was eliminated, the BT-15s and 17s were retained for doing instrument flight training *after* the AT-6 had been mastered. As was mentioned above, after the shift to two phases of training the twin-engined Cessnas were eliminated from the flight line.

The length of time spent in each phase of training varied over time. For the first class, with their very high levels of previous flying experience, the number of hours spent in primary training was as low as twenty-five, but this increased to seventy hours in the last classes, where incoming trainees had as little as thirty-five hours previous flying experience. When the middle phase of training was offered, it lasted between forty-four and sixty-five hours. Advanced training lasted between fifty and seventy hours at various stages. Instrument training varied from thirty to thirty-eight hours.

Noteworthy in the WFTD/WASP training programme was the amount of blind and night flying experience included. In fact, the women trainees received more blind-flying training than did male cadets. Trainees both 'flew under the hood' (i.e. in day time but with a canvass covering cutting off the vision of the trainee while an instructor or another trainee flew dual with full visibility) and at night.

It is unclear whether aerobatics was part of the curriculum or not. One WASP remembers as follows:

> Of course, we never got any aerobatics training. This was frustrating so one day, flying solo, I took the Six [AT-6] up to ten

thousand feet and tried a slow roll. Well, I couldn't manage to keep the nose from dropping and the plane fell into a 'split S', which means that it simply dropped nose first straight down out of the sky. I was sure glad I had gone up to ten thousand feet because I was below five thousand feet before I could pull out.[25]

However, other WASP pilots appear to have had considerable aerobatics training. The explanation is probably that the amount of aerobatics training received by any individual trainee was entirely up to the instructor – many of whom were men who enjoyed aerobatics themselves. Gunnery training was, of course, not part of training and nor, officially, was formation flying.

The amount of cross-country instruction increased over time in direct response to repeated demands from FERD for this aspect of training to be improved and expanded. In addition to 'hops' of two to three hundred miles, a thousand-mile solo trip requiring several nights away from home base was part of the training and later a second of these flights was added to the programme. These were the only flights given in training that really simulated ferrying duties in the United States.

Ground instruction was reputedly 'identical' to male cadet training and included: mathematics, physics, maps and charts, navigation, aerodynamics, engine operations and maintenance, communications, meteorology and first aid. In the final phases it lasted nearly 400 hours, and is described by one observer as the equivalent of a college degree in aeronautics. In addition to these more-or-less traditional aspects of pilot training, the programme specifically provided 'military training' in the form of lectures on military courtesy and customs, the Articles of War, security, Army organisation, Army correspondence and personnel files, and chemical warfare. In May 1944, the WASP curriculum was further expanded to include lectures on the responsibilities and duties of officers.

Last but not least, in addition to flying and classroom instruction, great emphasis was placed on physical education and military drill. Physical education was officially six hours a week and 'included callisthenics and muscle-building, with particular attention to increasing upper body strength'.[26] The military aspects of training started with a roll call each day before sunrise, and included being marched in formation to every activity. In fact, each class was organised into squadrons, with elected leaders, and subject to all aspects of military discipline.

Once the WFTD programme was transferred to Avenger Field in early 1943, training took place in a completely militarised environment. This meant that the women trainees were housed in military barracks, their quarters subject to inspection. They were given demerits for mis-behaviour. All extra-curricula activity was chaperoned, and trainees were confined to base except when granted leave or passes at the discretion of the commanding officer. Nor were the civilian women trainees spared any of the pettiness of military training, from white-gloved inspections of quarters to being expected to make up their beds so that a coin would bounce off the blankets. Trainees were warned on their first day that for the duration of training they 'would be told when to do what, how to do it and when to stop doing it'.[27] The day lasted from 6 am to 10 pm.

Yet, despite this military environment, the instructors for the WFTD/WASP were all civilians hired by Aviation Enterprises. Because of the overall expansion of the Army's training programme, it was not easy to hire qualified instructors. Training women was not considered as prestigious as training Air Force cadets. There was a constant turnover of instructors who quit or were fired. Some of the instructors in the programme, particularly in the early months when WFTD recruiting requirements were high, had less flying experience than their trainees. Many knew nothing about flying 'the Army way' and so were in no way qualified to help trainees pass Army flight checks. Furthermore, many instructors knew nothing about night flying.

Just six and a half months into the WFTD programme and shortly before the graduation of the first class, complaints about the quality of the instructors finally induced Cochran to request an inspection. The results: the Army Air Inspectors found that many of the civilian instructors flew with a 'so-called proficiency about like that of an entering student'.[28]

Despite this devastating assessment, no fundamental changes were made to the system. The contract was not taken away from Aviation Enterprises. Instructors continued to come and go at whim, resulting in a very high turnover and continued uneven quality of instruction. Some of the instructors were better than others, but none of them came from the Army and so none of them had ever done the kind of flying their trainees were expected to do on graduation – whether that was ferrying or any other military task.

In June 1944, another Air Inspector came to essentially the same conclusions as his colleague a little more than a year earlier. Namely: 'The flight instructors are inexcusably ignorant, not in the least familiar with the theory of how various airplane control systems operate. If they have an instrument rating, it is next to worthless because they do nothing to maintain proficiency. Their notions of navigational practice are foggy.'[29] By the time this report was issued, however, it was too late to salvage the programme anyway; it was about to be scrapped.

Despite the low standards of instruction, the failure rates for the WASP programme were extremely high. In her Final Report, Cochran bragged that the total washout rate in her programme *for flying deficiencies* was 'just' 30.7 per cent compared with a comparable washout rate for male cadets during the same period of 35.6 per cent. In making this comparison, Cochran conveniently overlooked the fact that male cadets entering USAAF training had *no* previous flying experience compared with the thirty-five hours required of WASP; it was therefore only to be expected that their failure rates for flying deficiencies would be higher than that of the women.

Furthermore, Granger's class by class statistics show that overall failure rates varied from a low of 23 per cent in the first (highly qualified class) to as much as 56.5 per cent for the class 44–7. Since the statistics for latter classes do not distinguish between the causes for non-graduation and there were always a number of 'hold-overs' and 'wash-backs' confusing the numbers in any one class, an average failure rate is probably more useful than Cochran's selective and non-verifiable claim regarding failure for 'flying reasons'. The overall failure-rate was 42.35 per cent for the classes with minimal entrance requirements (i.e. thirty-five flying hours) and 39.7 per cent for all classes. These failure rates are hardly suitable as evidence of particular aptitude on the part of women.

There is, however, considerable circumstantial and anecdotal evidence that suggests that the washout rate was kept artificially high. Many cadets may have failed not for lack of aptitude, but owing to a conscious policy of eliminating a high percentage (between one third and one half) of all trainees. For example, the standard 'welcoming speech' given to new trainees by the Commanding Officer included the statement that only one in three would graduate. One WASP reported: 'There seemed to be so much "luck" involved in the washouts. We later found out that many good pilots didn't make it.'[30] Another said: 'It wasn't fair because one of those girls could fly circles around me. She was a wonderful pilot. I'm beginning to see that maybe a lot of those who were washed out really weren't bad pilots.'[31] A third relates that when she asked her instructor why she had failed the check-flight, she received the blunt reply: 'I don't like your face now, and I won't like it any better when I check you again tomorrow.'[32] Ruth Adams, later a psychologist, claims that at the time she felt:

> If they're going to wash a bunch of us out, they can't tell who is really good or bad. They might be able to recognise the very

outstanding upper ten per cent, and they could probably pick out the really bad fliers – uncoordinated, bad judgement et cetera – but the whole middle mess of us, they would not be able to discriminate among at all. They were going to do it on personal prejudice.[33]

In short, the WASP training programme appears to have set out to fail between one third and one half of all candidates in every incoming class. The reasoning behind this policy is obscure. It may have resulted from the Army's desire to retain an 'elite' image for its pilots, or it may have sprung from the Army's need to siphon suitable candidates out of pilot training and into vitally needed but less prestigious (and so less popular) aircrew functions. Cadets who failed in pilot training frequently landed in these other specialities, such as navigator, bomb aimer, radio operator or air-gunner. Although there was no alternative employment within the USAAF for washed-out WASP, Aviation Enterprises appears to have simply adopted the statistical guidelines of the cadet training programmes and applied them blindly to WASP training.

Yet, despite the lengthy and comprehensive training combined with an apparently arbitrarily high washout rate that should have ensured first-class graduates, the graduates of the WFTD were far from the proficient fliers expected or needed by FERD. In a report to Cochran from the Assistant Chief of Staff Operations, Air Transport Command, dated 5 July 1943, the deficiencies in the programme are listed. These included: 1) too little practice landing on pavement, 2) too little navigation, 3) too little cross-country experience, and 4) too little grasp of flying.[34] In another report from General Tunner, Commanding General of Ferrying Command, dated 28 August 1943, Tunner complained that recent graduates of the WFTD demonstrated: 'an excessive accident and mishap record . . . too many ground loops, examples of poor judgement in flying into thunderstorms and bad weather, resulting in forced landings in unsuitable fields and cases of over or undershooting runways.'[35]

In September of the same year, FERD complained again about the quality of WFTD graduates. This report described the women graduating from Avenger Field as 'airport pilots' because 'unless their home base is in sight, they get lost'.[36] The situation was serious enough for FERD to recommend returning seventeen recent graduates of the WFTD to Avenger Field for fifty more hours of instruction. Throughout this period, FERD resisted hiring the graduates of the WFTD unless they met FERD's own standards as demonstrated in test flights.

Starting in 1944, FERD was no longer compelled to accept graduates from the WFTD, but even so the problems did not end. Ferrying Command expected its pilots to transition upwards from Class I to more difficult classes of aircraft. When by April 1944 half of the women already serving with FERD had not qualified on 'pursuits', Ferrying Command declared them superfluous and sought to transfer all these pilots back to Training Command for assignment to other duties.

Although Cochran and her defenders try to dismiss the complaints from FERD as 'prejudice', their case cannot be sustained. First, FERD was the first unit to request and use women pilots and it consistently supported and assisted the women in qualifying on more challenging aircraft. FERD's command was not prejudiced against qualified women pilots, but it was not prepared to lower its standards just because the pilots happened to be women. Second, there are numerous recorded instances where recent graduates got lost or responded irrationally to situations. Equally important, there were many officers in other Commands who were equally unenthusiastic about the quality of WFTD graduates. In fact, virtually all the women reporting for duty after graduation needed additional training before they were capable of replacing male pilots as the USAAF wanted.

In the USAAF B-17 training took an additional six to twelve weeks. B-26 training took nine weeks. Pursuit training, one of the shortest courses, required just four weeks. In consequence, by the time the WASP programme was discontinued, WASP were spending an average of nine and a half months in training, seven and a half at Avenger Field and a further two months in specialist training, before they were deemed capable of doing a job. Compared with the eighteen months needed to train a bomber crew, this was perhaps acceptable, but it was still very time-consuming and expensive. The costs of the training at Avenger alone ran at over $12,000 per pilot.

Further training costs and more time from operational flying was lost by the decision to send WASP, particularly those with the most experience or command responsibilities, to the School for Applied Tactics in Orlando, Florida. The purpose of this training was to prepare WASP for their anticipated commissioning, but the effect was a further four weeks spent in training rather than 'on the job'. A total of 450 WASP went through this training before it was cancelled at the end of September 1944. In a further reflection on the poor quality of WFTD training, one WASP compared the quality of (ground) instruction at Orlando to that at Avenger Field, Sweetwater, saying: 'Everything we were taught at Sweetwater amounts to about two hours in class here.'[37]

Perhaps the saddest commentary on WFTD/WASP training, however, was the indignant complaint of a former WASP:

... when I think they sent us out on those long cross-country flights, over mountains with no mountain experience, and very little AT-6 cross-country time, it makes me mad. Also, we didn't have what the FAA requires now – a forty-five minute gas reserve. I misfigured my course correction and almost ran out of gas, so there was only a short time of extra flying. There was very little room for error.[38]

Seven fatalities during training testify to the fact that WASP training was indeed dangerous.

It is, in fact, hard to avoid the conclusion that the training provided for the WASP was extraordinarily ill-conceived and poorly implemented. No one it seems – and certainly not the Director of Women Pilots, Jacqueline Cochran – sat down and tried to work out a programme specifically tailored to the needs of the WASP. Instead, WASP training copied cadet training, with little consideration for the fact that cadets would be going on to various types of operational training while WASP theoretically were supposed to replace men. The programme was in consequence bloated and slowed down by superfluous content (e.g. maths, physics, military law, chemical warfare, drill and firearms etc.) and by physical education that ATA pilots, to this day, feel were exaggerated. Furthermore, WASP training was a rigid programme, which rigorously held candidates to a set schedule and programme. Each trainee had to pass through the various stages of training within a narrowly defined time frame, regardless of individual aptitude, talent or previous experience and education.

As a result, although WASP training was much longer and more comprehensive than ATA training, it singularly failed to meet the programme objective of training women up to the standards required by the USAAF. Admittedly, male cadets graduating from other USAAF training establishments also received subsequent training before becoming operational. Perhaps it was acceptable in the United States' context – although a distinct point of inferiority compared with ATA training – that the WASP needed additional specialised training after graduating from Avenger Field. Nevertheless, it must be stressed that while the curriculum at Avenger Field was *modelled* on that of the USAAF cadets, the poor quality of the instructors resulted in substandard *implementation* of that curriculum. The WASP were confronted with flying instructors who sometimes had less experience than they did themselves. Furthermore, WASP instructors were all unqualified for the task they had been set, and their treatment of pupils was notoriously arbitrary.

In summary, ATA training stands out as remarkably efficient – particularly in contrast with the WASP training. ATA training produced exactly the kind of pilots required in a much shorter time with an incomparably lower washout rate and with the added benefit of enabling the trainees to 'earn their keep' from a very early stage. In short, ATA training efficiently produced ferry pilots in a minimum of time and at a minimum of cost. WASP training in contrast produced at great expense and over a lengthy period of time 'airport pilots'. It was then left to other units of the USAAF in Training and/or Ferrying Command to provide the WASP with the additional training necessary to make them employable in the tasks to which they were assigned.

Notes:

1   King, Alison, *Golden Wings*, 1956, 44.
2   De Bunsen, *Mary, Mount up with Wings*, 1960, 98, 100.
3   Walker, 68.
4   Cheeseman, 53.
5   Curtis, 90.
6   King, 110.
7   Genovese, G., *We Flew without Guns*, 1945, 125.
8   Sharland, Freydis, *The Air Transport Auxiliary*, Ross, A.E. ed., *Through Eyes of Blue*, 144.
9   Walker, 77.
10 Curtis, 309.
11   Lucas, 137.
12   Walker, 50.
13 Verges, 47.
14 Verges, 48.
15 Simbeck, Rob, 135.
16 Bartels, Diane Ruth Armour, Sharpie: *The Life Story of Evelyn Sharp, Nebraska's Aviatrix*, 1996, 184.
17 Bartels, 206.
18 Tunner, 27.
19 Tunner, 38.
20 Verges, 191.
21 Verges, 69.
22 Arnold quoted in Granger, 38.
23 Verges, 75; also Granger, 70.
24 Granger, 73.
25 Cole, Jean Hascall, *Women Pilots of World War II*, 1992. 60–61.
26 Merryman, 19.
27 Keil, 157.
28 Granger, 247.
29 Granger, 366.

30   Cole, 33.
31   Cole, 43.
32   Granger, 247.
33   Cole, 25.
34   Granger, 135.
35   Tunner, General William, quoted in Rickman, 214.
36   Granger, 181.
37   Granger, 388.
38   Cole, 69.

CHAPTER FOUR

A Woman's Work

DUTIES, AIRCRAFT, THEATRES OF OPERATION AND APTITUDE

The idea of women flying military aircraft in any capacity was very radical at the start of the Second World War. Those women who did so automatically became 'guinea pigs', and their every move was observed with great attention.

Of course, male reactions to the women often depended on what the expectations had been, and expectations were often very low indeed. WASP Anne Berry reported that when she made a courtesy call on her Commander at departure in December 1944, his comment was: 'Well, you didn't mess up too much.' She asks: 'What did he think we would do? Crash his airplanes or create general havoc? He seemed agreeably surprised to think we could fly there for three months without causing any trouble.'[1] Thus it was that often the greatest sceptics became the women's greatest admirers.

Regardless of expectations and attitudes, however, at every step along the way, the question was being asked whether women were performing up to standard and whether they were performing as well as – or in a different fashion from – their male colleagues. Real or imagined temperamental and aptitude differences were perceived and attested. This chapter examines exactly what jobs the women were given to do, what kind of aircraft they were allowed to fly and finally examines the observations made about their performance by their contemporaries.

DUTIES

ATA

The duties of pilots flying for the Air Transport Command were more diverse than is generally presumed. As stated earlier, although not initially envisaged, the primary function of the ATA soon became the ferrying of service aircraft, a function for which the ATA held a monopoly from 1 May 1940 until the summer of 1945. But ferrying was not, in fact, ever the *only* type of flying that ATA pilots might be asked to do.

Given its predominance, however, it is useful to look in greater detail at just what ferrying entailed before turning to the other tasks. First and foremost, because aircraft factories were a prime target for enemy bombardment, initial emphasis was placed on clearing newly produced aircraft from the factories as soon as possible after manufacturer flight-testing. This entailed collecting aircraft from the factory and delivering them to RAF Maintenance Units, where the new aircraft were then fitted with additional equipment, notably armaments and radios.

Once these modifications had been completed, the aircraft were ferried forward to the squadrons or training units where they were to be operated. Initially, and again towards the end of the war, this ferrying was often done by the RAF, but during the bulk of the war the ATA conducted this ferrying as well.

Other ferrying tasks involved the return of aircraft from squadrons to Maintenance Units for repairs that could not be handled by the squadron's own ground crews; the transport of aircraft due for shipment overseas to ports; and the last flight of aircraft due to be dismantled for scrap. Likewise, aircraft delivered from overseas either by ship or by the Atlantic Ferrying Organisation* needed to be collected at their point of arrival and delivered either to Maintenance Units for modifications or directly to squadrons. Aircraft might also be sent to Maintenance Units for fitting with special equipment such as photo reconnaissance cameras and the like, a task also assumed by the ATA. D'Erlanger was proud to say that every friendly aircraft in the skies over Britain had been flown by the ATA at least once, and probably more than once.

To support the ferrying mission, the ATA developed and operated its own fleet of taxi aircraft in order to bring pilots to and from their deliveries in the most efficient manner possible. The fleet of taxi aircraft started with just one Tiger Moth, but the inefficiency of requiring ferry pilots to

* The responsibility for flying Lend-Lease aircraft over the Atlantic was never part of ATA's mandate. A separate British organisation, composed almost entirely of BOAC pilots, was responsible for this work as long as the US was neutral. After the US entered the war transatlantic ferrying was a joint responsibility of the British Atlantic Ferry Organisation and the US Ferrying Division of Air Transport Command.

return to their Pool by ground transportation after a delivery – perhaps across the length or breadth of the country – was almost immediately apparent. In consequence, the Director General of Civil Aviation soon put an assortment of other light aircraft at the disposal of the ATA. Of these, the Anson, which could transport seven or eight pilots at a time, and the Fairchild, with a seating capacity of four, proved the most reliable and practical aircraft for taxi service; together they soon became the mainstay of the fleet. This taxi fleet eventually peaked in 1945 with no fewer than 218 aircraft.

Every morning taxi aircraft set off from each of the twenty-two Ferry Pools to bring pilots to factories, Maintenance Units or squadrons, where they collected their first delivery of the day. Taxis also transported pilots from one delivery point to the next, to the extent it had not been possible to link deliveries previously, i.e. for a pilot to collect an aircraft for ferrying onwards at the airfield at which he/she had just made a delivery. Last but not least, taxi aircraft collected pilots from their last delivery of the day and returned them to their own Pool.

Any ferry pilot qualified to fly Class III aircraft and upwards could be assigned to fly the taxi (and Class I and II pilots could fly taxis when empty). While some pilots were particularly suited to and happy flying the taxi, and consequently specialised in this duty, most of the taxiing work was shared out equally among the qualified pilots of any one Pool. Each day, based on the deliveries assigned to each pool, the Operations Officer worked out the taxi schedule. In effect, the taxi service was a highly flexible internal passenger charter service.

Charter passenger services were also provided to the Services and Government in response to not infrequent requests for the transport of VIPs about the country. This could take the form of a single or round-trip flight, or entail lending an aircraft and pilot to a particular Command, Ministry or dignitary for a week or even longer. One particular type of charter was supporting secret sabotage work in Scandinavia by flying personnel and materiel up to the north of the Shetland Isles. This entailed taking planeloads of detonators, explosives, electric wiring etc., as well as the Commandos themselves, north. The Royal Navy also often called upon the ATA to fly specialists from HMS *Vernon* at Portsmouth up to Scapa Flow or some other location where ships were in urgent need of specialist assistance.

The proximity of the Fifth Royal Canadian Hospital, near Maidenhead, to No. 1 Ferry Pool at White Waltham probably explains why the ATA soon developed an ambulance service as well. The ambulance aircraft employed in this service were specially converted Ansons and Rapides, and the patients, flown in from across the country, were often accompanied by members of the ATA's own medical staff. 'The ability of the Air Movements pilots to fly in almost any weather was a great asset as most of the cases were urgent, and [the ATA] undoubtedly saved many lives.'[2]

The ATA also operated its own Testing and Flying Training facilities, giving selected pilots experience in flight instruction and test-flying. The senior women pilots had conducted conversion training for newer, less experienced women pilots all along, and starting in 1943 the ATA's Flying Schools, providing every kind of instruction from *ab initio* training to conversion onto heavy bombers, were staffed by ATA pilots. Individual ATA pilots were also engaged in test-flying for the purpose of producing the all-important Handling and Pilot's Notes provided to all pilots of the ATA. All pilots were test pilots in as much as they were expected to be alert to problems and to file a report on aircraft performance at delivery.

While this latter task was usually just a routine case of filling out a form, occasionally it was more significant. Diana Barnato Walker describes the following incident:

On 27 June, just three weeks after the Normandy invasion, my CO at Hamble called me to Operations. 'Diana, your return job! I want you to be very careful and if you don't like it, don't take it. Go around it very carefully, run it up, test everything, then leave it if there is anything suspicious.' . . . the RAF were sending in a special ground crew for an aircraft which two naval pilots had disliked. The first pilot had done a precautionary landing there, while the second had aborted his take-off because, he said, something was wrong . . . .

. . . I found the aircraft in question was a gull-winged naval thing. In my memory I can see it now, with its elbow-bent wings, standing forlornly by a blister hangar with its ground crew, plus transport, waiting. I looked around it as I spoke to the senior airman. He told me that they couldn't find anything at all wrong with it. Now, they and the other ATA pilot who had flown me over were all waiting on my 'whims'. Will she, won't she? – I could almost hear them thinking.

What was it? . . . Reading my delivery chit to check the aircraft number (FN883), I saw it was a Grumman Avenger I, an American torpedo bomber, used by both the American Navy and FAA. It was a big aeroplane, weighing nearly 11,000 lb empty, 2,000 lb heavier than the Corsair . . .

I walked around it again, doing more than my usual 'kick-the-tyres-and-see-that-the pitot-head-cover-was-off' routine . . . .

I was very thorough, while keeping the ground crew waiting and anxious. I knew they would be keen to get rid of their 'Jonah' which had defeated other pilots, but which was also cluttering up an otherwise deserted aerodrome . . .

Everyone appeared a little bit more friendly when I climbed up into the cockpit. Was this a good sign, they wondered? The Avenger started up like a bird, running sweetly with no mag drops. According to the notes, an Avenger can only be run-up on the ground to a stated boost and revs . . . Therefore, there was no way to check the two-speed supercharger, which could only be checked above those stated revs and boost. It was used only above a certain height, in order to give more power in the rarefied air. If the blower was at the wrong setting and too much power was applied, the engine would blow up.

With great relief to everyone, I agreed to take it. Smiles all round. The take-off was dead into the wind off the narrow naval runway. I decided to use no more power than I had used on the run-up, hoping that would get me off the ground. Not using the higher settings for take-off and climb meant a much longer run as well as a slower rate of climb, but I had plenty of runway. I knew the engine was OK up to those power settings I had tested.

I opened up very slowly, not to mention gently, taking off while watching the speeds and temperatures closely. When I had reached 5,000 feet, I throttled back to cruising revs and boost and flicked the switch over to check the supercharger, whereupon the revs and boost disappeared downwards. So, nearly, did the Avenger and I.

I put a little more power to keep my altitude, then changed the switch over again, whereupon the rev-counter and boost gauges surged nearly off the clock while the double-row Wright Cyclone engine roared back at me in distinct disapproval. I tried again, with the same results.

Something, as the FAA pilots had reported earlier, definitely wasn't right . . . .

What was wrong was now obvious – even to me. The super-charger was linked up the wrong way around. Knowing this, I was able to fly all the way to Worthy Down, in Wiltshire, with the switch in its 'wrong' position (flying time an anxious 1 hour and 15 minutes), but we didn't blow up. On my snag-sheet I wrote, 'Supercharger U/S. Linked up wrong way around'.

Margot Gore, my CO, called me to her office the following day, telling me the 'authorities' had taken the trouble to ring through to her to ask her to commend the pilot (me!) on finding the fault on their Avenger that had mystified the male sex. I grew at least an inch in stature after that interview, thinking to myself, 'There you are, you see, the ATA training must be better than the Navy's.'[3]

Last but not least, although the ATA began transporting freight rather late in the war, it was a task carried out with increasing frequency as the war drew to a close. First, the ATA instituted an internal 'scheduled' transport service to carry urgently needed spare parts from the central stores at White Waltham to other Ferry Pools. This service operated daily to a strict schedule and it was a 'point of honour' for the pilots to get through almost regardless of the weather.[4] However, it was with the invasion of Normandy that the need for charter transport really developed on a significant scale.

The deeper the Allied Armed Forces penetrated into the Continent, the greater was the strain on the entire logistical system of the British Armed Forces. By September, with the opening of the Arnhem offensive, the Forces could no longer cope alone and the RAF turned to the ATA for assistance in getting urgently needed supplies to the Second Army, which was advancing into Holland.

All ATA Ferry Pools were immediately contacted and asked to release what they could spare in the way of taxi Ansons and to deliver these to White Waltham. At White Waltham during the night of [September] 16th, ground engineers worked unceasingly to strengthen the floors of the Ansons to carry loads of 1,500 to 1,700 lb, to paint them with black and white 'invasion' stripes and generally to ensure that they were fully serviceable.[5]

Some twenty pilots were then engaged in this mission, which lasted several weeks and up to thirty trips were flown in a single day. Although the bulk of the material was delivered to Brussels, some flights were flown 'right up to the front-line airstrips at Tilburg and Eindhoven and Nijmegen on the fringe of the Arnhem battlefield'.[6]

The newly established 'Overseas Freight Flight' of the ATA that sprang up to cope with the above also made itself useful to the Red Cross and other relief services, by bringing back personnel, wounded, refugees or released POWs and others in need of a rapid transit back to the United Kingdom. Gradually – and without any clear mandate – the ATA began to assume charter work for destinations all across Europe and even to the Middle East. In the last phase of the war, ATA pilots delivering supplies to any point on the Continent would simply inquire on arrival if there was any further work for them. The spirit of this service is best summarised by an ATA pilot who reported: 'On arrival in Algiers we delivered our cargo and manifests, and asked if they had any loads for anywhere. "What! Anywhere?" said the astonished Officer in Charge. "What a wonderful service!" '7

The women pilots in the ATA ultimately took part in all the activities of the ATA on an equal basis with the exception of test-flying. This equality was attained only gradually and in stages. Initially, women were confined to ferrying light training aircraft, but from the summer of 1941 onwards they were allowed to ferry all operational aircraft, including – once qualified – the heavy bombers. They flew the taxi aircraft and the ambulance aircraft. They served as instructors, first as instructors for women pilots and later as instructors for both men and women at the ATA's Flying Training Schools. Here, women were instructors on the heavy bombers as well as lighter aircraft. As pilots for the Air Movements Flight, they also engaged in passenger charter and transport duties.

One duty, however, was the exclusive privilege of the women of the ATA: morale building for the RAF. The story is best told in the words the participants. For example, Diana Barnato Walker, writes:

> On 29 December in the winter of 1944, Margaret Gore tannoyed for a few of us . . . telling us that a certain RAF squadron along the coast had suffered losses of aircraft so we were to take a batch of new Mosquito XXXs . . . to them from various MUs around the country. These new aeroplanes, which were a later Mark, would have slightly different flying characteristics to those which they had recently lost, so the RAF crews would no doubt welcome seeing girls bring them in without any problems.
>
> Margot said, 'You've got all day to do this one job..,' adding that she had chosen a good-looking bunch of us girls, so we should be sure to make ourselves as attractive as we could. 'Efficient and pretty, please,' she said finally, and added that she would later be sending a transport for us all. She also said we could stay for lunch in the squadron's Officers' Mess and chat to everyone.
>
> The plan was, of course, cooked up by Margot and the 'Mossie' squadron CO for the aircrews to see and talk to a load of girls who had flown in these new types, in order to allay some of the prevailing tension. It was most unusual for Margot to tell us to hang about, and even more so to be ordered to stay for lunch at

an RAF station instead of gulping the issue bar of chocolate as we were being fetched, or taking another aeroplane on, as fast as possible. We certainly all liked the idea of the proposed outing.

Every one of us except Lois arrived safely, being certain to make careful – and beautiful – landings. The squadron CO had sent an RAF transport with some of his officers up to the airfield, (a) to ensure they saw us land, and (b) to drive us back to their Mess. Whilst we were awaiting Lois' arrival, we joked and flirted with the young pilots, who asked us who was coming in next. Lois had married at 16, and her daughter, also 16, had herself a baby. So one of us chirped up, 'The flying grandmother!' The young men looked apprehensive but then we heard the sound of approaching Merlins, and said, 'Ah, here comes Grannie in her Mossie'.

Lois did a dainty landing, taxied in, then emerged from under the under hatch looking her usual immaculate self. She apologised for keeping everyone waiting. The RAF pilots, who had obviously expected some grey-haired, doddering old thing, were entranced by the apparition of femininity that had at last turned up.

We had a most enjoyable day. It was some days later before we learned that the Mossie crews had suffered severe losses and that the squadron CO had confided to Margot that his men could do with some bucking-up. This was why we were allowed so much leisure time on this delivery.[8]

A similar incident is reported by ATA Pool Commander, Hugh Bergel. Because the Typhoon had a long and stormy development period, it had acquired a bad reputation. In consequence, 'the CO of one Typhoon OTU [Operational Training Unit] rang me one day to ask if I would as far as possible arrange for any future Typhoons to be delivered by our women pilots, to reassure his nail-biting pupils'.[9]

A less deliberate kind of 'morale building', but a kind that was no less effective and also exclusively the preserve of the women pilots, is that described by an RCAF fighter pilot:

In August, 247 Sqn converted from Spitfire IXs to Tempests to chase 'doodle bugs'. My pilots were a little anxious about flying the new Tempest. However, the first aircraft was delivered to West Malling by the Air Transport Auxiliary (ATA), and the pretty young lady who piloted it powdered her nose and put lipstick on before she got out of the cockpit, so they decided that the Tempest was not that difficult to fly.[10]

Let me quote Guy Gibson, VC, DSO, DFC with regard to a similar incident:

> There is a story that one particular squadron in the north had got to the stage where they refused to fly [the Beaufighter]. They said it stalled too quickly and that it was unmanageable in tight turns. They were sitting about one foggy day on their aerodrome when there was no flying possible, and were discussing the subject heatedly, when suddenly a Beau whistled over their heads at about 100ft, pulled up into a stall turn, dropped its wheels and flaps and pulled off a perfect landing on the runway. Naturally, this attracted a lot of attention. They all thought that this pilot must have been one of the crack test pilots who had come up to show them how. As it taxied up to the watch office, they all crowded around to get the gen. However, a lot of faces dropped to the ground when from underneath the Beau crawled a figure in white flying-suit, capped by blond, floating hair; it was one of the ATA girls. I am told that this squadron had no trouble from Beaus from that day on.[11]

In summary, although the ATA was engaged primarily in ferrying work, pilots of the ATA also flew passengers, either internally as part of their taxi service or externally as a service to VIPs and as a humanitarian service for persons on the Continent in need of rapid repatriation. They flew as ambulance pilots and piloted both scheduled (internal) and charter cargo transport. Selected ATA pilots, including women, served as instructors at the ATA's own flying schools. Last but not least, the women of the ATA provided an invaluable service in maintaining the morale of the RAF by their example.

WAFS

The only duty performed by the WAFS was ferrying, as it was an integral part of the Ferrying Division (FERD) of Air Transport Command (ATC). FERD had responsibility for ferrying all aircraft of the USAAF, both domestically and overseas, from factories to airfields or ports, and from one command to another as required. As in the ATA, the WAFS were initially confined to flying light training and liaison aircraft, but it soon became evident that it was quite impractical to confine women to such flying as they thereby blocked the training opportunities for men pilots, who also needed to fly small, light aircraft as the first step of their training.

Furthermore, the founder and commander of the WAFS, Nancy Love, made use of the informal and decentralised system for converting to heavier aircraft to demonstrate the capabilities of women pilots. Thus Love was one of the first pilots of either sex to fly the P-51 Mustang, a fighter aircraft that was at that time (February 1943) not yet operational. Throughout the spring of 1943, Love continued to transition to heavier and faster aircraft, encouraged by ATC Headquarters, which urged her 'to prove what women could do'.[12] Thus six months after inception, a number of other women were also checking out on more powerful aircraft, notably the P-47 Thunderbolt. In April 1943 the policy of transitioning women upwards to more powerful aircraft became official and was applied to all women flying with FERD. In a directive from the ATC to the subordinate FERD, it was stated that: 'It is the desire of this command that all pilots, regardless of sex, be privileged to advance to the extent of their ability.'[13]

Unfortunately, the C-In-C of the USAAF disagreed with ATC on one point. General Arnold vehemently opposed the deployment of women 'overseas' – as FERD discovered when Arnold personally halted a high-profile transatlantic flight by Love and another woman pilot. Arnold's policy against the deployment of women overseas meant that women could not be used on the all-important transatlantic and India-China routes. Once it became clear, however, that the women could not be employed on the transatlantic (much less the India-China) route, FERD became reluctant to train them on heavy bombers.

In consequence, in September 1943 (the aborted attempt to use women on the transatlantic route had taken place in August of the same year), the decision was made to have the women specialise in 'pursuits'. For the next year, FERD sought to increase the number of women qualified to fly 'pursuits', and by the spring of 1944 wanted all women unable or unwilling to fly them to transfer out of the Command. When the WASP was disbanded in December 1944, there were 141 women serving with FERD and 117 of those were flying pursuits. Two of the women were based at HQ, and just twenty-two of the women were flying other classes of aircraft, presumably Class I and II in preparation for transitioning onto pursuits.

WASP

By far the greatest diversity in duties was enjoyed by the WASP. Jacqueline Cochran had convinced General Arnold to establish her Women's Flying Training Detachment (WFTD) with the argument that women pilots could be put to use at more tasks than just ferrying. Thus, from the start, the WASP were intended to perform a variety of duties, but here too they got off to a rather slow start. The first class of trainees did not graduate until April 1943 and all these graduates were absorbed into FERD, which was still desperately short of pilots. It was therefore not until July 1943, ten months after Cochran had won approval for her organisation, that Cochran was able to try her first 'experiment'.

With a great show of secrecy and urgency, Cochran selected twenty-five WASP to be the first women to fly target-towing missions for anti-aircraft artillery. The women themselves were neither told what task they had been selected to perform, nor given any opportunity to decline. They were simply told that they 'were about to be given the opportunity to serve in one of the most crucial and central domestic functions performed by pilots of the AAF. Their performance on this mission would determine the future of women pilots in many other capacities'.[14] (Note: in the UK target towing was the task of Army Co-Operation and was carried out, at least in some instances, by civilian contractors. At least four of the ATA's women pilots, Amy Johnson, Mona Friedlander, Rosemary Rees and Lettice Curtis, had flown such missions prior to joining the ATA.)

Beginning in October 1943, at roughly the same time that FERD's complaints about the quality of WFTD graduates were reaching a fever pitch, Cochran began to pursue a systematic diversification of the assignments for women pilots. The graduates of the next three classes were all sent to Training Command and General Yount, the Commanding General of this Command, took over the responsibility of finding useful jobs for them.

The tasks eventually assigned to WASP were indeed very diverse and took them to nearly 125 different USAAF installations across the Continental United States. The tasks included the following: target towing for anti-aircraft and air gunners; flying target aircraft for radar calibration and searchlight tracking; glider towing to train glider pilots; smoke-laying and simulated strafing to train ground troops; engine and maintenance testing; flying as co-pilots on aircrew training bases (where bombardiers and navigators were trained); flying the control aircraft for radio-controlled target drones; collecting meteorological data; instructing on instruments; and the transportation of personnel and spare parts. Altogether, these various assignments for the WASP meant that by 1944 more than half of all WASP on active duty were serving in capacities other than ferrying aircraft.

And like the women in England, the American women pilots had an 'unofficial' duty as well: building morale for male pilots. Thus one WASP reported:

The story, as we all heard it, was that the men were complaining about flying B-26s. Many of them were afraid to fly it. The B-26 was a hot plane, difficult to fly, and the landing gear was narrow, contributing to danger in landing. The answer to the problem was to send a group of us women up to fly them, and it certainly worked. One other class of WASPs had completed B-26 school successfully. The men could hardly refuse to fly an airplane women could handle, and time proved that the women could handle it very nicely.[15]

Likewise with the Airacobra*:

P-39 Airacobra was proving to be treacherous. Its 1700 horse-power engine was mounted behind the pilot ... and directly under the cockpit were large fuel tanks . . . An alarming number of Tunner's pilots had not followed the tech orders precisely while taking off or landing ... they had spun in, crashing to their deaths. Calling the Airacobra a 'flying coffin', the pilots were contriving excuses not to fly deliveries of them. Then a WAF Stationed at Romulus wangled her way into the cockpit. For a day she practised take-offs and landings, experimenting with various airspeeds, and found that the plane had to be landed at a higher speed than the men had been using . . . From June, women had delivered three P-39s from the Bell factory to Great Falls, Montana. Since then, miraculously, landing and take-off accidents in the Airacobra had virtually stopped.[16]

Again, when the new B-29 Superfortress was greeted with less than enthusiasm by the aircrews assigned to fly them, WASP were put into the cockpit and a series of demonstrations were laid on for aircrews preparing to fly this aircraft in the Pacific.[17] This exercise, however, backfired:

The men could not get over how well the two WASP beauties flew the bomber that had the reputation of being such a fiery beast. They flew so well, in fact, that word reached Washington ... and the Chief of Air Staff ... wired that the two WASPs must stop flying the Superfortress immediately. To boost morale was one thing, . . . but the girls were 'putting the big football players to shame'.[18]

In summary, while the WAFS and WASP of FERD increasingly specialised on 'pursuits', thereby flying fewer different types of aircraft than did the individual ferry pilots of the ATA, the WASP as a whole tackled a much wider variety of tasks than did the ATA. Cochran effectively demonstrated that women could be employed in many diverse domestic capacities, particularly within Training Command.

TYPES OF AIRCRAFT

Air Transport Auxiliary

Owing to the ATA's monopoly on ferrying during the peak years of crisis, the ATA moved literally every type of aircraft, training or operational, new or obsolete, that was in service with the RAF and/or FAA in whatever capacity. This came to a total of 147 different types of aircraft, of which eighty-seven were single-engined, forty-six were twin-engined, eleven were multi-engined and three were flying boats.[19]

The flying boats were the only class of aircraft on which women ATA pilots did not qualify. Curtis explains that it was not until March 1943 that a serious demand for ferrying flying boats surfaced, and indeed during the entire war only 967 deliveries of flying boats were made by the ATA compared with, for example, 171,934 deliveries of single-engined aircraft. Furthermore, training on flying boats (which had to land on and take off from water) was very time-consuming, dangerous and expensive. The large flying boats were especially difficult to handle in any kind of sea. After an early training accident, which resulted in loss of life and severe injury to the flight engineer and pilot respectively as well as the loss of the aircraft, the ATA left training on flying boats exclusively to the RAF. Only the most experienced, with experience four-engine aircraft, ATA captains were sent to this training. None of the women were sufficiently senior on multi-engined types to qualify.[20]

The women of the ATA did, however, fly the first operational jet aircraft of the RAF, the Meteor and the Vampire – and entirely without any fuss. No special training was required for conversion to jets. The ATA had the best relations with the aircraft manufacturers after so many years of clearing the factories of new aircraft and, of course, knew the manufacturer's test pilots. The ATA's own test pilots had, furthermore, handled the jets and produced the necessary Handling and Pilot's Notes. Meteors were being produced by Gloster Aircraft Company at Moreton Vallance, so it was the pilots from the nearest Ferry Pools at Aston Down and Bristol who had the opportunity to fly them first – regardless of sex. The first woman happened to be Veronica Volkers, an ATA pilot since 1941 and a Flight Captain.[21]

[Ms Volkers] discovered to her surprise that it wasn't very much different from any other fighter delivery, except it *was* rather surprising to see 16,500 rpm on the run up, instead of say 2,700 as in a Tempest . . . Where she did get a definite impression of the extra power and speed was on the take-off . . . The landing she found easy and quite uneventful, in fact much less complicated than a Mosquito.[22]

The combination of high quality, specialised training and the excellent Handling and Pilot's notes devised for them enabled the pilots of ATA to master the wide variety of aircraft assigned to them with a very low accident rate. Nevertheless, certain aircraft had very unsavoury reputations, most notably the Airacobra, which killed two ATA pilots before the Handling Notes were completed and issued.[23] The Flying Fortress, in contrast, the epitome of masculine prowess to USAAF officers*, was described by one of ATA's women pilots as 'very easy to fly – a sort of American Lancaster . . . .'[24]

All in all, there is no evidence today that the women pilots of the ATA had any particular difficulty with any particular aircraft, although undoubtedly individual pilots had individual preferences – as did the men.[25] For example, Mary de Bunsen described the Barracuda as follows:

The Barracuda was rather a joke . . . [like] the Duck-Billed Platypus which . . . was Nature's attempt to fulfil an impossible specification. The Barracuda was festooned with so many excrescences, and had to do so many things that were clearly unreasonable, that it flew like a waterlogged ship, though I liked it because it had a comfortable heating system and was easy to put down in bad weather in a hurry. You got so deafened and dazed by the noise of the stub exhausts that I fell asleep in a Barracuda while I was flying solo, in beautiful weather, at a safe height, after a very good lunch. It was the sort of freak aeroplane, for which one developed rather an affection, but none of us could resist making fun of it.[26]

Walker, disliked the Walrus. She said of it, 'The Walrus was my least favourite aircraft. I would not have liked to be killed in one: a most unglamorous end. Every Walrus I flew knew I didn't like it'.[27]

* General Arnold personally expressed doubts about whether 'a slip of a young girl could fight the controls of a B-17.' Keil, p. 330.

WASP

Both the WAFS and the WASP, like the women of the ATA, gradually expanded the types of aircraft they were allowed to fly, steadily overcoming entrenched prejudice against the ability of women to handle powerful and, particularly, heavy aircraft. Altogether, Granger claims that seventy-seven different aircraft types were flown by WASP. Unlike the pilots of the ATA, however, most of the women specialised in one or at best a class of aircraft (such as the 'pursuit' pilots of FERD) after completing the WFTD training. Nancy Love stood out because she qualified on fourteen different types of aircraft in a relatively short period of time and later qualified on the B-17 and C-54 as well.[28] But she was exceptional in her diversification. For comparison, Diana Barnato Walker had seventeen different types of aircraft in her log-book *before* she flew her first Spitfire – and that was while she was still only qualified for Class I and II aircraft![29] Mary Wilkins lists seventy-three different types flown by the time she left the ATA, Rosemary du Cros reports having flown no fewer than ninety-one types and Marion Wilberforce allegedly flew more than a hundred types.[30]

THEATRES OF OPERATION

ATA

The ATA's official theatre of operation was the UK, and at no time did the ATA have responsibility for ferrying aircraft across the Atlantic. However, as early as May 1940, the demands of the war took ATA pilots (on an entirely voluntary basis) over to France to deliver urgently needed replacement aircraft to RAF squadrons supporting the BEF. These operations can best be described as improvised and the pilots as intrepid or foolhardy. They crossed the Channel without life-vests, radios or maps. They were greeted with curses as often as thanks on arrival. The taxi aircraft sent to collect them were often besieged and commandeered by passengers with 'higher priority'. Thus, more than one ATA pilot was left to his own devises to find his way back to Britain. Three pilots returned in Hurricanes that were so unserviceable (no brakes, no hydraulics, non-functioning instruments etc.) that they were about to be destroyed, and one of the pilots flying one of these dubious machines had never flown a Hurricane before! In the end, all the ATA pilots who had volunteered to fly aircraft to France managed, after many trials and adventures, to evade being caught in the debacle or killed, but it was certainly a near thing.

By the time Operation *Overlord* was being prepared, however, the

ATA's role had become so vital and well integrated into the operations of the RAF that the participation of the ATA in the invasion of the Continent was assumed, planned and prepared. The RAF established two Group Support Units (GSUs), which were expected to advance onto and across the Continent in the wake of the operational units. The ATA was given the responsibility for flying replacement aircraft to these GSUs, from which the RAF itself planned to ferry the aircraft onward to the front-line squadrons. Two ATA Ferry Pools (White Waltham and Aston Down) were designated 'Invasion Pools' and tasked to support the GSUs at Redhill and Aston Down respectively. Because of the high demand for ferrying anticipated, volunteers from other Ferry Pools were temporarily transferred into these 'Invasion Pools'. The pilots of these pools were given inoculations and dinghy drill and fully expected to be flying to Normandy in the near future.

In the event, however, the RAF did not move the GSUs forward as planned. As the Allied troops pressed deeper and deeper into France, however, the strain on the RAF pilots flying from the GSUs to the front-line squadrons became ever greater. The ATA could deliver to the GSUs far faster than the RAF could deliver the aircraft onwards to the advancing squadrons. After the breakthrough in August, RAF pilots were sometimes flying 300 miles or more in one direction and could be absent from their home base for several days.

In early September 1944 eight ATA pilots, who had just delivered aircraft to a GSU, learned that a number of aircraft were desperately needed in France and the RAF had no pilots to ferry them. Sources vary on the details: either the pilots – with the blessing of d'Erlanger – volunteered to take them, or the Wing Commander at the GSU requested their help. In any case, it was soon agreed that the ATA would 'lend a hand'. The RAF Wing Commander requested only that he receive a letter from the ATA stating that it 'would be helpful for our [ATA] pilots to have experience of landing on the forward strips'.[31] The Wing Commander was prepared to view this letter as sufficient coverage 'in face of the wrath of his superior officers should anything go wrong'.[32]

The very next morning the Wing Commander had his letter and two pilots of the ATA were ready to ferry aircraft to a forward airfield near Abbéville. First Officer Maurice Harlé, a Frenchman, was specially chosen for the honour of being the first ATA pilot to set foot in France since its fall in the summer of 1940.

At it turned out, he and another ATA pilot were dispatched to deliver Spitfires to an airfield still under construction, from which the operational squadron had been operating only three hours at the time they arrived. The Germans, they were told, had pulled out of the nearby village only five days earlier and some snipers were still reported in the surrounding woods.

After this first foray onto the Continent, the ATA undertook an increasing number of cross-channel flights so that 'by the end of October the ATA was well and truly established in the business of continental flying'.[33] Notably, however, it was 'not until December 24, after the ATA had been ferrying on and off to the Continent for nearly three months, that the Second Tactical Air Force – reluctantly one must assume – legalised the situation and gave formal approval for the ATA to undertake overseas ferrying tasks'.[34]

While the ATA found its way back to the Continent in a – for it – typically non-bureaucratic, spontaneous and creative manner, the breakthrough for women was even more unique. In early October 1944, very shortly after the ATA had started flying *un*officially to the Continent and months *before* such flights were officially sanctioned, one of ATA's women pilots, Diana Barnato Walker, also delivered a Spitfire to 2nd Tactical Air Force. As it happened, her husband, Wing Commander Derek Walker, was Personal Assistant to the CO of the 2nd Tactical Air Force (after serving four front-line tours of duty). The story is best told in her own words:

> One morning, Derek arrived back at Hamble from Belgium with his invasion-striped Spitfire . . . Derek told me he had a problem that I would be able to solve . . . a photographic reconnaissance aircraft was needed in Brussels to take pictures of the latest German lines, but . . . he had no pilot to fly it over. Would I like to take it there for him the next day, whilst I was officially on leave? . . . I jumped at Derek's suggestion, but then said, 'I can't go. We're not allowed to'.
>
> 'Aha,' said Derek, 'you will be on leave, so this won't be an ATA job, it's an RAF one.' With a flourish he produced a letter signed by his boss [Air Marshal Sir Arthur Coningham] . . . It read:
> > *Headquarters*
> > *Second Tactical Airforce*
> > *Royal Air Force*
> > *25th September, 1944*
> > *This is to certify that First Officer D.B. Walker, Air Transport Auxiliary, has permission to travel to Brussels and to remain there for a period of four/seven days, as from 1st October.*
> > *She is proceeding by air and will be in uniform.*
> > *Coningham*

Air Marshal Commanding
Second Tactical Air Force

. . . Derek's plan was for me to formate on his Spitfire as we flew to Brussel's Evere aerodrome. 'Whatever happens,' he warned, 'don't land anywhere else. If anything crops up, get yourself back to England.'

As mentioned earlier, the ATA did not fly in formation, we flew alone, so my idea of formation flying was practically nil. Still, it was a lovely sunny day, and my left wing was tucked in well beside Derek's right wing. It was exciting, to say the least, to see the White Cliffs of Dover being left behind after so long, then to see Cap Gris Nez ahead. Looking down, I could see the masses of bomb craters in the sandy strip of coast lying north-south up from Boulogne. I wanted to sing, throw the aircraft about in celebration of my freedom from my English bonds, but desisted as I had to watch my left wing-tip. I certainly didn't want to bump into Derek.

As we headed out over the Channel, I marvelled at the scene. This had to be a unique event: a husband and wife flying two operational Spitfires across to the Continent in wartime. Other husbands and wives may have flown together, but our set of circumstances left them all standing.[35]

After a very enjoyable and exciting leave in the newly liberated Belgian capital (during which the Spitfire was used for the task for which it had been intended), Diana Barnato Walker flew the Spitfire back to England – but not without incident. The weather was very 'murky' (as she describes it) and she became separated from her husband, on whom she was again 'formating'. Although the Spitfire she was flying had a radio, her helmet had no attachment and she had no instruction in radio use. Since she could not map-read and formate at the same time, she had no idea where she was when she lost her husband in cloud. By the sheerest good fortune, she managed to locate and land at Tangmere – the only airfield anywhere in Britain that was still open to flying at the time.[36]

The incident furthermore had repercussions. The press got wind of it and it was reported (inaccurately) that: ' . . . the beautiful daughter of the millionaire racing motorist, and her husband, Wing Commander Derek Walker DFC, have flown on a honeymoon trip to Brussels and back, each piloting their own Spitfire.'[37] There was an inquiry and W/C Walker was docked three months' pay – but all women pilots of the ATA were soon authorised to fly to the Continent.

After that, it seems, there was no stopping the ATA. Admittedly, these early flights to the Continent were not all sight-seeing, cheering crowds and fresh food that had not been seen in Britain for years (although they were often that too). Flying in winter weather was difficult, dangerous and bitterly cold. King points out that:

> Setting out on a trip to the Continent in those days meant more than ever that [a pilot] might be saying goodbye to her pool for quite a long time. Many times Spitfires, destined for some airfield in France, would have to be flown on to the forward airfield to which the squadron had advanced. And then, of course, if a machine needed flying back for repairs to England, the ATA pilot would have to wait for it.[38]

Furthermore, telephone communications to the Continent were unreliable at best, accommodations uncertain, and the enemy still active. Four ATA Ansons, for example, were lost to enemy action during the start of the Ardennes Offensive – fortunately on the ground without loss of life.

But neither the risks nor the hardships discouraged the pilots of the ATA. Undaunted by the danger, ATA pilots flew within five miles of enemy lines when delivering aircraft to a Free French Air Force squadron at Colmar on the Rhine. Two ATA pilots delivered Spitfires beyond the Rhine shortly before V-E Day.[39] With evident eagerness, they took on more and more flights, extending their reach as far as they could. In addition to the already described 'cargo charter' flights that took ATA pilots via Marseilles and Rome to Naples, Algiers and Cairo, they also flew passengers to Copenhagen and Oslo. After the end of the war in Europe, during the early days of the Occupation, the ATA delivered aircraft to Pilsen and Prague, and in August 1945 the ATA reached Berlin itself.[40] Women, too, flew to these destinations. Zita Irwin, from the Invasion Pool at Aston Down, was photographed with Red Army Soldiers in Hitler's shattered Chancellory in Berlin.[41]

WAFS and WASP

The women flying for the WAFS and WASP were confined throughout their service to the Continental United States. General Arnold personally ensured that no women flew the Atlantic and he prevented them from flying to either Alaska or Hawaii as well. The official reasons for this policy are unconvincing. On the one hand it was considered too 'dangerous' for the women to fly in 'combat zones'. But the delivery of aircraft to the United Kingdom was hardly more dangerous than flying battered, old aircraft due for scrapping, or target towing for gunners with live ammunition, or maintenance testing aircraft that had crashed. The official reasons why women were not allowed to fly to Alaska are even more absurd. Allegedly, 'the men stationed there and elsewhere in the territory of Alaska had not seen a woman of their own race for over two years'.[42] This 'explanation' surely needs no comment, and the real reasons for the prohibition against women flying to Alaska will probably never be known. That said, the Continental United States is far from small and the women who served with FERD flew, literally, tens of thousands of miles, sometimes in the space of just a few days. For many of these women, who had never left their home towns or home state before joining the WASP, seeing New York or California was almost as exciting as the Continent was to the women of the ATA.

Assessment of Women's Aptitude for Particular Tasks

The ATA's system of converting pilots to more advanced aircraft at a pilot's own pace, being very individualised, makes a comparison of men and women's aptitude for flying in the ATA context difficult. In the early years, for example, the women joining the ATA had much more pre-war flying experience than some of their male colleagues, and so could be expected to transition upwards more easily. Nevertheless, the ATA's instructors found that even after the flying experience of women recruits fell to minimal levels, the women required no more conversion training than the men – once they were recommended for that training by the Pool Commander. There is, however, no available information on whether on average the women required more practice flying with their Pools before being recommended for conversion training.

When *ab initio* training was introduced, however, it was found that women did have a significantly higher washout rate than did the male trainees. After their very positive experience with the women previously, this higher failure rate surprised the instructors of the ATA. Looking for an explanation, they discovered 'that many of the women who failed had never driven a car nor had any mechanical experience at all'.[43]

On the other side of the Atlantic, when the instructors at Avenger Field were asked to evaluate and compare women trainees with male cadets by an Air Inspector, they claimed that women and men had roughly the same overall aptitude. However, it is important to remember that the women training at Avenger Field had to have thirty-five hours of flying time already and so those with absolutely no mechanical experience/aptitude had already been eliminated. Furthermore, the instructors at Avenger Field went on to differentiate very finely, claiming that:

> women need more explanation and more instruction, possibly due to not having the same confidence men have. Men do better in aerobatics too. And men respond faster and more instinctively in emergencies. But women excel on solo landings. Their co-ordination is generally better. So is their judgement. They are smoother on the controls. Women are better in forced landings from high altitudes. Men excel at low altitudes.[44]

The performance of women 'on the job' was most comprehensively assessed in the ferrying context, since this was the job for which all ATA women and nearly half of the WASP were engaged. General Tunner, the CO of FERD, stressed in his memoirs that a ferry pilot was not meant to be a hero – just get his job done. Yet, many of the pilots initially available to FERD were 'barnstormers, stunt pilots, crop dusters – men who flew on the edge, took chances, showed off'.[45] Later, many of the men were combat veterans. But here again, in Tunner's words, 'the combat pilot is not supposed to be cautious, or conservative, or sparing of his ship. But in the Ferrying Command we had to have different standards . . . Our pilots were not supposed to risk their lives or their ships, but to fly skilfully and safely and deliver those planes in good condition'.[46] Only the former airline pilots were really trained and mentally schooled to place the highest priority upon the safe delivery of an aircraft without incident. In this environment, the women by almost universal consensus appear to have done exceptionally well.

The ATA's Director of Training argued that women made better ferry pilots because they had the right qualities, 'not the dashing impatience of the fighter pilot but just the desire to fly well and do the job pro-perly'.[47] Specifically:

> They took more trouble over the cockpit drill, for instance, were more careful about finding out beforehand where the bad weather was and going around it, and they never showed off. They somehow did not have the urge to beat-up, fly low or in any other way 'show Mother what they can do'.[48]

General Tunner also felt that women pilots were particularly good ferrying pilots. 'They paid attention in class, and they read the character-istics and specifications of the plane they were to fly before they flew it.'[49] It was these qualities that made him order a group of girls to be checked out on the P-39 when troubles developed with it. He had looked into the fatal accidents that had occurred and come to the conclusion that all could be attributed to pilot error. In his own words:

> Sure the P-39 was a hot ship, all right, but it was perfectly safe if it was flown according to specifications. It was plainly written in the literature on the plane . . . that this plane needed speed, at least 150 miles per hour, to maneuver. It had the glide angle of a brick . . . These accidents occurred when the plane got out of control on the first turn after taking off or the last turn coming in. The reason was obvious. On take-of, pilots would put the plane into a steep bank before reaching the required speed; on landing they'd reduce speed too much before making the last turn. But anyone who read the specifications and characteristics of the plane . . . knew that it would go into a high-speed stall under such conditions . . . The solution to the P-39 problem was a natural one . . . With no doubts whatsoever, I had a group of girls checked out on P-39s and assigned them to make P-39 deliveries. They had no trouble, none at all. And I had no more complaints from the men.[50]

Alec Matthews, one of the ATA pilots, likewise attributed to his female colleagues a greater degree of conscientiousness in delivering their aircraft in perfect condition. He claimed that the men tended to want to put the machines 'through their paces' and inevitably accidents occurred, while the women – too anxious to prove they could do the job at all – avoided unnecessary risks.[51]

Anthony Phelps appears to have been speaking for the vast majority of his male colleagues, when he states:

> Officially Ferry Pilots were not encouraged to do aerobatics, but I think most of us kept in practice. I don't think anyone with real blood in him could take up a Spitfire on a fine day and consistently fly it straight and level. It would be inhuman to expect it.[52]

J. Genovese is even more blunt. Referring to the women pilots of the ATA he writes:

> They were a competent group of flyers, those women, and for the most part extremely conscientious. None of them, so far as I ever heard, was subject to the same tendency toward horseplay that most of the male contingent displayed, and for that reason they

were more of a joy to the Air Ministry and to the individual field officers than many of the men.[53]

He also provides some vivid examples of this kind of 'horseplay'.

When three Hurricanes in fighting formation put the heat on a flock of ducks . . . you have something unique in the way of sport. Actually, you don't hit very many ducks . . . but the accuracy required even to draw a bead on a slow-moving mallard through the gun sights of a Hurricane doing 250 miles an hour is enough to make it a truly competitive proposition.[54]

He also recalls:

Al and I were flying a couple of Beaufighters up to a field near Aberdeen . . . one day in January 1942, and Al made the happy discovery that his machine guns were loaded . . . He promptly dove, all guns blazing, and knocked off two of the mines on the first try. I dove and picked off two more.[55]

He describes his feelings equally tellingly:

It was a thrill to feel the offensive power of the planes, to feel the guns blasting under our fingers, to escape for a few brief moments into the imaginary world of combat and action. It was easy to imagine that the mines were enemy tanks churning down a dusty road on the way to the front, that they were German transports and landing craft bearing down on the English coast – and we were the knights in shining armour who destroyed them as they came.[56]

Although a fellow ATA pilot who knew Genovese has expressed serious doubts about the accuracy of the above accounts,[57] what is important for this study is not the accuracy of his claims but the attitude toward flying Genovese's account epitomises. This is in sharp contrast to, say, Mary de Bunsen, who writes: 'I found the Oxford very easy, for I am a bus-driver by temperament and have always liked twin-engined aircraft.'[58] Rosemary du Cros, unlike Phelps, could indeed resist the temptation to do aerobatics in a Spitfire. She writes:

It may sound priggish but I couldn't see why the fact that a Spitfire can do lovely contortions with an RAF pilot in a dogfight (and I believe them superb for that) was any reason why we should impose on them the strain of aerobatics . . . .[59]

Freydis Sharland explains the women's point of view simply:

We tried very hard to fly safely and to keep our aircraft at the correct speed so as not to strain an engine needed for combat. Thus on some aircraft the throttle was only opened enough to get airborne and then brought back to ATA Cruise.[60]

The women of the ATA noted a variety of ways in which *they* felt women differed from men. For example, Mary de Bunsen wrote: 'I always found that far the best way to start any engine was to do exactly what was said in the handling notes, but the men pilots generally thought they knew better.'[61] On another occasion she noted:

The way we each tackled this trip reflects a difference between masculine and feminine psychology. The men – creatures of habit and braver than ourselves – all blinded off up the west of England via Liverpool, which was the way we knew best, ignoring the fact that there was an east wind and the weather was worse on the west side of the Pennines. Lucy and I tried to find a better way round. We studied the map and the weather reports thoroughly and realised that we would get much better weather east of the Pennines . . . the women got there first and the men had a very sticky time west of the Pennines.

Lettice Curtis writes of flying Halifaxes at a time when there had been a series of unexplained accidents:

. . . we were warned to avoid violent manoeuvres, something which, with due regard to the limitations in their physical strength, women pilots would in any case have been very unlikely to attempt. Certainly it was always my instinct to avoid situations from which the only way out was the use of brute force . . . Foresight and good anticipation are in my opinion far more valuable qualities.[62]

On the whole, the women of the ATA demonstrated a remarkable degree of reliability and safety, which was at least in part attributable to the fact that they were aware how closely they were being watched. Curtis certainly felt her success on four-engined aircraft would impact on all women in the ATA:

To me it was a very harassing time. Not only was I faced with the possibility of personal failure which I would have minded quite inordinately but at the back of my mind there was in addition the knowledge that as always, any mistakes or failures in the early days even if not of my own making, could result in a decision that four-engined aircraft were not for women.[63]

But the senior women pilots of the ATA appear to have consistently set a good example 'with their steady flying and a hard core of common sense'.[64] They certainly built up a reputation and established a standard of trustworthiness that the younger women pilots sought to emulate and maintain.

In the United States as well, women pilots proved to be reliable ferry pilots. For example, early in 1943 when the WAFS were still very much viewed with scepticism and even suspicion, six WAFS were tasked to fly six of twenty-three PT-17 (light, primary training aircraft without radios) from Great Falls in Montana to a training base in Tennessee.

After taking off from Great Falls, the flight scattered, each pilot taking his or her own pace for the long cross-country flight. The morning of the second day, the PT-17s began to arrive in Tennessee. One by one, the six WAFS landed, but two days later only six of the seventeen men pilots had appeared. As radio reports filtered in, it became clear that the others had got lost, a couple had damaged airplanes, others were suspiciously late, presumably paying visits along the route . . . The Air Transport Command was horrified at the under 50 per cent safe delivery rate of the flight. But headquarters could not avoid noticing who had accomplished their missions successfully.[65]

Ferrying Command, in fact, was convinced of the value of *trained* women pilots very rapidly. It was Ferrying Command that suggested women fly the Airacobra and fly a B-17 across the Atlantic as an example to the men. Ferrying Command actively promoted the specialisation of women in flying fighters as well. Ferrying Command, however, insisted that all ferry pilots – men or women – be highly trained particularly on instruments and cross-country navigation. It insisted on at least 300 hours' flying experience, and it was not prepared to accept under-trained pilots whether they were women or men. This stand caused considerable friction between Cochran and Tunner, but it was in no way a reflection on the women flying for FERD. It was FERD that made the greatest efforts to retain its women pilots even after the WASP programme was scheduled for closure.

Turning to look at other flying duties, the great diversity of tasks assigned to the WASP provides an opportunity to discover a number of other apparent differences between the natural talents of men and women with regard to flying. One WASP reports on flying as a gun-sighting pilot:

> For us they used cameras, and it was so dull. They said they didn't think men would do it. It would take a woman to have that much patience. We had to fly at a certain altitude, at a set airspeed, over a set pattern, and not deviate from it so the gunnery students could practice.[66]

Another account describes it as follows:

> The air force had been losing a pilot on gun-sighting runs about once every two weeks. This was tedious work, looping over and around artillery emplacements while the crews set their sights on their huge weapons. At Las Vegas young men regularly became hypnotized by the desert terrain or got lost in dreams of a hot P-47 Thunderbolt and flew right into the ground. The WASP were eager for any piloting chore and did much better at this repetitious assignment. During their ten months in Las Vegas not one woman was lost on the gun-sighting mission.[67]

Keil claims that the male pilots doing this work not only crashed, but 'would break out of the pattern and fly off to practise acrobatics'.[68]

Yet, the record of the WASP was not unequivocal. Although Jacqueline Cochran unabashedly claimed in her Final Report that:

> The WASP according to the overwhelming opinion of station commanders where they were on duty, were as efficient and effec-tive as the male pilots in most classes of duties; and were better than the men in some duties, as for example towing of targets for gunnery practice.[69]

In fact, the assessment of the various station commanders is by no means as unambiguous as Cochran makes it sound.

It is true, that WASP generally seemed to have done particularly well in ground school, at instrument flying, and at tedious tasks like the gun-sighting and tracking missions. Given the accidents and lack of conscientiousness among male target-towing pilots it is also not surprising that officers commanding these installations were particularly enthusiastic about the women. At March AFB, the CO reported that the women were significantly better than the average male pilot. Lt-Col Walters at Buckingham AFB in Florida wrote an official commendation drawing attention to the excellent job done by the WASP on his base. Another commander at a target-towing base, Colonel Bundy at Eagle Pass, was so enthusiastic he officially requested an all-woman towing squadron.

But the response to the WASP was not universally so positive. For example, Colonel Root, the CO at Dodge City, Kansas, a training base for B-26 pilots, reported that 'the experiment' with women pilots had been 'reasonably successful'. He added: 'these women displayed a most co-operative attitude and were enthusiastic and tried harder than the normal student.'[70] Tried harder?

Even at Camp Davis, the first of the target towing bases on which the WASP were employed and so Cochran's first 'vitally important experiment', the CO reported after seven full months of WASP service that they still could not fly the B-34 or the P-47. He thought, however, that most of the women would 'eventually become first pilots on the twin-engined medium bombers used for towing and tracking missions'.[71] Eventually?

At the B-25 school at Mather AFB, it was noted that while the women were particularly good on the Link trainer, they had 'difficulty in grasping the instruments as readily as men pilots, less disposition to look around while flying, and need[ed] far more dual transition prior to soloing'. Furthermore, they demonstrated 'over-cautiousness, poor judgement, and difficulty in retaining what was learned' in addition to having more difficulty than usual 'in grasping beam orientation and let down procedures'.[72] Even FERD's Pursuit School reported that while the women pilots had above-average ground-school scores, in flying they had a much higher washout rate than the men, 37 per cent versus 12 per cent.[73]

The Commander of the glider towing installation at South Plains AAFB near Lubbock, Texas, reported even more serious difficulties. Not only did the women require extra training before they could start their duties, only six out of sixteen successfully completed this training 'and they were rated with minimum skills – under ideal conditions'.[74] In his report he went on to say that the only reason there were no accidents during training was because of the precautions taken against them by the instructors, 'In fact, the women were often not even aware of their danger'.[75]

A major problem with the WASP programme was that due to the fact that Cochran wanted to prove the versatility of women pilots, they were assigned a wide variety of tasks for which they had specially to be trained. However, it took time to train women for these various duties and the WASP were rarely given that time; the programme was discontinued just eighteen months after the start of the first 'experiment', and on many installations the WASP were not on duty for more than a few months. Furthermore, with very few exceptions, the number of women performing any one task was in both absolute and proportional terms too tiny to be statistically significant.

Furthermore, like ferrying, the various tasks called for various specific skills. Drone control called for a very sensitive response to the drone and the ability 'to know at once what an airplane is up to, almost before the change in flying occurs'.[76] 'Slow-timing' of engines required above all patience, and tracking missions demanded precision. Not all WASP could be equally adept at all tasks, but the women were assigned to their duties randomly, with very little effort to match skills and temperament to task. It was therefore inevitable that not all women would be equally suited to the duties to which they found themselves assigned. Because there were so few of them, however, the personal failings of one or two women could quickly cause sceptical commanders to draw conclusions about women pilots generally. It is also hard to estimate the extent to which prejudice among conservative commanders, who opposed women pilots categorically, affected judgement.

One last point of interest is that when comparing the ATA to FERD, it is striking how very different the attitude toward fighter aircraft was. The ATA put all single-engined fighter aircraft from the legendary Spitfire to the infamous Airacobra into Class II – the second easiest category. Pilots were expected to master these *before* going on to light twins such as the Anson and Dominie. FERD segregated fighters into a separate category primarily because they could not be flown across the Atlantic, but also because the accident rate was triple that of other categories of aircraft and a certain aura appears to have surrounded them. Words like 'hot', 'dangerous', and 'macho' are frequently used by American pilots in connection with the fighters. General Tunner himself described pursuits as 'the most difficult of all ships' in his memoirs.[77] Most important, it is reported that: 'Not all the women in the Ferry Division wanted to fly pursuits. They were hot, perilous aircraft that required an aggressive, venturesome spirit – even for a flyer.'[78] Nancy Batson, one of the WAFS with over 500 hours flying time prior to joining the USAAF squadron and fourteen months' experience with FERD, still 'felt as if she were in a barrel about to go over Niagra Falls' the day she

flew her first P-47 Thunderbolt.[79] There were clear exceptions, Evelyn
Sharp was enthusiastic about flying pursuits and found the P-51 and
even the feared P-38 'beautiful'. Yet, the rule was reluctance rather than
enthusiasm. WASP Ruth Adams remembers that when the call came for
volunteers to go to pursuit school in Brownsville, Texas, 'nobody
wanted to go because that was hard. It was a pretty tough experience
and a little dangerous, with pursuit planes'.[80] What is more, 37 per cent
of the women pilots who *did* attempt to convert onto fighters were
washed out in training. In contrast, there is no recorded case of an ATA
woman pilot failing to qualify on fighters.

Furthermore, the British women do not appear to have been intimidated by fighters in the same way. Diana Barnato Walker describes the
attitude as follows:

> Light or training aircraft were one thing, but the types many early
> ATA cadet pilots dreamed of, quite naturally, were the Hurricane
> and the Spitfire fighter types. . . . Every ATA pilot longed for the
> day they might fly one of these machines, and not just the men,
> but me too.[81]

Peggy Eveleigh, a former WAAF who joined the ATA far later than
Walker, had very similar feelings. She describes her first flight in a
Spitfire as follows:

> I could hardly believe it. I had realised one of my life's ambitions
> and was actually flying a Spitfire!
>
> I thought 'I'm going to make the most of this so that even if I
> crash on landing, I will have known what it is like to fly.' . . .
> Gradually it dawned on me that perhaps I was staying up longer
> than I should. I looked around for the airfield and saw it some
> distance away, so I flew back and made a very correct approach
> and landing . . . I taxied in, pleased with myself – only to be met
> by my rather irate instructor, who ticked me off for being so long
> and leaving the circuit. I was completely honest with him. I told
> him I was determined to make the most of my first Spitfire flight
> in case it was my last! He laughed and all was well.[82]

Even the Beaufighter, distrusted by the RAF as Guy Gibson so graph-
ically described, did not particularly distress the ATA. Mary de Bunsen,
never one of the most adventurous women, described her first
encounter with the Beaufighter as follows:

The Beaufighter was a comparatively small aircraft with two very powerful engines, and nothing in our previous experience had the smallest resemblance to it, so we were all a bit pensive. I asked Ursula, who had already flown one, to tell me about it. 'It's a *lovely* aeroplane,' she said, 'and it's very easy to land, but you want to watch the take-off. The engines sort of take charge if you apply the power unevenly. But you'll love it.' . . . The take-off was a bit breathtaking, but in the air I found it a beautiful aeroplane – stable and manoeuvrable and very comfortable to sit in, being apparently tailored round someone about my size.[83]

In fact, in the ATA – both men and women – flew even the most notorious American 'pursuits' without any apparent trepidation or special training; they simply checked their Pilot's Notes and got on with the job.

Another, and far more telling difference between the women of the ATA and the WASP, however, are the accounts of WASP behaviour that are in stark contrast to the universally praised common sense of the ATA women. For example, more than one WASP enjoyed and engaged in mock 'dogfights' with USAAF and Navy cadets. A large number of WASP engaged in 'buzzing' of one kind or another, including stampeding cattle or buzzing the 'tourist court' where other WASP were known to be staying. Teresa James describes her adventures in her diary as follows:

I flew about 15ft over the highway scaring the hell out of everyone. Then I followed the train track for 50 miles. Headed straight for a train, then hopped over him. I expected the engineer and fireman to leap right out of the cab. Then I went and pestered the farmers. Scattered them in every direction. Boy, what a rip-roaring time I had. Good thing there are no numbers on the ships.[84]

Fun it might have been, but it was irresponsible and dangerous too. WASP Mary Trebing died when a telephone wire caught on the tail of her aircraft while buzzing on 4 November 1943.

Aerobatics could be dangerous too – which was why it was officially discouraged. Unfortunately, official disapproval failed to stop it. Marion Toevs attempted to do a slow roll at 300ft over a relative's house. Fortunately, no one in the house was killed. Marion Toevs was. Of the thirty-eight women who died while in service with the WASP, several were victims of their own irresponsibility rather than misfortune.

Notes:

1   Cole, 131.
2   Cheeseman, 181.
3   Walker, 149–50.
4   Curtis, 251
5   Curtis, 252.
6   Cheeseman, 187.
7   Cheeseman, 197.
8   Walker, 177–8.
9   Bergel, Hugh, *Fly and Deliver: A Ferry Pilot's Log Book*, 1982, 70.
10   Edwards, James F. 'Eddie', quoted in Oliver, David, *Fighter Command 1939–45*, 2000, 146.
11   Gibson, Guy, *Enemy Coast Ahead*, 1946, Reprint 2001, 113.
12   Verges, 89.
13   Verges, 96.
14   Keil, 211.
15   Cole, 72.
16   Keil, 245–6.
17   Verges, 216–17.
18   Keil, 282.
19   Cheeseman, 247–8.
20   Curtis, 258–64.
21   Lucas, 109.
22   King, 175.
23   Welch, Ann, Lecture before the History of Air Navigation Group, Royal Institute of Navigation, 23 Sept. 1998.
24   Curtis, 207.
25   All women ATA pilots who responded to my questionnaire indicated that they had not felt that strength was required to fly any particular aircraft. Phelps describes vividly in his memoirs his dislike of the Lysander, 59–62.
26   De Bunsen, Mary, *Mount up with Wings*, 1960, 146–7.
27   Walker, 152.
28   Verges, 108.
29   Walker, 68.
30   Du Cros, 78, Mary Wilkins, Letter to the Author, 20 June, 2004, Obituary of Marion Wilberforce in the, 12 Jan. 1996.
31   Cheeseman, 166.
32   Cheeseman, 166.
33   Cheeseman, 169.
34   Curtis, 249.
35   Walker, 164–6.
36   Walker, 167–9.
37   Walker, 170.
38   King, 173-4.
39   Cheeseman, 175.

40   Cheeseman, 190–203.

41   King, 174.

42   Keil, 249.

43   King, 178.

44   Granger, 352.

45   Rickman, 132.

46   Tunner, 29.

47   King, 179.

48   King, 179.

49   Tunner, William, *Over the Hump*, 1964, 38.

50   Tunner, 37–8.

51   Fahie, 151.

52   Phelps, 82.

53   Genovese, 95–6.

54   Genovese, 98–9.

55   Genovese, 97.

56   Genovese, 97.

57   George, Peter M, Letter to the Author, 21 Jan 2005.

58   De Bunsen, 110.

59   Du Cros, 84.

60   Sharland, 143.

61   De Bunsen, 85.

62   Curtis, 185.

63   Curtis, 171.

64   Bunsen, 96

65   Keil, 136–7.

66   Cole, 103.

67   Verges, 196.

68   Keil, 233.

69   Cochran, Final Report, 2.

70   Cole, xv.

71   Verges, 197.

72   Granger, 275.

73   Verges, 197.

74   Verges, 154.

75   Verges, 154–5.

76   De Bunsen, 187.

77   Tunner, 38.

78   Verges, 197.

79   Keil, 237.

80   Cole, 124.

81   Walker, 66.

82   Lucas, 56–7.

83   De Bunsen, 126–7.

84   Rickman, 147.

CHAPTER FIVE

The Wonderful
(or Not so Wonderful)
World of the
Woman Pilot

DAILY LIFE FROM 'ZOOT SUITS' TO FLYING BOMBS

Anthony Phelps, who had flown Spitfires in the Battle of Britain for the RAF, admits: 'subconsciously, like many RAF pilots, I had inclined to the view that after Service flying this ferrying would be a 'piece of cake', but I soon discovered just how much there was to learn about it . . . .'[1]

The key difficulties for the ferry pilot in wartime Britain were the diversity of aircraft they were expected to fly, navigation without radio and the unpredictable weather. For the women flying with the WAFS and WASP, the greatest difficulties resulted from the vast distances they were expected to fly; trans-continental flights were not uncommon in the later years and flights of several hundred miles were viewed as 'short hops'.

In addition to these flying-related challenges, the women pilots also faced risks above and beyond the normal risks associated with flying. In Britain these risks stemmed primarily from the fact that throughout the war the ATA was flying in a war zone – either in British airspace or over the Continent as the ATA followed in the wake of the advancing RAF. The pilots were thus vulnerable not only to the *Luftwaffe* both in the air and on the ground, but also various hazards resulting from the air defences of their own country. The women of the WASP, in contrast, were kept scrupulously clear of all war zones and any possibility of encountering the enemy – only to face equally fatal hazards at the hands of their colleagues in the USAAF.

This chapter examines the day-to-day realities faced by the American and British women flying military aircraft in the Second World War, including a closer look at the risks that were part of their daily lives.

WORKING CONDITIONS AND DAILY LIFE

ATA

The ATA flew seven days a week, fifty-two weeks of the year, and the pilots had a duty cycle of ten days on and two days off, with two weeks' holiday a year. They were never posted to ground duties for a rest (as was standard practice in the RAF), which meant that by the end of the war, ATA pilots had been flying as much as six years straight. During the long hours of daylight in summer, a ferry pilot's working day might last twelve to thirteen hours. However, since ATA regulations restricted flying to the hours of daylight, during the short days of winter, the working day might be a little as six or seven hours even in good weather, and on many days flying was impossible altogether.

Summer or winter, the working day for an ATA ferry pilot began at 9 am when all pilots reported to their respective Ferry Pools irrespective of weather. By the time they reported, the Pool Operations Officer had worked out the day's programme of deliveries based on the dispositions of Central Ferry Control (CFC).

CFC was a small staff located directly at the Headquarters of No. 41 Group, RAF, the unit responsible for 'the maintenance and movement of all His Majesty's aircraft'.[2] On any one day, there could be anywhere from 400 to 1,400 aircraft in need of ferrying, and CFC allocated these aircraft to the various Ferry Pools. The Pool Operations Officer at each pool then worked out the duty roster, matching aircraft to pilots qualified to handle them (i.e. qualified on that particular Class of aircraft or above). The objective was to optimise the schedule of each pilot to minimise the time spent on the ground getting from one job to the next.

The pilots received their 'chits', i.e. delivery forms, for the aircraft they were scheduled to ferry in the course of the day and were told whether, where and when they would be transported by taxi aircraft. The pilots were then individually responsible for checking on the weather report from the Pool Meteorological Office and checking with Maps and Signals regards changes with respect to flying hazards (such as barrage balloons, Restricted Areas etc.). If a pilot had never or only infrequently flown a particular type of aircraft, it was also his/her responsibility to check up on the characteristics of the aircraft in his/her Handling and Pilot's Notes.

Assuming the weather was good enough for the airfield to be open, shortly after 9 am the pilots would be taken by the available taxi aircraft or (if the distance was short) by motor transport and dropped off at the factories or Maintenance Units (MUs) at which they were to collect their first aircraft for ferrying that day. At the larger Ferry Pools, as many as six or seven taxi aircraft might take off one after the other. Each taxi would drop pilots at one or more different destinations and then, once the last pilot had disembarked, hurry on to start collecting pilots from delivery points in order to take them to their next job.

If the weather was very bad, of course, a Pool Commander might close down the airfield. This did not mean, however, that the pilots were released from duty. On the contrary, they had to wait around in the Mess in the hope of the weather improving. Only if by mid- to late-afternoon, depending on the season, it became evident that the weather would not clear enough for even a single delivery before darkness were the pilots released.

On good weather days, the delivery of the first aircraft was only the start of a series of deliveries. As often as possible, a ferry pilot would have a new aircraft delivery originating at his/her first destination airfield. Alternatively, the pilot would be collected by taxi and taken to his/her next task, or – if the distances warranted – he/she might be expected to use ground transportation between one delivery and the next. As a rule, a pilot would deliver two to three machines per day and up to (but rarely) as many as five machines on good, long summer days. On one occasion, however, two pilots working together and using a Fairchild 'taxi' to shuttle back and forth delivered seventeen aircraft in one day.

Flying a vast variety of aircraft was, as was noted previously, the primary challenge of both the ferry pilot and the ATA as an organis-ation. To cope with the problem, the ATA developed the system of categorising aircraft into Classes, which had similar characteristics, and then developing concise, comprehensible notes on each individual type (and Mark thereof) for quick reference by the pilots. The ATA, in fact, developed two sets of notes: the Handling Notes and the Pilot's Notes.

The Handling Notes ran about thirty pages long per aircraft type and contained all essential specifications condensed down from more comprehensive manufacturer's handbooks and technical drawings etc. They contained useful diagrams, for example, of the fuel system or key pieces of equipment. The key feature of the Handling Notes was, however, that they were written for pilots, not engineers, and they were written with the ATA's function in mind. Thus, extraneous information (from the ATA perspective) such as combat and or aerobatics perform-ance parameters were omitted. Instead, the ATA's own test pilots developed recommendations for optimal ATA cruising speeds and suggestions for flap and engine settings for slow flying in particularly bad weather. The Handling Notes also drew attention to any unusual features 'such as a pronounced trim change when the flaps were lowered, or a tendency to swing on landing – features which might embarrass a pilot on a first delivery flight, but pass unnoticed by one flying a particular type continuously'.[3]

These Handling Notes contained everything a ferry pilot needed to know about any particular aircraft, but despite being vastly abridged compared with the usual technical data provided by a manufacturer, they were still far too comprehensive and bulky to be used on a daily basis. For day-to-day flying, therefore, the ATA provided its pilots with a loose-leaf notebook of 4 in x 6 in cards on which were printed (in very fine print) all the essential data for getting an aircraft from A to B without incident. They contained in further condensed form such data as take-off, climbing, cruising and landing speeds, rpms, boost, mix, pitch, temperatures, fuel consumption and the like.

The compact, handy and durable format of the Pilot's Notes was designed to enable them to be carried around and consulted in the cockpit itself. Walker admits that she could never remember all the relevant speeds etc. so she 'used to mug up the take-off, climb and cruise details and then, when I got to the other end, read up on the landing details whilst in the circuit'.[4] The practice appears to have been widespread. Peggy Eveleigh reported the following incident:

My first flight in a Barracuda I shall not easily forget. I had to take one from Worthy Down up to a Fleet Air Arm Station in Scotland, from where I had another aircraft back again.

I was sitting in the aircraft checking to see where everything was, when two naval officers approached me. One of them climbed up to the cockpit and I saw he was a Fleet Air Arm pilot. He told me that both of them had got leave and that their home was in Scotland. They had permission to fly with me if I would take them as passengers . . . Very reluctantly, I agreed. They both climbed into the observer's seat and, when ready, we took off. I decided to make a half-way stop to refuel and when I got to the circuit, I joined it and then got out my little book 'Ferry Pilot's Notes' to check how many degrees of flap I should use on the approach. I came into land very carefully . . . I managed to make a quite reasonable landing and taxied to control and got out. I asked my passengers how they were and they said 'Fine, but we were a little bit worried when we saw you reading a book going around the circuit! Do you always do that sort of thing?' I explained that it was, in fact, quite frequent practice amongst us when flying strange types as it was not always possible to keep everything in one's head and it was much better to check and be sure![5]

Navigating in wartime Britain was another unique skill that ATA pilots had to master. Because ATA pilots flew without radios, all navigation was a combination of visual navigation and dead reckoning. This meant they could not 'fly the beam' – the standard means of commercial navigation at this time, by which a pilot could locate his position relative to a point on the ground by listening for distinctive radio signals. Nor could an ATA pilot call in for a 'fix' as did RAF pilots who were unsure of their location.

Rosemary du Cros highlights some of the difficulties in navigating by visual aids alone when she remarked:

At the beginning of the War a lot of American men came over to join ATA. They were very welcome and useful, once they realised that this is a small island and one had to be careful to stay on it, and not get over occupied Europe by mistake, and when they had learnt that there was no question of 'flying North until you hit a railroad', because the whole place is a criss-cross of railways in every direction.[6]

The remark about not flying over occupied territory is not hypothetical. One Polish pilot, who disobeyed regulations and flew above the overcast, got lost and flew over Germany before eventually landing in France.[7]

Dead reckoning was further complicated by the fact that owing to barrage balloons and other restricted areas such as flying, anti-aircraft and artillery schools, coastal defences and the like, it was almost never possible to fly a direct route. In densely populated parts of the country, particularly the industrial Midlands, there were so many roads and railways that pilots found it very easy to get confused. Nor should it be forgotten that during the War the burning of coal for both domestic and industrial purposes was still standard and hence the degree of air pollution was far in excess of current levels. The Midlands, for example, usually lay under a thick layer of dirty, industrial smog, which obscured visual references from the air. Visual navigation was further complicated by the fact that many of the destinations to which the ATA pilots flew were intentionally camouflaged to be unidentifiable from the air.

To make matters worse, the maps on which the ATA had to rely, in the absence of radio aids were, at best, incomplete. In her talk before the History of Air Navigation Group, former ATA pilot Ann Welch vividly described the state of air maps at this time. Using examples, she showed that airfields were routinely omitted – but which ones were omitted varied from issue to issue. The maps never contained information about barrage balloons or air defences. They did, however, carefully include the useful disclaimer: 'Areas dangerous to flying are not marked on this sheet'.[8]

ATA pilots were officially prohibited from marking hazards on their own maps, in case they – and hence their maps – should fall into enemy hands. In theory, the pilots were supposed to consult the master map kept under lock and key at their Ferry Pool and memorise the features (that could change daily). It appears that a great many pilots ignored this regulation, however, and in fact pencilled in those features of most immediate danger to them on their own maps.

Even if the pilots of the ATA successfully found the aerodrome for which their aircraft was destined, the hazards were not over. Anthony Phelps points out in his memoirs that very many of the aerodromes to which the ATA delivered aircraft were still under construction, being modified or expanded. For example, he describes delivering Hurricanes to an aerodrome where the runways were still being built and having to land on the grass strip between them. Lettice Curtis gives another example of unsuitable fields:

> For a Lib[erator] the run must have been absurdly short, for this aircraft was heavy on the controls and, like all tricycles, needed very positive urging to get off the ground. It also had a very moderate after-take-off climb performance even when lightly loaded. I have, in fact, never ceased to be amazed that it should have been considered feasible . . . to make routine take-offs in an aircraft such as that from that short, uphill grass run . . . But in those days we were not yet conditioned to the use of runways . . . Moreover we were still accustomed to choosing take-off and landing paths strictly according to wind direction, as befitted the majority of tail-wheeled aircraft.[9]

But by far the greatest hazard to the ATA pilots, dependent as they were on visual/dead-reckoning navigation, came from the changeable and unpredictable English weather. It must be borne in mind that weather forecasting – never an exact science – was particularly difficult during the War. Whereas during peacetime ships to the west of the British Isles routinely sent wireless messages with weather conditions, such communications were strictly prohibited during war. Because of the U-boat threat, ships did not broadcast their position for any reason.

Particularly on the west coast, the weather was notorious for changing very abruptly. Taking off in clear – much less question-able weather – by no means assured pilots that they would find suitable weather at their destinations. Without radios, the ATA pilots could neither obtain weather forecasts while *en route* nor request alternative airfields if their destination was 'washed out' on arrival. Dicing with the weather was therefore a perpetual game of chance played by ATA pilots. The weather probably killed more ATA pilots than any other cause. Mary de Bunsen cites two such cases:

> 'You don't want to let the weather worry you,' said one of the Milton brothers one day, as he pointed out to me on the map a short cut across the mountains to the east coast . . . A few months later this man was killed in a Beaufort when one engine failed cutting across that very bit of high ground . . . 'Chiri' was a charming and gallant gentleman and we had been together in training pool where he, too, used to tell me not to be frightened of bad weather. He hit a hillside, having crept up a valley under a low cloudbase until it became too narrow to turn around.[10]

During a particularly dismal period of the war, namely in the autumn of 1942, the ATA flew in very bad weather in an effort to deliver vitally needed aircraft, particularly Spitfires bound for Malta via an aircraft carrier. On 15 September no fewer than six pilots were killed, including two who were flying the urgently needed Spitfires. On another occasion, Diana Barnato Walker found herself caught out abruptly in cloud and barely managed to put down at an airfield not featured on her map. She learned when she reported in to her CO that she had encountered a so-called weather 'inversion': due to a slight drop in temperature on a day with very high humidity, 'the whole of the middle of England had suddenly condensed into cloud. Every pilot of the Training Pool had been caught out by the weather, and had had to put down somewhere. Several aircraft had been broken, and two of us had been killed'.[11] Anthony Phelps remembers another bad day:

> One of the two Hurricanes (both in the hands of ATA pilots) which passed me over the tops of the cloud spun in from many

thousand feet with several inches of ice on its wings.

. . . altogether in that area the freak weather conditions caused seven aeroplanes to crash, killing twelve pilots . . . .[12]

The problem for the ATA was that, particularly in the winter, the weather was often so bad for so long that aircraft accumulated in great numbers. Under the circumstances, the RAF often got impatient. There is an account, perhaps apocryphal, that Air Chief Marshal Harris complained to d'Erlanger about the failure of ATA to deliver replacement aircraft to his squadrons. D'Erlanger allegedly responded by asking how many sorties Bomber Command had flown in the previous week. Indignantly, Harris retorted that it was quite impossible to fly sorties in the weather they had been having – and only then realised what he had said. The meeting is said to have ended amicably.

The tendency of the experienced ATA pilots, however, was to *try* to fly even when the weather was very doubtful. Diana Barnato Walker reports: 'If the weather seemed nearly unflyable or beneath the weather minimum laid down, most of us would take off to have a look. We did a circuit. It often didn't seem so bad once we were up in it.'[13] The situation caused by the particularly bad weather at the all-women's Pool in Hamble, which had responsibility for ferrying some urgently needed Spitfires for Malta on their first leg north, is described vividly by the Pool Operations Officer, Alison King:

The first day we had these Spitfires, the whole of England was laid in a blanket of snow and fog, but although we knew, and the Met was forceful in its confirmation that it would not clear, we waited until dusk had set in and there was no more hope that day of flying. The flying for the next few days was bad, each day the pilots would go off by car to sit all day in a creaky, draughty hut and wait and look, and wait and sigh, and wait again . . .

When the morning of the third day came there was a very slight hope that at midday there might be a lift in the fog . . . It was most treacherous weather . . . the fog would lift for no apparent reason and only slightly it was true, for anything from two to ten minutes, then clamp down again . . . Anyway, two pilots would always be down in the aircraft, ready in case, with batteries plugged in and mechanics ready to start them . . . An hour later the phone rang and it was Margot again. Ann had taken off and gone – somewhere. She herself had frantically tried to beat the weather and had got off too, but . . . it had closed in. She did a circuit, she didn't quite know how and fell, simply fell, into what she hoped was the aerodrome . . . She said she had heard a Spitfire forlornly flying around, as if wanting to get back, but they could see nothing and soon it went away. 'It sounded pathetic going off in the distance,' she added.

When Ann took off the weather closed in around her again almost immediately. She stayed low, as low as she'd ever dared fly, only a few hundred feet above the ground. Even then she didn't see how she was going to get to any airfield, even back to the one she'd left. Low as she was, she was skimming over the almost obscured ground too fast to map-read, and although she had half-flap down to slow her up, she was still flying at 120 mph. She could only continue to keep her eyes on the murky white ground, her course in the right direction, and hope that she would eventually recognise some half-obliterated landmark.

Suddenly, after twenty minutes of this half-blind nightmare flight, she thought she saw the Savernake railway line and she followed the snow-blotted loop road . . . and then literally lane by snow-covered lane, she flew until through the yellow murk . . . she knew she had reached an airfield – and it had to be Colerne.

Not an aircraft moved, there was not a movement anywhere; as she approached the wide white airfield and as her wheels touched the clear-swept runway, she breathed normally for the first time since she had taken off. As she taxied up to the Watch Office, she was literally pulled out of her seat by the waiting engineers and she knew she was at Colerne all right! They had been waiting to fit and calibrate and load, to make the aircraft ready for the next stage of the journey.[14]

Although it was the responsibility of the individual Pool Commanders to open or close their airfields for flying, in general it was left to the discretion of the individual pilot as to whether he/she would actually fly. ATA guidelines were that there had to be a ceiling of 800ft and at least 2,000ft of visibility, but in fact pilots flew whenever they felt – subjectively – that they could make it. This meant that even if several ATA pilots were at the same Pool and heading in similar directions with identical or similar aircraft, in questionable weather some of the pilots might take off and others elect to remain on the ground. Alternatively, they might take off and some carry on while others turned around and returned to their point of origin to wait the weather out a little longer.

Clearly some pilots considered it a test – or proof – of courage, to fly in questionable or difficult weather. The American men, who had volunteered to fly for the ATA, had a particularly bad reputation in this regard. One presumes they had come to England for the adventure of being in a war zone, even if they did not want to risk their citizenship by serving in a foreign military, i.e. by joining the RAF. They were nevertheless on the whole young and anxious to prove themselves, in contrast to the older British pilots who formed the backbone of ATA.

The Pool Commanders naturally tried to discourage foolhardy flying, as it was in direct conflict with the ATA mission of delivering aircraft safely and in perfect condition to the RAF or FAA. One Pool Commander is quoted saying:

> When I first came here . . . pilots used to shoot a line about the weather they had been flying through. I have put a stop to that. If the weather was so bad that it was worth talking about after landing, then you should not have been flying without a radio. In this game always remember that it is a good pilot who gets himself out of trouble, but a better one who doesn't get into it.[15]

It would appear, however, that the above Pool Commander only put an end to *talking* about flying in bad weather rather than actually doing it.

The decision to fly or not was always the pilot's. ATA pilots carried what was known as an Authorisation Card, which verified their authority to fly at their own discretion – sometimes over the objections of senior RAF officers. One ATA woman pilot, for example, was flatly told by an Engineering Officer that he 'was not having a girl taking off in this weather, not in a Mosquito' – but she did.[16]

Mary de Bunsen, who early in her career with the ATA had often been criticised by her male colleagues for being too timid, gradually gained sufficient confidence to take calculated risks. She describes flying into the all-male Pool at Kirkbride after she had been with the ATA for a number of years.

> I arrived, however, to find all the Kirkbride pilots sitting gloomily in the mess. 'We've been washed out', they said. 'Bad weather over the Pennines.' (Another junior pilot had been killed the previous day and the administration was having one of its periodic panics.) 'And where did you come from?' they asked.
>
> 'Over the Pennines,' I replied, trying not to look too pleased, and went out and took another Oxford back the same way.[17]

Or more vividly, while serving as a taxi pilot Mary de Bunsen was tasked to collect a colleague at a FAA station on the northern tip on the

Firth of Forth. When she called ahead to see what the weather was like, he reported that the fog was rapidly closing in and the Navy had closed the Station to flying. He added: 'they won't give you permission to land. But I think if you make a determined pass at the place, I may be able to persuade them to let you in.' Mary de Bunsen continues the story:

> I decided to stay underneath it if I could, and crossed St Andrew's bay just above the waves in almost zero visibility, reflecting that I had just completed 500 hours in 'twins', the war was nearly over, I should be going home soon and this, in the current phraseology, was a bloody silly thing to be doing . . .
>
> I made my circuit half on instruments, plunging in and out of the fog, and put down on the first runway I saw. There were no signals out, and although they gave me no encouragement, they didn't actually shoo me away. Ron was probably holding them down. I taxied in, picked up Ron, stood not upon the order of our going but took off again like a scalded cat. I had never broken so many regulations all in one go, but taxi-pilots were allowed a good deal of latitude by our own people as long as they got the others home. A pilot in the hand was worth two stuck out for the night . . .
>
> The Navy, which had very sportingly allowed me to gatecrash, was now signifying its official disapproval of the whole business by firing off every red Very light it could lay hands on. They looked very pretty against the fog.[18]

The above reference to being 'stuck out' raises a very important aspect of the life of ferry pilots: the frequent necessity of spending the night somewhere far from home, often in completely improvised accommodation. Pilots, if they were wise, always carried with them their personal toiletries and a change of underwear just in case they had to put down somewhere unexpectedly and were 'stuck' somewhere until the weather cleared or the aircraft was again serviceable. Lettice Curtis points out that, in fact, the pilots never knew on departure, just how long they would be away – whether they would be home by nightfall or gone for a week. However:

> this could not be allowed to make a great deal of difference to the luggage we carried. Our overnight bag as well as being light to handle had to be small enough to be stowed in a spare seat, locker or sometimes beside one's seat in the cockpit. In the Hurricane

they were sometimes put under the gun panels in the wing. Inevitably then it had also to be flexible . . . How much easier it would have been with modern synthetic and drip-dry materials![19]

If the pilots did indeed find themselves 'stuck out' overnight, they were very much at the mercy of circumstances. In Cheeseman's words, having seen his aeroplane 'bedded down', a pilot would 'hike his way to the nearest town to begin the tiring tramp round, often in the blackout, to find a hotel'.[20] Phelps, too, describes the difficulty of walking to the nearest bus-stop or station wearing flying kit and lugging a parachute and overnight bag. An illustrative example of the difficulties of finding accommodation for the night follows:

> Leaving our parachutes with the RTO, we were fortunate enough to get a taxi and asked the driver to take us to the nearest hotel. It was full. So was the next. The third was able to accommodate us. Its sole claim to fame is, I believe, that it once housed for the night a high dignitary of the Church who, as a result thereof, was subsequently involved in a divorce case which created some public interest at the time.
>
> Having washed, I felt a little happier, although I wished that I had some shoes as my flying boots tucked under my trousers seemed to weigh about a ton and feel as though I had been wearing them a month. The thought of dinner did much to cheer me. The thought of it, however, was all we ever got that night.[21]

This situation improved for the men of the ATA more rapidly than for the women, simply because many RAF stations took a dim view of women in their midst for some time yet. In the first year or so, women pilots were generally sent off to find their own accommodation in a nearby town – which might in fact be miles away in the bitter cold, fog or pouring rain. They, too, were in flying kit and dragging a heavy parachute with them. And, just as Phelps describes above, having arrived in a provincial town or village without warning, there was no guarantee that there would be any accommodation – suitable or otherwise. What could be found might be very cold, lacking hot water and other amenities, and priced to the market (i.e. excessively expensive).

But things were not always this bad. The RAF could be very charming too. Mary de Bunsen reports the following incident from *before* she joined the ATA, when she delivered a Tutor Moth while still a civilian employee of an aircraft dealer:

A frosty moon was shining when I finally waffled in to Aston Down, parked the aircraft, and walked into the watch office in my 'County' tweed coat and skirt, jumper and pearl necklace.

They took me in their stride. 'You'd better stay the night,' they said kindly. 'We'll make up a bed for you in the ante-room'.

The war was yet young, and it was the only time I ever slept in the ante-room of an RAF officers' mess. A sergeant made up my bed and brought me soap and towels . . . [22]

June Farquhar tells of another kind of hospitality when she was stuck out over a New Year by fog:

It was a refit station for aircrew who needed to make-up a new team for bombers. I landed there in my little Tiger Moth and was stuck there for three days over the New Year. I was adopted by a Wellington crew who had lost their skipper. It was a highly emotional and marvellous time for one lived for the moment and discounted the lives lost. Those wonderful kids made me their skipper for that short duration and we did everything as a team, Church on Sunday, parties, the lot.[23]

Before long, as the number of WAAF increased rapidly, there was usually a 'Waafery' where the women ATA pilots could find accommodation – and by then the WAAF officers had largely broken down the barriers to women in Officers' Messes too.

Equally important, with time the ATA increased its efficiency too. There were more linked flights, and more taxis, so that the chances of being 'stuck out' decreased as the war progressed.

'Foraging' was another uncertain proposition throughout the war, although again things improved somewhat with time. In the early days, pilots – both male and female – were left to their own devises. As described above, after hitchhiking to the nearest town and looking for a vacant room in the blackout, it was often too late for a meal, so many pilots retired hungry. As the ATA became an increasingly familiar and appreciated partner, however, the RAF more-or-less 'adopted' the ATA. The men were, of course, integrated more easily. At first the women often found themselves in a stuffy, unused 'Ladies' Room' or sometimes completely excluded, but after the initial adjustment period the women too were accepted. They could then get a meal at most Officers' Messes, or, if they didn't want to take the time of going over for a formal meal, they could eat at the small canteens provided for ground crews in the hangars. Nevertheless, when time was short and pilots in a hurry, many carried on all day with nothing to eat but their bar of Cadbury's milk chocolate, which ATA's Chief Medical Officer, Dr Barbour, 'managed to persuade the Ministry of Food to allocate to ATA . . . .'[24]

Another hardship in the early days, before there were enough taxi aircraft or enough pilots to fly them, entailed returning to the home Ferry Pool by ground transportation after a delivery. In these early days, because there were only a very few Ferry Pools, the trips could be very long, sometimes all the way back from Scotland. This could mean spending all night in an 'unheated, darkened train, usually choc-a-bloc with troops, so that the only seat was on their parachute bags in the freezing corridors'.[25] By mid-1943, however, the number of Ferry Pools and taxis had increased dramatically, as had the ground support organisation. Rather than ferrying aircraft from one end of the country to the other, aircraft destined for distant points would be ferried only as far as the next appropriate Ferry Pool for ferrying onwards. The pilots would generally collect aircraft that were moving in the opposite direction at that Pool, and bring them back to their own Pool before nightfall. The need for ground transportation was thereby greatly reduced.

Even when a pilot was not lucky enough to land a return ferry job, there was always the chance of 'hitchhiking' with another ATA pilot going the right way in an aircraft with capacity for a passenger. As a rule, the more Classes of aircraft a pilot was qualified to fly, the more likely he/she was to have a return-ferry. By hitchhiking with senior pilots, however, junior ferry pilots often had the opportunity to co-pilot. Another alternative for getting where one wanted to go was hitchhiking with the RAF or FAA. This could take quite extensive dimensions. When the mother of a South African ATA pilot became very ill, the pilot received leave and permission to travel home by whatever means she could.

> The first stage of her journey was easy enough. It was an ordinary delivery Spitfire form Hamble to Lyneham in Gloucestershire . . . When she had delivered her Spitfire, she started to make discreet inquiries in the Watch Office and discovered that a Liberator was to leave for Cairo in a couple of days' time. Now Jackie is a very determined young woman, but she doesn't look it, which is the perfect combination for getting your own way! It didn't take her so very long to get permission from the squadron leader to go as second pilot on the trip to Cairo and she was duly briefed . . . The Liberator didn't get any further than Malta, as it went unserviceable there, but no sooner had Jackie said good-bye than she set about making arrangements for her next trip. She soon discovered

that there was a Dakota going east and managed to get a lift, purely as a passenger this time. When they landed at Cairo . . . she managed – miracle of miracles – to get aboard a Dakota going, of all places, to her home town of Pretoria . . .

She stayed with her mother only a few days and then she said good-bye, to get a lift in another Dakota bound this time for Khartoum. As they touched down, Jackie, quick as ever, noticed another just landing in front of them. She rushed over to the pilot as he taxied in and asked him where he was bound for. He was on his way to England with some Ghurka officers. Here she really did experience difficulty in getting herself included on the plane – and she didn't mind whether it was as a passenger, crew or cargo! However, just as it looked as though she really was going to be left behind on this heaven-sent flight, the trouble was sorted out by the RAF and, with not a moment to lose, she was off and on her way to Marseilles . . . At Istres the weather was so bad that the landing had to be made straight out of cloud under conditions of the greatest difficulty and hazard. The next day the weather was still bad, but on went the Dakota and finally Jackie landed in . . . England . . . .[26]

But it was above all the taxi aircraft that played the most important part in ensuring that pilots made more frequent deliveries, and also greatly reduced the number of nights pilots had to spend away from home. Getting them home at night not only assured that they would be available for duty the next morning at 9 am, but also had a significant impact on morale. Being 'home' for the night generally enabled ATA pilots to eat and sleep better than when scrounging in strange places. It furthermore ensured that they could have a semblance of private life, whether this was pursuing sport or hobbies or maintaining relationships. There can be no question that increasing the number of nights pilots spent at 'home' contributed to the health, efficiency and morale of the entire organisation.

'Home' for the ferry pilot might be any of a variety of accommodation. The ATA, being a civilian organisation, did not usually provide housing or quarters for its employees (although there was one living-in Mess at Thame, where Sir William Currie put one wing of his Tudor mansion at the disposal of the ATA[27]). As a rule, ATA pilots were free to choose where they wanted to live and what they were willing to pay for it, but there were also Billeting Officers, who helped foreign pilots or those on temporary duty at one Pool or another to find housing. This could be very good (Lady Astor, for example, welcomed the pilots of the ATA into her own home),[28] or it could be quite dismal. Emily Chapin, one of the American women who flew with the ATA, encountered very inhospitable conditions:

> When Emily and Bobby arrived at their new billet, it looked from the outside like a grand old English house. Inside it was like a barn. Their room had no heat, not even small heaters . . . so she put on her long underwear and socks and went right to bed to keep warm . . . . Her bed was barely wide enough to turn over in, and when she did, the blankets fell off. She got up and put on her gloves and laid her overcoat on top of her. Then she felt the cold coming up from underneath, so she got up and put two of the blankets on the mattress. When she pulled the remaining blankets over her, she realised they were only three and four feet long . . . .
>
> At lunch, Emily and Bobby went straight to the billeting officer. 'Oh, we're all cold,' he said. 'Is that your only complaint?'[29]

The next night Emily preferred to pay for a hotel. Fortunately, she also enjoyed ten days as the guest of Sir Lindsey Everard, Air Commodore, RAF, when she received hospitality and comfort that more than compensated her for the above experience.

Most of the British pilots found housing in clubs, with friends, or rented cottages or rooms near their respective Pool. The women ATA pilots often rented a cottage together. Whatever the accommodation, one of the ATA men observed, 'nobody complained too much . . . because, perhaps, we were secretly ashamed of enjoying ourselves so much when everyone else was having such a thin time'.[30]

For those who wanted, therefore, social life could continue much as before – to the extent that wartime conditions permitted this for anyone. Mary de Bunsen, for example, remarks that she 'saw little of the others off duty, because, in fact, we had very little in common outside of flying and most of the men wanted a different kind of feminine companionship'.[31] Lettice Curtis stresses that her circle of friends was not exclusively ATA, but rather included the test pilots, instructors, RAF and indeed anyone working on or near the airfields. Yet, Lucas felt that women pilots 'automatically had an affinity with other pilots . . . apart from that the RAF pilots were our heroes and the reason for ATA's existence'.[32] Certainly, the instances of romance between the women of the ATA and other pilots were numerous. Several were already married to or widows of RAF pilots when they joined the ATA. Other ATA women preferred ATA pilots and ground crew. One of the American recruits was engaged to one of ATA's ground staff within a month of arrival.

Other Americans found it more difficult to strike down roots, and 'learned to recognise those at the Red Cross club who, like [themselves] wanted spur-of-the-moment company at the theatre, a good dance partner, a friend with whom to share the interlude of war'.[33] For someone who did not intend to stay in the United Kingdom, the company was transient, and so were they. But even the transients like the American Emily Chapin had to admit she had never enjoyed life more'.[34]

Admittedly, by the end of the war, most of the ATA pilots – male and female – were very tired. Those who had been with the ATA from the start, or at least the early years 1940 and 1941, in particular had reached that point – as Mary de Bunsen put it – 'which seasoned pilots know well, when you are too tired to do anything but go on flying, which you continue to do with a kind of mechanical efficiency because it is your job'.[35] In retrospect, however, most agree with Freydis Sharland, who summed up her experience saying: 'Looking back I remember laughing more in the ATA . . . than at any time before or since.'[36]

WAFS/WASP in FERD

The American women who flew with the Ferrying Division of Air Transport Command had in many respects very similar working conditions to the women of the ATA. They, too, flew seven days a week, reporting to the Flight Line at 8 am, unless they had returned from a previous delivery after 10 pm the previous night. The WASP with FERD, like the ATA, flew from dawn to dusk, weather permitting, and were faced with the same difficulties of finding food and accommodation when away from their home base.

The similarities in working conditions were greatest during the early days of the WAFS, when the American women too were flying only small, light aircraft without radios and so were navigating by dead reckoning and maps. Yet, despite all the similarities, the defining characteristic of ferry work in the United States was distance rather than weather.

Of course, the weather could be very bad. It closed down flying for extensive periods of time, and thunderstorms and ice were two weather dangers that were far more common in the United States than the United Kingdom. There were also tornadoes, hurricanes, dust-storms and temperatures of over 100 degrees Fahrenheit to deal with – all phenomena unknown on the British Isles. But encounters with such extremes were rare, and on the whole the weather in the United States was much more predictable. There were therefore far fewer instances of pilots being abruptly 'caught out' in or by it.

The distances that had to be covered were, however, on a completely different scale than in Britain. In late 1942 and early 1943, when the WAFS were primarily tasked to deliver small training aircraft from the factories at which they were produced in the mid-Atlantic states to training establishments across the South and South-west, this meant covering well over 1,000 miles – one way. These aircraft with 65 hp engines, a fuel capacity of just 12 gallons and an average speed of 75 mph, took literally days to deliver.

Verges writes:

For the women of the 2nd Ferry Group, delivering Piper Cubs from the factory in Lockhaven, Pennsylvania, to flight schools in the South-west was a week's work. Just before sunrise they flew to the factory in the WAFS transport plane, hauling all their flying gear. In mild weather a flight of Cubs could usually get as far as Atlanta the first day . . . . By dawn the next day the WAFS were hopping across the South between fuel stops to Shreveport, Louisiana, the second night's stop.

The third day they landed in Dallas and then flew on to an AAF training field in some desolate place farther west. Once the paper-work on the Cubs was finished, the women put on uniform skirts, spruced up, and caught the late bus from the nearest small town. After riding several hours back to Dallas, the WAFS took the first American Airlines flight to Washington.

. . . It was eleven hours' flying time to Washington, where they boarded a train to Wilmington and then grabbed a taxi out to New Castle AAFB. They still had to file reports before they could wash their hair and get some sleep.[37]

Given the distances and the weakness of the engines of these tiny primary trainers, a good head wind could result in so little progress that not only the cars on the highway below were overtaking them, but fuel would not last even to the next airfield. The WAFS, however, proved resourceful and equal even to this situation, as the following incident involving two WAFS flying in tandem shows:

Either the wind information given me was incorrect or it increased mightily . . . After the gas gauge sat on empty for 10 minutes, I decided I had better choose a place to land before it was chosen for me. A lovely beautiful wonderful highway came rolling into view and it took me hardly a moment to realize just how particu-larly wonderful a highway it was. It ran into the wind and was totally without telephone wires but best of all it was long and flat and provided a view of traffic, something there was fortunately none of.

I landed gingerly and looked back with tremendous relief to see the other plane land beautifully and so up the road we taxied . . . We were so delighted to have the planes safely down we forgot to realise how ridiculous we looked. A truck almost went into the ditch at the sight of us prancing up the highway.

When I asked the filling station operator what octane his gas was he chewed reflectively on his cigar and finally said rightly, 'Octane! I don't know, lady. All I know is that it's mighty cheap car gas.' And it was. But it took us sputtering safely to our destination.[38]

Flying in these open-cockpit aircraft in winter over such vast distances was not particularly pleasant either. The temperatures were bitter cold even in fleece-lined flight suits, and the women had to lash their maps to their legs to keep them from being blown away in the wind. Navigation was more difficult too. One of the WAFS explains: 'What you usually use in spring, summer, and fall are the streams and rivers, and they were all frozen over. They were all white with snow on top of the ice. You could get so lost in that territory.'[39]

While this was a problem encountered in the United Kingdom as well, on the whole navigating by sight and dead reckoning (known as VFR for Visual Flight Rules) in the United States was quite different. First of all, there were relatively few restricted areas – and lots and lots of room to go around those there were – and there were absolutely no barrage balloons. Furthermore, the destination airfields were for the most part *not* camouflaged. Quite the contrary, the United States government had undertaken an extensive programme in the 1930s to make towns identifiable from the air by painting the names of towns prominently on the roofs of large buildings. Across most of the country there was also no black-out, and the farther west one went, the fewer roads and railroads there were, reducing confusion – provided one could find such a landmark at all, that is. The flat nature of vast portions of the country furthermore added to the ease of following these ground transportation routes, which generally cut across the country straight as arrows.

Conditions improved significantly once the women were allowed to fly larger, more powerful and closed-cockpit aircraft – all equipped with radios. In these aircraft, the WAFS could use the standard commercial and military procedures for navigation, in which they had been trained. This meant they were able to follow radio signals under blind flying conditions, and had radio contact with airfields as they flew over them and as they came in to land. It was possible to get weather checks and so divert to airfields that were not experiencing weather difficulties, much the same way as airliners did then and still do today.

Particularly satisfying for the WASP of FERD were long distance deliveries in the fast fighters.

> On a routine ferrying delivery flight in a P-51 from Long Beach to Newark, WASP Jean Landis flew from coast to coast in only nine hours and thirty-five minutes in the air, two hours faster than Jacqueline Cochran in her P-35 when she won the Bendix Race in 1938. For airline passengers, such a trip still took two, and often three, days.[40]

Or:

> Jill McCormick, at the controls of a P-47 en route from Long Island to North Carolina, kept finding check points ten minutes ahead of where she thought she should be. When she recomputed her ground speed, she clocked 401 miles an hour, faster than the pre-war international speed record.[41]

But it wasn't speed alone that made such flights exciting for the women. Because of America's sheer size, most women had not seen much of the country beyond their hometown, state or region before joining the WASP. Suddenly, they were travelling from one end of the country to the other, often stopping along the way for refuelling or because of bad weather.

Despite the excitement, these were often gruelling flights. They required careful planning: plotting a course in advance, planning re-fuelling stops, and getting the latest weather reports. Flying over these distances also meant flying with full tanks, and keeping these balanced. As the aircraft were usually new, the pilots were warned to watch for possible malfunctions, which were not infrequent. Every plotted course included alternative airfields for putting down in an emergency. In contrast to England, these could be few and far between and the inter-vening territory completely inhospitable desert, forest or wasteland.

There were also the Appalachians and the Rockies to be reckoned with, and these were formidable barriers indeed. They required flying at high altitudes and so dealing both with oxygen and the often violent wind currents and ice. Ann Craft remembered her first flight across the Rockies vividly:

I can remember that mountain coming closer and closer, but I just stayed on the same level and I think finally I only had about two hundred feet of altitude over the mountain and all of a sudden here we were at the Tuscon airport.[42]

Gini Dulaney had a more unnerving experience on her return flight across the Rockies during training:

When she gained enough altitude to clear the pass, however, the engine quit. Then, as soon as she descended to a lower altitude, it caught again. 'I went so far as to undo the safety belt, and I rolled back the canopy and was just about to jump.' After her engine caught, she went back up to higher altitude again and it quit again. 'By then I was a cot case . . . and I still hadn't cleared the pass!' The engine failed her three times . . . before she figured out it must have been carburettor ice . . . [She] finally did make it over the mountains, but then she had a dust storm blocking her vision . . . It was very dark and the flares were lit before she arrived at Avenger Field.[43]

Given the distances, the women ferry pilots flying with FERD spent a great deal more time 'stuck out' than did their English colleagues. Even routine flights, particularly in the trainers, but also with larger aircraft during the shorter winter days, required overnight stops. The return trip by ground transportation or commercial airline took even longer. Like the ATA pilots, American ferry pilots were also frequently given a new job when they delivered an aircraft, so that they never knew where they might be spending the night or when they would get back to their home base.

For example, WASP Barbara Erickson left Long Beach, California, one morning with a P-51 for Evansville, Illinois. The next day she was given a P-47 for San Pedro. The day after, she ferried a C-47 from Long Beach to Fort Wayne, Indiana, returning to California in a P-47. Altogether, it amounted to four 2000-mile trips in just five days of flying – a feat for which she was awarded an Air Medal.

More illustrative of the risks of getting 'stuck out', however, is the experience of Teresa James. She received orders one day to collect a P-47 from Farmingdale, Long Island, and deliver it to Evansville, Indiana, 'a quick 800 mile trip in the fast pursuit'. She assumed she would be getting another P-47 to fly back east, and so took off without a change of clothes. But on arrival in Evansville, she was handed orders to deliver a P-47 to Long Beach in California – on the opposite coast from the one at which she was stationed. To make matters worse, it needed repairs and then the weather closed in. She bought a toothbrush and tooth-paste, and waited nine days before the plane and the weather were ready and she could fly the 1,800 miles from Evansville to Long Beach. There, she was given a P-51 bound for Fort Meyers, Florida. She had never flown a P-51 before, but she checked herself out on it, flying circuits and bumps for twenty minutes until she felt confident. Then she set off east. Unfortunately, halfway across Texas, she ran into the outer fringe of a bad storm in the Gulf of Mexico that was causing rain from Louisiana to Texas. For days,

> Teresa could only make short hops from base to base during breaks in the overcast. Her loafers were permanently caked with mud from soggy runways. The humidity would not allow her socks and underwear to dry overnight before she had to put them back on in the morning. As she did not have her uniform jacket, she could not enter any air bases officers' clubs. She began to tire of sandwiches at operations canteens, and she desperately hoped that at Fort Meyers, she would be given a plane to fly home to New Castle. When she signed over the P-51 to Fort Meyers operations, however, the officer indicated an AT-6 out on the flight line that was due in Oklahoma . . . .
>
> Two days later, Teresa was in Tulsa . . . [Here she] received orders to take a P-39 Airacobra to Great Falls, Montana . . . .
>
> The next day, Teresa flew her P-39 over 1,200 miles from Oklahoma to Great Falls, Montana. As soon as she walked into the operations office, she was handed another set of orders. She could not bear to open them until she had found a cup of coffee. Then she sat down and began to read. For a minute she sat in disbelief. At last she was being ordered to fly a P-47 back to New Castle.
>
> . . . Her day's hop in a P-47 to Evansville had turned into a 4-week, 17-state, 6- airplane, 11,000-mile trip.[44]

Being 'stuck out' was a very mixed experience. The worst that could happen was that the young women pilots in their unrecognised uniforms would be arrested. One incident was described earlier, another is equally illustrative:

> In the early spring of 1944, bad weather grounded four WASPs in Americus, Georgia. They left their airplanes in the hangar at the airport and caught a bus into town to look for a hotel room. No sooner had they started down the main street, than a police car

pulled up beside them. Two policemen got out and demanded that they come to the police station. Women were not allowed on the street at night in slacks, one cop said sternly. No amount of insisting that they were Army pilots in uniform would do.

At the police station, the women were locked in a cell. They tried to persuade the sheriff to let them make a telephone call to the ferrying base. Instead, he decided to test their story by calling the commanding officer of the air base where they had landed. The CO was at a party. The WASPs listened to the sheriff's end of the conversation with growing alarm. 'We have a few girls down here impersonating officers,' he said. The mockery with which he enunciated the last two words showed clearly the genre of women he thought them to be. 'That's exactly where I've got 'em,' the sheriff said smugly, and hung up the phone.

Not until after 2:00 in the morning were the WASPs allowed to make one phone call. They decided to call Cincinnati and wake up Nancy Love. When they told her where they were, Love demanded to speak to the sheriff . . . The WASPs were released and driven back to the airfield, where they waited with agitation until dawn to take off and fly as far away from Americus as they could.[45]

Although not an isolated incident, such treatment was in fact rare. Far more common was simply to be denied accommodation at the huge AAF bases at which the women pilots put down to 'RON' (Remain over Night). USAAF installations tended to be located at some distance from the nearest town, to which the WASP then had to find their way (lugging their parachutes and overnight bags). They had to then find a hotel, often in obscure provincial towns with little accommodation for transients, and stay at their own expense. In many small towns this could be almost impossible, or highly unappetising. Bed bugs and unsavoury fellow guests were just some of the problems encountered. All WASP learned to iron shirts and collars on hotel radiators, to press their slacks under their mattresses and similar tricks. Many WASP preferred to spend the night sleeping in airport lobbies. In one case, an exhausted WASP, unable to find other accommodation in the middle of the night on a strange base, took herself to the base Sick Quarters and lay down fully clothed on an unmade bed in an empty ward.

Where available, the WASP were generally given accommodation in Nurse's or WAC quarters. But here too the reception might well be less than hospitable. Many nurses and WACs resented the WASP, whom they perceived as being over-paid and over-publicised 'glamour girls'.

At the better bases, particularly the Ferry Groups and airbases to which the WASP flew regularly or where WASP were stationed, accommodation was often provided in the Bachelor Officers' Quarters (BOQ). And military efforts at gallantry could have their humorous side.

> A flight of WAFs in Cubs was forced down at the Marine base in Quantico, Virginia, because of weather. The Marines were anxious to be hospitable. They partitioned off part of the barracks with a sturdy wall and posted a sign: KEEP OUT! LADIES PRESENT. Regardless, the officer on duty posted an armed guard, who also personally escorted each of the WAFs to the latrine.[46]

Similar problems arouse with regard to meals. At some bases, WASP enjoyed the 'officer's privileges' they had officially been granted on inception, entitling them to eat at the Officers' Mess and enter the Officers' Club. Some bases restricted WASP to Nurses' and WAC Messes. Others sent them to eat with civilian contractors and employees, if there were enough of these to have their own canteen. At particularly hostile bases, the WASP would be sent out to eat at civilian restaurants and snack bars off-base.

Once a delivery was finished and if no new job awaited at the delivery point, FERD regulations required pilots to find the 'fastest way back to base'. Where practical, the USAAF tried to provide transport. For example, when batches of deliveries from one factory or another required many WASP to report at the same time for collection, they would often be brought there in a transport plane. Already in December 1942, for example, New Castle AAFB had a 'regular shuttle' to bring the women to Hagerstown, Maryland, to pick up PT-19s bound for training establishments in the south. The women had their own Lockheed Lodestar to take them to the Piper Club factory in Pennsylvania for the same purpose. Later, when the WASP were carrying out multiple P-47 deliveries every day between Long Island and Newark, New Jersey, they were allocated a C-47 to pick them up at Newark and bring them all back to Long Island to collect the next delivery. In other instances, where the distances were shorter and multiple pilots were shuttling back and forth, ground transportation would be provided.

There was also a military 'airline' (MATS) run by FERD to move pilots around, but in sharp contrast to the taxis of the ATA, this service only figures very rarely in the accounts of the WASP. Furthermore, it was almost always referred to as 'SNAFU' Airlines for 'Situation Normal:

All Fouled Up'. It had a reputation for taking unnecessary risks and for sloppy flying, as well as never being on time. More significantly, it does not appear to have been sufficiently large to meet the demand. Far more frequently, therefore, the WASP found themselves on commercial airlines, for which they (and all ferry pilots) were officially authorised to 'bump' any other passenger short of the President of the United States.

Unlike the women of the ATA, however, the WASP were initially expressly forbidden from hitching rides with the Air Force. The reason appears to have been 'concern' for the women's 'reputation'. This strict segregation, however, meant that the women were more dependent on civil air transportation, which was generally over-crowded, slow and, most important, serviced large cities rather than the obscure places in which the Army Air Forces usually located their bases. WASP usually had to take public buses and trains to the nearest town with an airport and then wait an indefinite period for the next flight going the right direction. Because their male colleagues could hitchhike rides on military aircraft, the women were clearly disadvantaged by this ruling and their effectiveness inhibited. Gradually, however, the policy against hitchhiking on military aircraft was undermined, so that by 1944 this regulation had faded into obscurity, ignored if not repealed.

Once they had returned, by whatever means, to their home bases, however, the women serving with the USAAF were again treated as members of the Armed Forces. From 30 August 1943 onwards the WASP were *required* to live on base. By this point, special barracks had been provided for the WASP of the FERD at all the four Ferrying Groups where they were permanently stationed. At installations in Training Command as well, the women were provided with housing on base – and ordered to live there. In fact, henceforth they needed passes to be *off* the base.

Teresa James describes the WAFS quarters in New Castle Army Air Base in her diary:

> Our new home was built from two-by-fours, planks and boards. One window per room, two if you had a corner room. I think . . . I had to be crazy for leaving my comfortable home and lucrative job as flight instructor. I never expected to see such a barren struc-ture, because I had been informed that the men who had occupied BOQ14 had moved to another building. I was expecting furnish-ings. As I strode through the first floor, layered with mud, I passed the vacant rooms and was astonished at the sunlight peeking through the cracks in the walls.

I thought maybe the second floor might be better. I proceeded to the stairs in the rear of the building, climbing the fourteen steps. I immediately picked out a room with the least daylight peeking through the cracks. Furnishings consisted of one sagging cot and one iron chair.[47]

Another WAFS pilot, Nancy Batson, found: 'A ten by ten cubicle with a metal Army cot, dresser, mirror and a rod from which to hang her clothes . . . . This is the Army, Miss Batson, she thought to herself, paraphrasing a popular song of the day.'[48] Another problem was that initially the barracks had no curtains or blinds. The women therefore had to dress and undress in the dark or the hall if they did not want to be a spectacle for the men going to and from the Officers' Club next door. The Army was as little interested in the women providing that kind of entertainment as the women themselves and venetian blinds were soon fitted. The Army was less concerned about dealing with the frequent difficulties with boilers and plumbing; the women were often left without heat or hot water long enough to feel the need to wear their bulky flying kit to bed. Not all reactions to the accommodation were negative, however. Betty Gillies found in retrospect:

As I remember, my reaction to the physical properties of the base was mainly AWE! The huge airport with all the fantastic flying machines scattered about. Our quarters were rather drafty. My room was on the north-west corner and one could see daylight through the cracks. But I loved it! BOQ 14 was right in the centre of the base and next to the Officer's Club, which we were privileged to enjoy.[49]

Yet, even Gillies' positive attitude might have been strained by the conditions faced by the WAFS at Long Beach Army Air Base on arrival:

. . . the unpartitioned second floor allowed no means for privacy. At one end, in open space, a row of toilets squatted in full view of God and everybody. The women later learned the place had been used as a psych ward.[50]

Fortunately, better accommodations were soon built, and there were 'entertainment advantages' at this base as well; owing to the proximity to Hollywood, radio shows were broadcast direct from the Athletic and Recreation Hangar and various well-known personalities performed at the Officers' Club.[51]

WFTD

During the early days of the WFTD, when training was still being conducted at Howard Hughes Airport in Houston, the women trainees were housed individually in hotels or in groups at motels specially rented for them. These arrangements lasted only a few months. The dominant experience of women who learned to fly with the USAAF was that of Avenger Field near Sweetwater, Texas, where starting in March 1943 an entire airbase was put exclusively at their disposal. The vast majority of WASP went through part or all of their training there.

At Avenger Field the women again moved into accommodation recently vacated by male cadets. They thus lived in barracks, which for some reason known only to the USAAF, were known as 'bays'.

> The bays were a series of one-story rooms, two rooms connected by a smaller room with showers and toilets. Six girls were bunked in each room, so twelve . . . shared the two showers and two toilets.[52]

At Avenger, women trainees were subjected to the same discipline as male cadets at similar installations across the country: reveille at 6.15 am; breakfast formation at 6.45 am; march to the Mess hall for a cafeteria-style breakfast; march to the flight-line or to the class rooms for ground instruction. There was also a daily PT drill, parades and inspections. Trainees could only leave the base on weekends, and only if they had been given a pass. Passes were denied if a trainee had accumulated too many 'demerit' points, and even when in possession of a pass, the girls were required to be on base at night unless they had a 'weekend' pass. Throughout the roughly seven months of training, trainees were entitled to only one such pass.

While at Avenger, the women pilots were under the direction of the female 'Establishment Officer', Mrs Deaton, her small staff of (female) assistants and a cadre of about a dozen USAAF officers, who were responsible for the administration of the base and the trainees. Flying and Ground Instruction, as described previously, was in the hands of a civilian contractor, Aviation Enterprises.

Compared with other USAAF and Army installations, the base was small; by August 1943 there were five to six classes of WASP at Avenger at any one time, which meant roughly 600 women in various stages of training. Avenger was also very isolated. For social life the trainees were dependent on organised events (such as Saturday night dances with cadets brought in from other bases) or invitations from local families to barbecues and the like. The trainees were for the most part effectively cut off from civilian life, and so they were largely responsible for their own amusement.

> Skirmishes and pranks between adjoining bays kept morale high when the weather caused training delays and boredom set in. Soap chips and nutshells scattered between the sheets or alarm clocks planted in enemy territory, set to go off at intervals during the night, erupted into rousing pillow fights.[53]

The women in training were also very adept at writing new lyrics to popular tunes in order to build up morale while marching and drilling.[54]

Notably, and in contrast to the women with the ATA, during their training the WASP were largely cut off from men. As a matter of policy, the army officers on the staff were married men, and the civilian instructors were officially 'off-limits'. Even the efforts of other Air Force cadets to establish contact with the women fliers were strictly discouraged. Shortly after Avenger Field became the first all-female flight school in the history of the USAAF, their unique form of courting became a problem:

> For several days dozens of eager cadets from neighbouring AAF training facilities made 'forced' landings at the base. In a single afternoon thirty-nine men taxied up to operations reporting mechanical difficulties with their aircraft. Within a week Avenger's commanding officer was obliged to close the field to all outside air traffic.[55]

Of course, where there is a will there is way. Despite the official prohibition against 'fraternisation' with instructors, for example, several trainees married their instructors after graduation.

Once the women pilots graduated from the WFTD and were posted to their various duties, the situation reversed dramatically. After the women left the nearly all-woman environment of Avenger Field, they usually found themselves assigned to bases with several thousand enlisted men, a few hundred male officers and only a handful of WASP. Sometimes there were nurses and WACs at the base, often there were not. Even when there were other women, the WASP had a marked advantage with flying officers because they shared the same interests and spoke the same jargon.

Nevertheless, the situation created could be uncomfortable. On one base, a particularly attractive WASP caught the attention of the CO and the men came to believe that the fastest way to get shipped overseas was to risk dating the object of their commander's affections; the WASP was thus sharply inhibited in her own freedom of choice. At Camp Davis there were roughly 50,000 men stationed, of which 600 were pilots, while the number of women pilots sent here was just twenty-five to start with. The WASP at Camp Davis reported feeling 'beleaguered'. Other WASP found it difficult to adjust to being treated as equals by male colleagues, encountering and being uncomfortable with camaraderie rather than courtship. And still others intentionally avoided relationships, which appeared to have no future. For example, at the B-17 school at Lockbourne Army Air Base the other trainees were mostly destined for the US Eighth Air Force, and 'forming strong relationships with them seemed like playing with fate'.[56]

But most of the attention was welcome and much of it mutual. Incidents of affairs, even with married officers, were not unknown. As one commentator worded it:

> Far removed from the stern gazes of their hometown neighbours, relatives and preachers, and consistent with the highly charged wartime atmosphere and extraordinary adventurousness of this choice to fly and join the WASP in the first place, the WASPs often had a more uninhibited attitude toward relationships than many Americans.[57]

At any event, a very large number of WASP left to marry men they had met while on active service.[58]

Risks

ATA

Flying is a dangerous profession, and a great deal has already been said about the risks of being caught in weather, however, the pilots of the ATA faced exceptional hazards quite aside from weather and the ever-present risk of mechanical failure. These additional risks originated primarily from the fact that, except for the last couple of months, the ATA was operating within a war zone.

Particularly during the early years, the RAF was understandably nervous about any unidentified aircraft flying in British air space, and since the ATA aircraft were not equipped with radios or IFF (Identification Friend or Foe), there was always the risk of them being mistaken for the enemy. The RAF, therefore, required that all aircraft flying, particularly in areas readily accessible to the *Luftwaffe* and/or containing tempting targets, be reported to it. In certain 'Defended Areas' such as around Portsmouth and Southampton, for example, 'Fighter Command reserved the right to shoot at any unidentified aircraft first and ask questions afterwards'.[59] It is to the credit of both the ATA and the RAF that there are no recorded incidents of aircraft flown by the ATA becoming victims of mistaken identity; no ATA aircraft were shot at – much less down – by the RAF.

The record of the Anti-Aircraft units is unfortunately less perfect. To be sure, no aircraft are recorded lost to friendly ground-fire, but there were a number of incidents of aircraft – clearly marked with RAF roundels and flashes – being shot at by 'Ack-Ack'. Lettice Curtis reports:

> Suddenly over the sound of the engine I heard a dull WHOOMP – then another. For a moment I was puzzled, then I saw puffs of smoke appearing above me and the realisation dawned that the airfield anti-aircraft guns were firing . . . .[60]

Diana Barnato Walker describes another incident or rather incidents:

> We used to take Hurricanes regularly from Langley to Cardiff and I don't know what the ack-ack boys were up to with their aircraft recognition, but frequently when I was flying across the Bristol Channel at between 1,500 and 2,000 ft, there would be a shudder by the aircraft as little blackberry-shaped puffs of dark smoke suddenly appeared, very close, all around it.
>
> . . . One day a notice appeared on the No. 1 Pool's board, requesting any pilots who thought they had been shot at over the Bristol Channel to report to the CO . . . there was quite a long queue.[61]

The ATA faced another kind of 'friendly fire' as well. ATA pilot Barbara Lankshear reported the following incident when delivering an aircraft to an RAF fighter station:

> . . . impossibly strong wind 90 degrees to the runway and fighters coming in right, left and centre made me decide to land on the grass. My aircraft was swarmed over when reaching the tarmac. 'Was I alright and was the aircraft alright?' Seems that the guns of a Spitfire were being tested and I had taxied right across the line of fire! . . . . an extreme example of the frustrations of our radioless flying. The Tower felt the same I am sure.[62]

Another form of 'friendly' hazard came from the barrage balloons. Walker describes them vividly as:

> enormous hydrogen gas-filled silver balloons on very heavy cables which went up to the cloud base or to 5,000 ft, placed around sensitive areas such as factories, certain aerodromes, towns and cities to keep Germans aeroplanes high up . . . The cables were dangerous to fly into; I think they got more of us than the Germans.[63]

Nor should it be forgotten that in the early years, when a genuine fear of invasion gripped the country, open fields were filled with barriers and spikes designed to stop the Germans from landing gliders – and equally intimidating to friendly aircraft trying to make a safe emergency landing!

Particularly during the Battles of France and Britain, the ATA was drawn to the very brink of the cauldron of war. The 'adventures' of ATA pilots delivering aircraft to France in 1940 have already been described earlier, but during the Battle of Britain the ATA again found itself 'at the front' – without ever leaving home. One ATA pilot delivered a Hurricane to North Weald during this period to find:

> . . . the aerodrome was burning and the whole field pitted with bomb craters. As the aircraft was urgently needed, he decided to try and land rather than go on to some other landing ground. Seeing a relatively straight course between the holes, he chanced it, and by luck brought the aircraft to a standstill in one piece . . . the airfield had been attacked only ten minutes [earlier], delayed action bombs were still going off, hot pieces of shrapnel were sizzling on the ground on every side, while on the runway a Spitfire burned fiercely, its exploding ammunition pinging in all directions.[64]

One of ATA's engineers at the time, a professional from BOAC, reported:

> How we admired the early pilots, whom we had almost to lift from their planes at the end of the day. We did almost everything for them but 'take off'. They were often simply 'all in', having had no time to eat or even think during these Battle of Britain days.[65]

From the fall of France in early summer 1940 until the Germans had been pushed back out of Northern France following the Normandy landings in the autumn of 1944, virtually all ATA flights took place within reach of the enemy. The intensity and nature of enemy air activity over the British Isles varied across these four years, but throughout the period the ATA, flying in unarmed aircraft without radios, were at high risk from enemy action in two forms. Like the rest of the British population, they were vulnerable to bombing and strafing while on the ground. In addition, they were subject to air attack while flying their unarmed aircraft in British airspace.

The 'Blitz' or bombing offensive of the *Luftwaffe* was, of course, a widespread phenomenon, which took over 50,000 civilian lives in the course of the war. The number of injured and homeless exceeded a hundred thousand. The ATA pilots working in and out of airfields at aircraft factories and at RAF stations, both of which were high-priority military targets for the *Luftwaffe*, were arguably even more at risk than the average citizen. There are many recorded incidents of ATA installations and pilots being subjected to enemy bombing. The airfield at Hamble, between Southampton and Portsmouth, was a 'front-line' airfield that received repeated enemy attention, including strafing raids that caused casualties among the staff. The airfield at Hatfield was bombed, October 1940, by a Ju 88 flying at low altitude. Lettice Curtis describes the incident:

> As so often happened, the air raid warning and the bombs came at the same instant and one bomb fell very near indeed to those running from the office to shelters. Luckily for them it did not explode on impact, otherwise we would almost certainly have lost, amongst others, Pauline Gower, our Commanding Officer, who was nearest to the bomb at the time.
>
> One of the bombs, however, did land on a factory workshop and twenty-one people were killed and some seventy injured. The bombs had been dropped from around 100 ft and the pilot had machine-gunned workers running to the shelters.[66]

In the summer of 1941, the Ferry Pool at White Waltham was bombed, and a Hurricane was destroyed on the ground while a hangar took a direct hit. The Ferry Pool at Kirkbride was the victim of a particularly clever attack as described by the American ATA pilot J. Genovese:

> The German was flying a Messerschmitt 110 . . . and from a distance it looked exactly like the British Hampden . . . Then, when the plane got close, it lowered its landing gear, wiggled its wings a couple of times, just like the ferry pilots and RAF boys

always did to signal they were going to land. Jerry got in just close enough to make a bad target for the AA gun when suddenly he gave his plane full throttle, retracted his gear, and roared down across the field at about 100 ft, machine guns and nose cannon blasting. At the center of the field he dropped one bomb, then he cut straight at the hangar and threw two more right through its roof. To put the finishing touch on his maneuver, he kept his plane just above the treetops, at an impossible level for the embarrassed gunnery officer to get another bead on him until he was well out of range.[67]

But if the ATA was a more frequent target for bombers than the average citizen, they also had the satisfaction of being exceptionally well protected. Operating as they did from RAF MUs and stations, they enjoyed the protection the RAF gave its own, and Ferry Pools were often located adjacent to RAF aerodromes such as at Aston Down. Genovese describes one incident:

> ... seemingly before the sound of the explosions had died away, there was a multiple roar at the far end of the field and two Spitfires shot out of a beautifully camouflaged nowhere, raced one behind the other down the field, and took off after the raider.[68]

Even after the *Luftwaffe* had been pushed out of France and the risk of bombing within England had been virtually eliminated, the ATA, advancing just behind the RAF, remained at risk. Thus on New Year's Day 1945, no fewer than four ATA taxi Ansons were destroyed on the ground when the hangar they were stowed in was set aflame in the surprise air attack that opened the Ardennes Offensive.

Nevertheless, the risk of being caught in an air raid was something the entire British population faced with varying degrees of stoicism, but the risk of being shot down while flying was unique to the RAF, FAA and ATA. The risks were serious enough and the instances of encounter frequent enough for the ATA to mount guns in its taxi aircraft and hire air-gunners for a brief period during the height of the Blitz. As it was against the Geneva Convention to arm civilians and the utility of the old Vickers guns mounted in the taxis was questionable, the practice was soon discontinued, but the risks remained.

Admittedly, the encounters with the enemy often ended entirely harmlessly, with no more than the nerves of the ATA pilot damaged. One ATA woman pilot reported seeing three Germans flash past under her while flying one of the cumbersome Walruses.[69] The American pilot,

Emily Chapin, watched two German aircraft fly underneath her without, apparently, being spotted by the enemy. (To her horror, she also saw the clouds of smoke erupt upwards from a nearby city, as the bombers made their attack.)[70] A third woman pilot was badly shaken when she was overtaken by a V-1 flying bomb; the V-1 passed just 100 ft overhead.[71]

Not all the encounters with the enemy in the air were so benign. Diana Barnarto Walker describes flying in a taxi Anson with no fewer than eleven other ATA pilots. She writes:

> Passing over the railway yards [near Reading], I saw a spume of smoke coming up from them . . . Suddenly, from the mass of cloud in front of us, out popped an aircraft . . . I saw tracer coming out at us from what appeared to be the gunner of the silvered aircraft. I then noticed the huge black cross on the fuselage and swastika on the tailplane. An Me 110!
>
> Jim saw it too. 'Jeese!' he yelled, 'it's a Jerry!' He yanked the Anson up into the overcast to hide as the German flashed past, very close, on our port side, its guns still blazing.[72]

Mary de Bunsen describes an even more dangerous encounter while flying in a small Fairchild taxi:

> One day four of us took off in a Fairchild four-seater during an alert, and guns opened up as we turned on course. We could see shell-splinters splashing in the mud and were rather frightened, so we came down low and skedaddled up the Hamble River at nought feet.[73]

The ATA did not always get away unscathed. Cheeseman reports that in one case:

> . . . a pilot saw two Spitfires attack four German planes. Judging the odds to be about right, he thought he'd stay around to watch. Unfortunately, he never noticed a fifth Jerry just below his tail and before he knew what had happened he got a burst of machine gun in his engine.[74]

Perhaps the most dramatic description of encounters with the enemy in the air, however, comes from Genovese. He writes of ferrying a Hampden bomber in late 1941:

I was just levelled out when I heard the crack of bullets and felt a jarring succession of holes ripped into the tip of my right wing. I couldn't believe it at first . . .

I tried to outclimb it but couldn't, and being out in front, every move I made either to the side or upwards gave him a better target . . . I was at about 700 ft and he was right on my tail. It was a serious question whether I had room enough between me and the ground to try another dive; on the other hand it was a far more serious question whether I would live another two minutes if I didn't . . .

A few miles to the west of Abbotsinch there was a secret RAF base, and the only thing I could think of as I started hedge-hopping on a beeline toward that base was the possibility of attracting the attention of a couple of RAF fighters . . . I managed to lead him directly over the RAF base – and I don't believe it was more than a matter of seconds before a pair of Spitfires were in the air chasing that German out over the Channel.[75]

Last but not least, during the latter stages of the war when the ATA was delivering aircraft and freight to the Continent, the pilots did run the very real risk of going off course and being shot at by German flak batteries. At least one ATA aircraft was so badly damaged by enemy fire that it had to make an emergency landing, fortunately on the Allied side of the lines. One Polish pilot, flying against regulations above cloud, managed to get so lost that he actually flew over German airspace before making a landing in France. Being and flying in a war zone, with all the dangers that implied, was very much part of 'daily life' in the ATA.

WAFS/WASP

The WAFS/WASP by contrast were at no time allowed near a real war zone, yet they faced a number of unusual risks nevertheless. One clear source of danger for the WASP was quite simply their inadequate training. Many WASP were released to perform duties without being fully prepared for the job they were expected to do. While much could be learned on the job, the complete lack of training in parachuting caused at least one death. After this incident, twelve hours of parachute instruction were added to the curriculum at Avenger Field.

More significant was the utilisation of women pilots for such tasks as target-towing. Clearly at those installations where live ammunition was used, the women were at risk, and there were several incidents of WASP aircraft being hit, although fortunately no injuries or fatalities resulted. The bulk of the women employed in target-towing were, furthermore, at units that used cameras rather than live ammunition to measure results.

Maintenance test-flying was another inherently dangerous task, since every aircraft flown had in some way been damaged or reported unserviceable. Some of the aircraft had crashed and been patched together again. Other problems ranged from exploded engines to broken propellers. The women therefore had to be alert for every irregularity in the sound of the engine, every deviation from an aircraft's normal trim, and every abnormality in the functioning of flaps, ailerons and rudders and so on.

It should also be remembered that unlike pilots flying with the ATA or FERD, who generally flew new aircraft straight from the factory, the WASP assigned to Training Command were often flying machines that had been withdrawn from combat or been in service for an unusual length of time. Whatever task the WASP were performing with these weary machines was made particularly dangerous by the fact that the maintenance crews at the training bases were notoriously under-trained and seriously over-worked. One WASP said retrospectively, that most of the problems with aircraft (and there were many) stemmed from the fact that the ground crews of the USAAF's training bases were 'overworked, underpaid and under-appreciated'.[76]

At some bases the condition of the aircraft was worse than at others. Camp Davis had a particularly bad reputation, and two WASP were killed while on active duty here, apparently owing to maintenance deficiencies. The mechanics tended to concentrate on 'essentials' – such as engines and airframes – not 'incidentals' such as instruments or hood-handles. One WASP died because her cockpit hood could not be opened from the inside. After a crash in which she was not fatally injured, she was incinerated in her cockpit because she could not release the canopy from the inside and no one reached her in time to release it from the outside.

Last but not least, the WASP were confronted with a unique form of risk in the shape of their colleagues. One WASP complained about having to fly co-pilot in a C-47 with a man who was completely out of practice but needed to fly in order to retain flight pay. Such senior officers could always 'out-rank' a WASP on a flight and so take the controls, no matter how incompetent. Other WASP claimed 'the most horrendous flying we ever went through was flying as co-pilot to some Eighth Air Force pilots with battle fatigue'.[77]

While any pilot feels a little nervous with someone else at the controls and possibly the WASP cited above were merely over-reacting, there is little excuse for the behaviour of one instructor as described below:

We were up in the AT-6 and suddenly, without any warning at all, he flipped the plane into a manoeuvre that was so violent that I was knocked unconscious almost instantly. In that brief moment before unconsciousness, I realised that I was not 'blacking out', but experiencing a 'red out'. I saw red just as I went unconscious. That meant, I later figured, that we had been thrown into either an outside loop or an inverted spin. Such manoeuvres force blood to the head, rather than from the head . . . When I finally regained complete consciousness . . . my nose was bleeding and there seemed to be blood oozing from my eyes. I was nauseated as well.[78]

With all due regard for and indulgence toward the 'high-spirits' and 'dare-devilry' of dashing young men, the behaviour ascribed to ferry pilots of FERD below was equally inexcusable:

A percentage of the men flying these [ferrying missions] were young, inexperienced and sometimes reckless, and the presence of women could bring out the worst in them. All the WAFS experienced or heard of incidents in which male pilots, showing off or attempting to frighten the women, would play fighter pilot, rolling and weaving near them, buzzing them or coming suddenly alongside . . . .[79]

Tragically, the first American woman pilot killed in the service of her country, Cornelia Fort, was the victim of exactly this kind of behaviour. She was killed while ferrying aircraft in formation with several male pilots. One of these, in an apparent effort to attract her attention by cavorting around her, knocked off the tip of her wing. Cornelia Fort had been instructing in a small training aircraft over Hawaii on the morning of 7 December 1941. She had been shot at by strafing Japanese aircraft as she landed. Yet, such were the risks of being a WASP, that it was not the enemy but an American pilot, seeking her favour, who killed her.

Notes:

1   Phelps, 43.
2   Cheeseman, 60.
3   Curtis, 73.
4   Walker, 52.
5   Lucas, 77-78.
6   Du Cros, 74.
7   Cheeseman, 89-91.

8   Welch, 23 Sept. 1998.
9   Curtis, 158.
10   De Bunsen, 118.
11   Walker, 77.
12   Phelps, 91.
13   Walker, 54.
14   King, 101–104.
15   Phelps, 55.
16   King, 160.
17   De Bunsen, 118.
18   De Bunsen, 143–4.
19   Curtis, 89.
20   Cheeseman, 95.
21   Phelps, 45.
22   De Bunsen, 87–8.
23   Lucas, 67.
24   Curtis, 160.
25   Walker, 43.
26   King, 97–8.
27   Cheeseman, 57.
28   Genovese, 58.
29   Keil, 91–2.
30   Bergel, 75.
31   De Bunsen, 146.
32   Lucas, 67.
33   Keil, 101.
34   Keil, 101.
35   De Bunsen, 148.
36   Sharland, 144.
37   Verges, 91.
38   Simbeck, 189–190.
39   Simbeck, 190.
40   Keil, 251.
41   Keil, 252.
42   Cole, 68.
43   Cole, 69.
44   Keil, 261–2.
45   Keil, 259.
46   Verges, 54. See also Simbeck, 177.
47   Rickman, 64
48   Rickman, 75.
49   Rickman, 56.
50   Bartels, 204.
51   Bartels, 212.
52   Cole, 24.

53   Verges, 176.
54   For examples of these lyrics see Keil, 148, 154, 183, 279, Verges, 79, 175, and Granger, 78, 82, 223.
55   Verges, 113.
56   Keil, 190.
57   Keil, 278.
58   Granger names many individual examples: 266, 291, 289, 308, 324, 331, 381, 384.
59   King, 73.
60   Curtis, 63-64.
61   Walker, 82
62   Lucas, 66.
63   Walker, 51.
64   Cheeseman, 34–5.
65   Cheeseman, 103.
66   Curtis, 47.
67   Genovese, 77–8.
68   Genovese, 55.
69   De Bunsen, 113.
70   Keil, 90.
71   Sharland, 144.
72   Walker, 81.
73   De Bunsen, 113
74   Cheeseman, 113.
75   Genovese, 79–82.
76   Cole, 110–111.
77   Cole, 94.
78   Cole, 57.
79   Rickman, 159.

CHAPTER SIX

Broken Wings

THE DEACTIVATION OF THE ATA AND WASP

The war in Europe was approaching its climax, with frantic preparations for the invasion of the Continent running at full steam, when a bill was brought before the American Congress requesting the creation of a separate service for women pilots flying in the service of the USAAF. The bill was advocated and supported by the Commander-in-Chief of the Army Air Forces, General Arnold, and by the Secretary of War, Henry Stimson. But when the bill came up for debate in the House, the gallery was filled with jeering and hooting GIs. Their hostility to the women pilots was so intense that they did not stop short of offensive and rude language and gestures. Offended by the means of expression, the worthy members of Congress had the GIs evicted from the galleries – and then proceeded to follow the advice of the hostile GIs by voting to kill the bill for a woman's flying service within the US military.

The existing civilian programme under which American women were then flying for the USAAF soon followed in the wake of the ill-fated bill; the programme was killed by order of the US Air Force Staff less than six months later. Thus, while undelivered military aircraft urgently needed by the USAAF waited in increasing numbers at the factory airfields, the women who had been trained to fly them at great expense went home against their will.

The women felt betrayed. Their feelings ranged from shock to shame. One spoke of being 'devastated' by the news, others volunteered to fly for just $1 a year, and still others took to the bottle, drowning their sorrows, regrets, frustration and hopelessness in alcohol. Their future prospects as pilots were dim. Returning combat veterans were given precedence everywhere, and the commercial airlines felt 'the public' was not yet ready for women in the cockpits of commercial airliners anyway. Meanwhile, the last graduating class at Avenger Field summarised their feelings in a song:

They taught us how to fly
Now they send us home to cry
'Cause they don't want us anymore.
You can save those AT-6s
To be cracked up in the ditches
For the way the Army flies
Really clears them out of the skies,
We earned our wings now they'll clip the gol darned things
How will they ever win the war?[1]

Meanwhile, in Britain, the women flying for the ATA were still actively involved in helping to win the war, flying along with their male colleagues all the way to Berlin. They were not sent home until more than six months after V-E Day. Nor did anyone in the British government or Forces doubt the contribution that the ATA – including the women pilots – had made to that victory. Battle of Britain fighter pilots openly acknowledged that 'the legendary few in the Battle of Britain would have been hard put to do what they did without the still fewer of the ATA who kept up the supply of new aircraft and never let them down on deliveries'.[2] Prime Minister Winston Churchill personally thanked the men and women of the ATA in a letter at roughly the same time that the WASP were undergoing the indignity of being coarsely ridiculed by GIs from the gallery at Congress. The Lords of the Admiralty, the Marshals of the Air Force and Sir Stafford Cripps, the Minister of Aircraft Production, all thanked the ATA in their own way for the ATA's contribution to victory. Lord Beaverbrook praised them publicly, and the Board of Directors of BOAC sent an official victory message to ATA, specifically referring to the women.

In short, in few areas are the contrasts between the experience of the women who flew with the ATA and WASP greater than with regard to the way their services were terminated. This chapter provides details of the premature and ignominious deactivation of the WASP and the business-like way in which the ATA was disbanded after a mission successfully accomplished. The search for an *explanation* of the different fates is left to the second part of this book, where an examination of critical issues such as military traditions, organisational structures and the key personalities involved will be undertaken.

THE AMBIGUOUS STATUS OF THE WASP AND THE EFFORTS TO REDEFINE IT

In a very real sense, the WASP was flawed from inception and its very creation contained the seeds of its destruction. Whereas the Air Transport Command had clear authorisation from Congress for the use of civilian pilots (gender non-specific), at no point in time did the extensive training programme for women pilots established at Avenger Field ever obtain Congressional approval. Indeed, 'no one ever asked for Congressional approval or funding of the WFTD'.[3] Equally dangerous: in the military appropriations bill for 1943 the existence of Avenger Field was not even mentioned. Thus, while the original WAFS was fully covered by existing legislation, the WFTD was not. With the merger of the WAFS and WFTD into the WASP, the entire programme became liable to the accusation of 'illegitimacy'. Furthermore, General Tunner warned General Arnold as early as August 1943 that the *employment* of the civilian woman pilots in other capacities besides ferrying aircraft could well cause problems in Congress. Given the widespread publicity the women pilots had received, it is hardly surprising that Congress eventually got around to investigating and questioning the legitimacy of the entire programme that had been slipped past them with a conscious 'sleight of hand' on the part of the Air Force Staff.

But Congress was very slow to act, and the actual drama, which ended in the premature deactivation of the WASP was in fact set in motion by none other than Jacqueline Cochran herself. The issue that precipitated the crisis was militarisation of the women pilot's organisation. Both Cochran and the USAAF were in favour of inducting the civilian pilots of the WASP directly into the USAAF.

The pivotal issue was that as civilians, the women serving with the WASP could literally quit at will. While the WAFS earned their keep almost from the day they joined, the women who entered the WFTD cost the USAAF roughly $20,000 dollars in training per head (including the costs of subsequent training on operational aircraft, instruments etc.) – and they could leave at whim long before the Army benefited from them. Furthermore, uncomfortable as the Army was with women in its midst, it was considerably more comfortable with women over which they had disciplinary control. The Army wanted to be able to dispose over the duties, schedule and assignments of the women just as they would over soldiers. They wanted women who wore uniform, who drilled and saluted and who could be housed in military barracks on bases where the Army could keep its eye on them twenty-four hours a day. Thus from the very start of the WAFS and WFTD, the women – despite their civilian status – were as much as possible *treated* (and expected to behave) as if they were members of the military. They were also told to expect official militarisation 'soon'. (Fortunately for the American women, the very dangerous issue of their civilian status if taken prisoner by the enemy was not relevant, since they were never near the enemy.)

The search began almost at once for a means of implementing the desired transformation of the civilian women pilots into soldiers. There seemed to be a variety of options. For a start, there were direct commissions as offered to the male civilian pilots hired by the ATC. This had the serious drawback, at least from Cochran's viewpoint, of only applying to pilots engaged in ferrying work. It was uncertain whether the provisions under which pilots were commissioned directly into ATC could be expanded to cover women still in training or on other kinds of duties. The idea was therefore never forcefully pursued.

Ways of incorporating the women pilots into the Congressionally approved Women's Army Auxiliary Corps (WAAC) were explored more vigorously. As early as November 1942, General Arnold had approached the Senior Officer of the WAAC, Colonel Oveta Culp Hobby about the integration of the women pilots into her organisation. However, the fact that the WAAC at that time was also only an auxiliary service, where women would still be free to leave at whim, made it seem hardly worth the effort to get the women pilots incorporated into it.

After the WAAC became the WAC (Women's Army Corps) and thereby became a component but separate part of the US Army in February 1943, the USAAF revived the idea of merging the WASP into it. The WAC commander, Colonel Oveta Culp Hobby, welcomed the notion, but Cochran vehemently opposed it. Individual WASP report that Cochran told them bluntly that she had 'no intention of being a major to Oveta Culp Hobby's colonel'.[4] She consistently slandered the WAC and its commanding officer at every opportunity, and she was not in the least ashamed of her attitude. On the contrary, in her memoirs she describes with apparent pride and relish the following exchange with General Arnold:

'How would you like to have your girls become part of the WACs?' he asked.

'How would you like to be back in basic training?' I answer.

'Don't get fresh with me,' he says.

'Those girls will become part of the Women's Army Corps over my dead body. No way. And I *am* fresh with you. I thought I was here today to discuss legislation to make my girls part of the Army Air Corps, not this. Hobby has bitched up her program and she's not going to bitch up mine.'[5]

The reasonable and professional tone of Cochran's approach needs no commentary.

Despite Cochran's opposition, the USAAF continued to try to find ways of merging the women's programmes because the Chief of Staff of the US Army, General George Marshall, personally favoured this solution. Cochran was, therefore, asked to meet with Hobby personally to discuss the proposal. Given Cochran's attitude toward Hobby and the WAC in general, it is hardly surprising that these talks came to nothing.

Furthermore, despite its best efforts, the US Army ran up against three major stumbling blocks. First, there were no provisions for flight pay for WAC. Second, the enlistment requirements were different. WAC members had to be twenty-one years old and older; WASP could be as young as eighteen and a half. According to Cochran, the younger candidates did better in flight training. Also, WAC were not allowed to have dependent children; 20 per cent of all WASP had such children.[6] On the other hand, the WASP had more restrictive physical requirements than the WAC and the requirement of thirty-five hours' flying experience. While these first two problems might have proved 'manageable', the third stumbling block, the issue of rank, was more ticklish. Pilots in the USAAF were *always* commissioned, but to commission all the existing WASP would have exceeded the total contingent of WAC officers approved by Congress in the WAC legislation.[7] And Arnold wanted still *more* WASP – 2,500 rather than the slightly more than 1,000 women that were then enrolled. Rather than try to rewrite the WAC legislation and resubmit it to Congress, it was decided to apply to Congress for the militarisation of the WASP as a separate unit.

Once the USAAF decided on this route, it developed a bill to transform the WASP from a civilian organisation into a component part of the Air Forces, directly under the Air Forces' (not the Army's) control. Congressman John Costello of California was happy to sponsor the bill, and no difficulties with passing the bill were anticipated. General Arnold was used to getting everything he wanted for his Air Forces approved by Congress, and he almost certainly underestimated the opposition that would arise to this seemingly innocuous proposal. Congressional approval was viewed as a foregone conclusion.

Some commentators believe that if the bill for WASP militarisation had been taken to the floor of the House without delay shortly after it was introduced on 30 September 1943, that it would indeed have passed. The bill, however, languished in the Committee on Military Affairs for roughly six months – probably due to more pressing business related to the forthcoming invasion of Europe and the still very critical situation in the Pacific. In early 1944, Costello himself submitted a longer and more detailed version of the bill, which superseded the first bill, and it was on this second bill that the Committee held hearings in March 1944.

These hearings were very short (roughly one hour) and there was only one witness: General Arnold. He laid out the case for the utilisation and militarisation of women pilots in the USAAF and the Committee members accepted his arguments without demur. On the same day they issued a report recommending passage of the bill. Two days later a parallel bill was introduced in the Senate.

As soon as the Costello Bill had passed out of the Military Affairs Committee, the USAAF began to prepare for militarisation of the WASP, treating Congressional Approval like a rubber stamp. Cochran's chic uniforms were distributed at last, and, more important, the USAAF started to send WASP to Officer Training School (OTS) at Orlando, Florida.

Unfortunately, by now, April 1944, the mood in Congress had changed substantially from a year or even a half-year earlier. It should be noted that the earlier bills authorising the formation of women's services (WAC, WAVES etc) had all encountered stiff opposition from certain conservative elements in Congress, which categorically opposed the enrolment of women in the military. What made the climate in Congress more difficult at this point in time was that in addition to this entrenched, bigoted faction, other mainstream Congressmen were increasingly cost-conscious and infected by growing confidence about winning the war. Both moods militated against giving 'the Generals' blank cheques any more.

Added to this was the fact that casualties in the air war had fallen far below expectations. The USAAF had anticipated 20 per cent casualties among aircrew in the European Theatre and training programmes had been geared up to replace casualties at this rate. But in the campaign in North Africa the actual casualty figures had been as low as 7.5 per cent and in the raids over Europe itself the average losses were below 13 per cent.[8] In consequence, training programmes were being scaled back and even discontinued. In January 1944, General Arnold closed all Primary Flight Schools and the Civil Aeronautics War Training Service, previously CPT. Suddenly, large numbers of formerly draft-exempt civilian, male pilots were facing the prospect of being drafted into the 'walking army'.

In fact, General Arnold had argued his case for the militarisation of the WASP on the very grounds that the Army needed foot soldiers for the impending invasions of Europe and Japan. His entire argument before the Congressional Committee had been based on the infantry's need for manpower, needs that could in part be met by allowing the WASP to assume more, rather than less, flying duties, and sending males in flight training back to the infantry. Arnold is quoted as stating: 'It is not beyond reason to expect that some day all of our Air Transport Command ferrying within the United States will be done by women.'[9] The *New York Herald Tribune* meanwhile reported that: 'The need for young infantry soldiers has become so acute that 36,000 men in the Army Air Forces pilot training pool are being returned to the Army Ground Forces . . . .'[10] (One begins to suspect the identity of those GIs heckling the WASP from the Gallery of Congress . . . .)

The civilian flight instructors also set up a howl of protest against the WASP bill. On the assumption that every WASP took a safe, State-side job away from them, they began intensive, well-organised and loud lobbying efforts to get the bill defeated. The fact that the protesting pilots often did not meet the USAAF's requirements was a fact they either did not know or chose to ignore. Off the record, Arnold had confided to friendly members of the Military Affairs Committee that he much preferred the WASP to the civilian males, who had up to now studiously avoided joining the Army. 'Not only did the WASP meet the AAF's highest physical and intellectual standards, they were loyal, dutiful and grateful for any flying job Arnold had allowed them to do.'[11] Arnold knew the WASP had done and were still doing jobs that even his trained Air Force pilots disliked doing or did poorly (like tracking missions, slow-timing engines etc.) Last but not least, the very aversion to serving their country in uniform, which the protesting civilians displayed, did not exactly endear them to Arnold or his fellow senior officers. But the decision was no longer in the Pentagon's hands, and the civilian members of Congress saw things differently.

First and foremost, they saw the apparently terrifying prospect of women stealing jobs away from men. The spectre that haunted the Halls of Congress was one of returned veterans finding their jobs taken away from them by trouser-clad, emancipated 'Rosie the Riveters' and 'career girls'. It was quite all right that these women had jumped in to fill the empty places left by their patriotic men during the war frenzy that followed Pearl Harbor, but it was now time for a 'return to normalcy'. For the vast majority of the Members of Congress that quite simply meant women belonged in the kitchen, kindergarten and church. Hitler agreed.

The shift in popular mood with respect to 'a woman's place' was reflected more than created by Congress, and it was very evident in the media at this time. Advertising representations of women in the military underwent a noticeable and abrupt change in 1944; increasingly even these women were portrayed doing domestic tasks. In her analysis of the portrayal of women in the US media, Merryman claims that: 'For *Life* the critical issue in the latter half of 1944 was not winning the war but returning to pre-war domesticity and productivity.'[12] In short, the American public, media and their Congressional representatives in 1944 no longer wanted American women to be soldiers and workers, but rather 'wives and girlfriends who welcomed home the decidedly male victors' of a war, already considered won.[13]

Against this backdrop, not only was the WASP bill already an anachronism when it came up for debate, but it had the added negative effect of provoking the Chairman of the Civil Services Committee to take a closer look at the WASP. Because of the publicity aroused by the public debate on the militarisation of the WASP, the Civil Services Committees launched an investigation of this unauthorised programme. It is hardly surprising that the Committee members, whose mandate to legislate on the employment of civil servants had been so contemptuously ignored, should be hostile to a programme about which they had never officially been informed.

Their natural outrage about being hoodwinked in turn made them very vulnerable to manipulation by that lobby of male pilots. The lobby of male pilots facing conscription into the 'walking army' were only too happy to provide the Committee with 'facts' about the WASP – provided, of course, that these facts reflected poorly on the women and the WASP programme generally.

It is therefore not surprising that the report issued by this Committee, widely known as the Ramspeck Report after the Committee Chairman, made numerous allegations about the incompetence of the WASP that were not founded, and concluded that the programme as a whole was a waste of money and effort. Undoubtedly, the Committee was prejudiced against the WASP from the start, and it 'presented facts about the program in a distorted and negative manner, with misleading and negative headings'.[14] But, like it or not, the core of its findings were in fact correct.

The Committee correctly focused its criticism on the training part of the programme, not on those women already on active service. In fact, the Committee 'took pains to indicate it was not attacking the women pilots already on duty', but rather 'objected to Cochran's extravagant flight school for inexperienced girls'.[15] It correctly pointed to the fact that the training programme and its budget had never been approved by Congress, that the costs of training were high and that its success was dubious. (With two Air Inspectors complaining about substandard training and Ferrying Command refusing to accept graduates, the Committee had the facts on its side.)

Most important, the Committee's findings suggested that the entire training programme was by this point in time superfluous. Given the number of male pilots returning from combat and all those male pilots making such a fuss about losing their jobs as civilian instructors, there was simply no need to train more pilots from scratch. The Committee was only drawing attention to the facts when it stated that:

> At the end of the war there will be tremendous surpluses of trained and experienced pilots throughout the world. Utilization of these surpluses will constitute an acute post-war problem. To now seek out and train, at Government expense, additional inexperienced personnel would add another surplus to this recognized post-war surplus.[16]

Furthermore, on the basis of General Arnold's figures (taking into account an expansion of the WASP to 2500 women), the Committee estimated total flight training costs at over $50 million, and suggested that expenditures of this magnitude surely needed separate and specific legislation.

The Committee's cost estimates were not seriously exaggerated. Cochran and most modern chroniclers of the debate, who provide lower training figures, are focusing exclusively on the costs of the initial training at Avenger Field. The Committee rightly pointed to the need for most of the WASP also to train on operational aircraft before they could be effectively employed. After all, even the pilots of Ferry Command were expected to go through Pursuit School in order to meet FERD's requirements. Nor is it in any way relevant to point out that male training cost roughly the same as WASP training; the Committee's conclusions suggested opposition to footing the bill for the flight training of inexperienced pilots at this point in time *regardless* of sex.

The Committee also – legitimately – questioned the costs of Officer Training for women, given the fact that they were still civilians and the prospects of them being granted commissions were getting slighter all the time. The OTS course lasted four weeks and hundreds of WASP were being sent through this training. (A total of 460 would eventually graduate.[17]) Such training looked very much like 'contempt of Congress' to sensitive Congressmen tired of having Generals do what they liked without asking permission.

Albeit petty, even the Committee's complaints about Cochran's designer uniforms were not completely unfounded. The uniforms may not have been as expensive as they looked, but why did the WASP need something so special when all the other women's services got along with much less flashy uniforms?

Last but not least, the Committee conducted interviews with a number of WASP and discovered that – very much in contrast to what Cochran claimed – apparently many of the women *opposed* militarisation. The feeling against militarisation was strongest among those who had been at the job longest and were best qualified – among the original WAFS.[18] For a good year-and-a-half these women had been serving without difficulty under the same rules and regulations as the male civilians of the ATC. They saw no significant advantage in militarisation as such and certainly resisted the idea of being directly subject to 'transfer at Cochran's whim'.[19] Cochran's arbitrary and high-handed style of command had caught up with her.

The Committee issued a report that concluded with three recommendations:

> The proposal to expand the WASP has not been justified. Therefore, it is recommended that the recruiting of inexperienced personnel and their training for the WASPs be immediately terminated.
>
> That the use of the WASPs already trained and in training be continued and provision be made for hospitalization and insurance.
>
> There exist several surpluses of experienced pilot personnel available for utilization as service pilots. Therefore it is recommended that the service of these several groups of experienced air personnel be immediately utilized.[20]

The impact of this report was significant. One of the Congressmen opposed to the militarisation of the WASP entered the entire report into the public record of the debate just one week before the Costello bill was scheduled for a vote. The report appeared to provide objective and balanced evidence of WASP deficiencies, which fuelled the fires of the frenzied media campaign against the WASP.

In short, as Congress deliberated on the Costello bill, it was subjected to pressure by a very vocal and apparently powerful lobby opposed to the WASP. Likewise, press commentary against the WASP *without* any basis in sound research was also being cited and quoted in the Congressional debate. Yet, no counter-lobby in favour of the women pilots was in evidence. The WASP themselves had been ordered by Cochran to refrain from all comment; they were forbidden to speak either to the press or to exercise their rights as citizens and to write to their own Congressmen. Meanwhile, the most important advocate of the women pilots, General Arnold, was recovering from a heart attack and trying to run the air components of the landings in Normandy. (The bill went to the Floor of the House less than two weeks after D-Day.) It is understandable that General Arnold did not have much time or energy to devote to this battle in Congress with regard to a couple of thousand women pilots, who constituted less than 1 per cent of all the pilots flying for the USAAF.

Given this imbalance of forces, it is surprising that the margin of defeat for the WASP bill was in fact so narrow. Fully 169 Congressmen supported the WASP, while seventy-three Representatives abstained from voting on the issue. Just 188 Congressmen were responsible for defeating the bill to militarise the WASP when it came to a vote on 22 June 1944.

With the defeat of the militarisation bill, the WASP was effectively back where it had started in September 1942. It was a quasi-legal, civilian organisation, whose members were not subject to military discipline nor covered by military benefits regarding hospitalisation or insurance. While the situation was not ideal, it had been working more-or-less effectively for close to two years. The defeat of the Costello bill did not in itself affect the existing WASP programme.

Not so the recommendations of Ramspeck Committee. These clearly stated that the training programme should be discontinued. In the prevailing atmosphere surrounding the defeat of the Costello bill, Arnold and Cochran accepted their defeat. Just four days after the defeat of the bill, telegrams were sent to all women scheduled to start training 30 June. They were told to stay home. But the status of the women already in training and on active service were nominally unaffected.

COCHRAN'S CRUSADE AND ITS CONSEQUENCES

Four options now remained open to the USAAF with regard to the WASP. As if to prove that the left hand of Congress didn't know what the right hand was doing, the House Appropriations Committee had meanwhile approved $6.4 million to fund the WASP programme. This meant that the WASP could have continued on the same basis as before, except for the gradual phasing out of training as those women already in training graduated. Alternatively, an effort could have been made to follow the positive recommendation of the Ramspeck Report and obtain by separate Act of Congress hospitalisation and insurance benefits for the WASP without altering their civilian status. A third option would have been to press forward the Senate bill on militarisation, which was identical to the Costello bill but had not yet gone to Committee. This, in effect, would have re-opened the battle for militarisation in Congress with uncertain success. A last option was to simply discontinue the entire troublesome programme.

Both the second and third options required going back to Congress. Given the fact that the media campaign against the WASP continued, and the lobby of male pilots was still active, neither of these options offered serious prospects of success in the short term. Inertia and other priorities therefore make it probable that the USAAF would have opted for the first solution, just carrying on as before and letting the public furore burn itself out, if it hadn't been for a report on the WASP programme issued by Cochran.

On 1 August 1944, Jacqueline Cochran produced an eleven-page, single-spaced report on the WASP programme. On the one hand she tried to make a case for its success and on the other hand claimed that 'the only effective means by which the AAF can obtain efficient and economical use of the women pilots is through a militarized program which makes the WASP a part of the AAF'.[21] Cochran's report was not a balanced or objective review of the options now facing the programme, with the pros and cons of militarisation and civilian status carefully weighed against one another, but a heavy-handed renewed bid for militarisation. Nor did Cochran keep the report confidential, as would have been appropriate if it was intended to serve as an internal discussion paper. Instead, as if to force the Air Force's hand, Cochran released her report to the press on 7 August.

If the report had been issued and publicised prior to the Congressional debate, it might have been useful. It provided many facts and figures, particularly a catalogue of the wide variety of tasks the WASP were successfully performing. It might even have made the entire public and Congressional debate on the WASP more factual and thereby helped to counter the image of spoilt females being granted privileges at government expense. Cochran's report specifically made the point that: 'The usefulness of the WASP cannot be measured by the importance of the types of planes they fly, for their job is to do the routine, the dish-washing flying jobs of the AAF, that will release men for higher grades of duty.'[22]

But coming as it did less than two months after the Costello bill had failed to win Congressional approval, Cochran's report seemed at best ill-timed and at worst tactless. Even this blunder might have been ignored or forgiven, if it had not been coupled with her concluding recommendation as follows:

Under a civilian status, so many elements of the experimental project are lost or weakened, and there is such a lack of control over permanency of work by individual WASP after they are trained, that serious consideration should be given to inactivation of the WASP program if militarization is not soon authorized.[23]

No effort on the part of Cochran's apologists to claim that the press blew this 'one sentence' out of all proportion can alter the fact that it was Cochran's own concluding suggestion to disband the WASP if the – politically impossible – goal of militarisation was not obtained 'soon'. Cochran was not willing, it seems, to let things lie for a bit and make a new attempt at a later date, when public sentiment against the WASP might have died down. She did not give the lobby against the women pilots time to disperse. By insisting on militarisation and insisting on it 'soon', she played into the hands of her enemies in a manner so foolish it is hardly comprehensible.

Immediately after the release of Cochran's report, the press jumped on her recommendation in what can best be described as a gleeful fashion. Headlines such as 'WASPS Ask General Arnold for Bars or Discharge', or 'Miss Cochran Would Commission Wasps or Junk Organisation' were typical.[24] More damaging, the report was widely interpreted as an ultimatum. As such, it left the USAAF no choice but WASP deactivation. The USAAF did not control militarisation, Congress did. Given the fact that the USAAF was still fighting a war in two theatres, it is understandable that it did not have any interest in fighting a war with Congress about a handful of women pilots. Whatever Cochran's intentions when she concluded her report with this wholly unrealistic 'recommendation', the effect was to put the de-activation of the WASP on the agenda.

Barely three weeks after Cochran had issued her report/ultimatum, the USAAF outlined plans for disbanding the WASP. The argument for disbanding was simple: given the hostility to the WASP in Congress and the media, 'any campaign to obtain militarization could result harmfully for AAF public and legislative relations'.[25] Quite aside from the war, the USAAF was anxious to gain independence from the Army, for which it would also need Congressional approval; it had no desire to make enemies in Congress or with the press for the sake of a few of women pilots.

Nevertheless, when one considers the arguments Arnold had tabled in favour of the WASP just five months earlier, it is surprising how readily the USAAF moved to eliminate the WASP. Cochran's report suggesting militarisation or deactivation had come out 1 August. The Air Staff memorandum looking into deactivation was dated 24 August. The official recommendation to deactivate went to Arnold's desk on

12 September. Arnold informed Cochran officially that the WASP had successfully 'completed their mission' on 1 October.[26] The deactivation deadline was set at 20 December 1944.

The Air Force Staff moved so fast, in fact, that the ATC was caught completely off guard. It should be remembered that it was the ATC that had gone to Arnold with a proposal to employ women pilots in early 1941. The ATC had also won approval for its WAFS before Arnold authorised Cochran to establish the WFTD. For almost a year the ATC's FERD had been the only 'customer' for WFTD graduates. Despite complaints about the quality of the graduates from Avenger Field, the ATC had been a consistent proponent of the employment of *qualified* women pilots. It had enabled WASP to transition onto all kinds of aircraft, including four-engined bombers and transports. It had been prepared to let women fly the Atlantic until Arnold stopped them. After that it developed and implemented plans to employ the women as specialists in pursuits. To be sure, the high standards required by FERD had resulted in the number of WASP being returned to Training Command. In consequence, the number of women employed in FERD had fallen from a peak of just over 300 in early 1944 to 141 in the autumn of 1944, but these remaining women pilots were considered vital.

Just one month after the deactivation of the WASP was announced, the new Commanding General of ATC, Brigadier General Nowland*, sent a memo to Arnold drawing attention to the impact of this decision on his command. He argued that: 'The Ferrying Division has 117 women "frozen" on pursuit deliveries. They comprise 82 per cent of the WASPs in the Air Transport Command. The pursuit WASPs are 49 per cent of the total pilots doing this all-important flying. The ATC needs its women pilots.'[27] The ATC also pointed to the costs of training male pilots to replace the women already qualified on pursuits, and came to a figure of slightly over $1 million – far from an insignificant sum at that time.[28] The Air Force Staff endorsed the suggestion of Brigadier General Nowland, stating:

> It is recommended that further consideration be given to retaining these 117 trained pilots in a civilian status after 20 December 1944 to meet the immediate needs of Ferrying Division, and to avoid the duplication of effort and expense of training male pilots to replace them.[29]

---

* General Tunner had gone on to take command of the India-China Division of the ATC, with responsibility for keeping open the supply lines over the Himalayas.

But long before the request was official, Nancy Love had been warned explicitly that Cochran was 'determined to take the WASP program down with her . . . .'[30] At all events, the official answer to ATC's request from Arnold was 'no'. Not even the offer by the women to fly for free could make him change his mind. The WASP ferrying squadron at Long Beach, California, wrote to ATC HQ, arguing as follows:

> Due to the shortage of pursuit ferry pilots at this station and the excessive amount of aircraft to be ferried the WASP Squadron Sixth Ferrying Group hereby offers their services as ferry pilots on a volunteer dollar a year basis without other remuneration . . . until such time as the present necessity for pilots is alleviated and sufficient pilots are trained to replace us.[31]

The answer remained 'no'.

Arnold did not state his reasons. One can only speculate that he was fed up with the entire issue of women pilots. General Tunner wrote in his memoirs: 'I suppose that General Arnold, with far more important problems to worry about, was sick of the whole thing.'[32] Or perhaps he really did bow to Cochran's wishes not to allow Love's WAFS to continue flying if 'her girls' were grounded. Whatever the reason, at deactivation on 20 December 1944, Arnold made only one exception with regard to dismissals and that was for Cochran herself. She was retained on his staff, although her function in the absence of any women pilots is mysterious.

On 7 December 1944, a date chosen to coincide with the third anniversary of the Japanese attack on Pearl Harbor and which entailed shortening the training programme, the last class of WASP graduated from Avenger Field. The Air Force made a small fuss about the graduation; no fewer than four commanding generals* and Cochran herself flew in for the ceremonies. Graduate WASP had been invited to attend,

---

* General Arnold, General Yount, CG Training Command, General Williams, CG 2nd Air Force, (80 WASP flew target-towing missions in his command), and General Kraus, Central Flying Training Command (where Avenger Field was located). The absence of any General from Ferrying Division/ATC is curious, but the preponderance of representation from Training Command appropriate. At this point in time a total of 916 WASP were on active duty, 620 of them in Training Command, 141 in ATC. The exact distribution is as follows: Training Command: 620, ATC: 141, Second Air Force: 80, Fourth Air Force: thirty-seven, First Air Force: sixteen, Weather Wing: eleven, Proving Ground Command: six, Air Technical Service: three, Troop Carrier Command: one and HQ AAF: one (Cochran).

and many made the trip to Sweetwater, Texas, for the event. The band of the Bombardier School played. The sixty-eight graduating women paraded and saluted. Speeches were held praising them. Their wings – finally standardised – were pinned on their chests. Everyone cheered.

Generals Yount and Arnold particularly had a lot of nice words for the girls. They possessed 'courage', General Yount testified.[33]General Arnold confessed to his initial doubts about 'whether a slip of a young girl could fight the controls of a B-17' but insisted that the WASP had proved him wrong.[34] He declared that 'the entire operation has been a success. It is on record that women can fly as well as men'.[35] To Cochran was left the task of stressing that: 'As much as the WASPs want to help by flying, we can all be happy that our Air Forces are now so built up and the progress of the war is so favourable that our services are no longer needed'.[36] It was all very moving, but strictly internal. After the last strains of the National Anthem had died and the dignitaries had flown away, the WASP were left with reality.

They had been dismissed – 'not', as one of them put it, 'because of any lack of efficiency, need or willingness on [our] part, but almost without reasonable explanation or justification'.[37] They had to find their own way home at their own expense (although, in fact, many commanders and sympathetic officers did unofficially fly – or even let the women fly themselves – to the Air Force base nearest to their home towns). They were not veterans. They were not entitled to any kind of benefit, whether GI bill, disability or pension. They were superfluous pilots in a market that greatly disadvantaged women employees, particularly in flying capacities.

Furthermore, despite the pretty speeches, the USAAF did not follow through with any commendations. On 17 October Air Force Headquarters had asked their subordinate commands to name any WASP who had served in such a distinguished manner as to make them eligible for a decoration. A total of fifty-eight WASP were duly recommended.[38] But nothing came of it. Only Nancy Love and Jacqueline Cochran were decorated subsequently; Barbara Jane Erickson had been awarded the Air Medal in March 1944. These were the only three WASP ever to receive official recognition for their services from the Army.

Disbanded early, the WASP were also soon forgotten.

When Germany surrendered in May 1945, no one remembered the WASPs. When Japan surrendered in September, thus ending the war, the AAF did not mention that WASPs had been part of the top secret planning missions of the crews who had dropped the atomic bombs. In hundreds of pages of stories in magazines and newspapers across the country that celebrated the soldiers of the US armed services, none remembered the WASPs.[39]

Even the impact of the WASP upon women in military aviation appears to have been nil. Arnold's claim for the programme, that it had proved women could fly as well as men, was spurious from the start. Amelia Earhart, Amy Johnson, Jacqueline Cochran herself, not to mention the women combat pilots of the Red Air Force, had all long since proved that fact – and in more spectacular fashion than the WASP in their 'dish-washer' jobs. And if Arnold was right in claiming that the Air Force would never again question the ability of women to fly military aircraft, then why did the US Air Force (USAF) at its inception in 1948 offer the former WASP only *non-flying* commissions? Even in the 1970s, when there was intense pressure to increase female recruitment to meet the demands of an All-Volunteer Force, the USAF still found it necessary to *investigate* whether it was wise to give women flight training. The record of the WASP was apparently *not* viewed as definitive.

More ironic still, when Jacqueline Cochran was invited before the Board of Investigation to give her assessment of the WASP, she testified that:

> ... based on her experiences, women would be unlikely to make careers in aviation. They would leave the service after their initial commitment was over for personal reasons, and the expensive education would be wasted.[40]

Cochran seems to have forgotten that ordinary WASP (who were not all married to muliti-millionaires as she was) could *not* make flying their career if no one – military or civilian – was willing to employ them in that capacity. Many WASP had indeed sought careers in aviation after the war, and almost all failed due to the prejudices against women in aviation and the surplus of male pilots returned from the war. Unfair though it was, Cochran's testimony twisted the legacy of the WASP from a positive example of women's capabilities into a negative example of unreliability. Fortunately, despite her testimony, the USAF's need for personnel and the 'women's liberation' movement were together sufficient to induce the Air Force to ignore Cochran's testimony and again give women a chance.

Meanwhile, public memory of the WASP had faded so completely that the press touted the 1976 decision to admit women to flight training as a 'first' in American aviation history – until the former WASP rose up in outraged protest. Confronted by young women doing what they had done and receiving so much praise reawakened resentment of the humiliating treatment they had received years before. Because militarisation had been the issue on which the WASP appeared to have been broken thirty years earlier, it became the focus of former-WASP attention thirty years later. Encouraged by the then active and successful Women's Movement, the former-WASP banded together and with strong support from Senator Barry Goldwater (a former pilot of FERD) and General Bruce Arnold (the son of the Second World War C-in-C of the USAAF), they launched a new campaign for recognition.

It was not the first. There had been sporadic attempts to win veteran status over the years, but these had all failed, usually killed in Committee without ever reaching the Floor of Congress. The opposition in Congress and from the powerful veteran's lobbies (the American Legion, the Veterans of Foreign Wars and the Veteran's Administration) was still strong. These organisations viewed the recognition of the WASP as in some way an insult to their own constituents and accomplishments – it not quite clear how.

By the late seventies, however, public mood had shifted. The media portrayal of the WASP was predominantly positive, while their lack of official recognition and benefits was commented upon negatively. The active military also weighed-in behind the WASP; they did not want any negative impact on recruiting women to the volunteer forces or on those women then in flight training. The Assistant Secretary of the Air Force for Manpower, Reserve Affairs and Installations testified in favour of the WASP before the Congressional Hearings.

The balance of lobbying forces was thus reversed from what it had been during the debate on the Costello bill thirty-three years earlier. On 8 March 1979 the WASP were officially granted veteran status. It was undoubtedly a satisfying victory after the humiliating defeat of the Costello bill, and for one or two of the surviving WASP the benefits were probably very welcome, but it is a curious victory all the same.

All the 1979 bill did was to recognise the fact that the WASP had been *de facto* members of the US armed forces. Congress recognised that all the drill, the parades, the living in barracks on twenty-four-hour notice, etc. had made the WASP soldiers in fact if not *de jure*. But that was *all* the bill did. For all the high hopes and claims made for the programme at its inception and since, it seems a rather paltry achievement.

The Deactivation of the ATA and its Legacy

The improvised ATA never made any particular claims about proving something as fundamental as the ability of women to fly as well as men.

It did not view itself as an experiment or a precedent. It was simply there to get an urgently needed job done as best it could. That job was to help the RAF and FAA win the war, and so – like the WASP – the war situation had a direct impact upon its future.

On 20 August 1944 or almost exactly at the same time that the USAAF was preparing to deactivate the WASP, the ATA was instructed to stop recruiting. Developments on the Invasion Front (Paris would be liberated just five days later) made it evident that current operational strength would be sufficient to meet needs in the foreseeable future. The degree of Allied Air Superiority over the Continent was by this time so overwhelming that casualties among pilots and aircraft were running far below expectations. This meant that not only were there fewer aircraft to ferry, but also that the RAF's now substantial manpower resources were increasingly able to cope with demands. It was foreseeable that the RAF would at the latest by the end of the war be in a position to meet all its own ferrying needs.

As a result of the halt on recruitment, the number of pilots serving with the ATA started to decline due to normal attrition. Particularly after the defeat of Germany in May 1945, pilots started to quit the service to return to their homeland or to civilian life. Thus, from a pilot strength of 675 at the time the decision was taken to stop recruiting, the number of pilots was reduced by normal attrition to 525 by the time ATA closed down at the end of November 1945.[41]

In addition to the halt on recruiting, the ATA set about closing down its training schools progressively. The first to close was the Initial Flying Training School at Thame, which closed in early 1945, but conversion and refresher courses in the more advanced classes of aircraft continued until after the victory over Japan. Furthermore, with an eye to helping their employees transition back into civilian life, the ATA made an effort to ensure that ATA pilots who wished to were given the opportunity to gain the licences necessary for commercial flying in the post-war world.

Nevertheless, on 2 June 1945, almost a month after the unconditional surrender by Germany, the ATA was officially informed that its services would not be required after the end of the war. Although prospects were held out for a number of individual pilots to be commissioned into the RAF as ferry pilots, the decision had been made that the organisation itself should be terminated at the latest by 31 December 1945. Since the RAF had no women in flying duties, the prospect of an RAF commission did not apply to the women pilots of the ATA. Meanwhile, plans were drawn up gradually to downsize the organisation in a systematic and sensible manner.

The first step was to turn over all ferrying from MUs on to active squadrons back over to the RAF. In accordance with this policy, some 148 RAF pilots who had been seconded to the ATA as ferry pilots, were returned to the RAF; they carried on with the same job they had been doing but thereafter under Service auspices. The next step was gradually to reduce the number of Ferry Pools, starting with the Invasion Pool at Aston Down, where 'black crows perched on the motionless airscrews of the abandoned Lancasters, which lined the boundaries of the silent airfield'.[42]

For a few months, however, the war in the Pacific continued, and the needs of the FAA, which was more active in that Theatre and which had fewer personnel than the RAF, kept those who chose to remain with the ATA busy. In addition to jobs for the FAA, there were also an increasing number of old aircraft that had to be flown to the scrapyards. Thus, there was sufficient work to be done so that no one had to be forced out of the organisation against their will. As each pool was closed down, those pilots who wished to continue flying with the ATA were transferred to one of the pools still operating. Those who left were allowed to purchase their uniforms at nominal cost, and – more important – were given a written testimonial summarising all hours flown on various aircraft. They also received a letter of thanks from d'Erlanger, and a blue and gold 'Certificate of Service'.

With the surrender of Japan, however, the days of the ATA were clearly numbered, and it was decided officially to terminate the organisation on 30 November 1945. During September and October all the subordinate pools were closed down, leaving only the HQ at White Waltham opened to the last. The last flight was made into White Waltham by a taxi Anson bringing home the pilots who had made the last deliveries.

Before that last flight, the ATA staged an Air Display and Pageant. The official purpose was to raise money for the ATA's Benevolent Fund, a fund established to look after the widows and orphans of the 174 aircrew who had given their lives while serving with the ATA. In best ATA tradition, the ATA 'managed to find a way around' the fact that the 'Authorities' had not 'strictly speaking' given their permission for an air display. Without official approval, they went ahead and offered their paying guests 'a display of flying which had not been equalled since the days of the Hendon pageant'.[43]

Not that the Authorities were otherwise mean. Official letters of thanks had already been sent to the ATA by the Minister of Aircraft Production, the Prime Minister and the Board of Directors of BOAC. The Air Pageant itself was opened by Lord Beaverbrook, who not only

1. Pauline Gower.
   (*Courtesy Michael Fahie*)

2. The first women recruits to
   the ATA in early 1940.
   (*Courtesy Michael Fahie*)

3. Women pilots at the ATA Ground School in White Waltham.
(Unknown)

4. Pauline Gower and two of her women pilots in early 1940.

(Courtesy Michael Fahie)

5. Two ATA pilots in their flying kit. *(Courtesy of Michael Fahie)*

6. *bottom:* The first women pilots waiting to board their private taxi – an Avro Anson.

(Courtesy Michael Fahie)

7. An ATA woman pilot in the cockpit of a de Havilland Tiger Moth.

(Courtesy Michael Fah

8. The Operations Officer calls pilots to their Avro Ansons.

(Courtesy Maidenhead Heritage Centre)

9. Women ATA pilots plan their flight on the tail plane of an Avro Anson at Hatfield in March 1941. *(Courtesy Michael Fahie)*

10. Cleared for take-off. *(Courtesy Ann Wood Kelly)*

11. ATA Headquarters at White Waltham. *(Courtesy the ATA Association)*

12. *centre:* Pilots of the Hatfield pool outside their mess. *(Courtesy Michael Fahie)*

13. Women of the Hatfield ferry pool having tea in the mess. *(Courtesy Maidenhead Heritage Centre)*

14. Ratcliffe ferry pool. *(Courtesy Maidenhead Heritage Centre)*

15. The staff of Ratcliffe ferry pool. *(Courtesy Ann Wood Kelly)*

16. Ratcliffe Hall served as the mess for the Ratcliffe pool. *(Courtesy Ann Wood Kelly)*

17. *Above:* Pilots of the Sherburne pool pose before a Fairey Barracuda torpedo bomber. *(Courtesy Ann Wood Kelly)*

18. *Right:* Pilots of the Hamble pool pose before a Spitfire. *(Courtesy Ann Wood Kelly)*

19. ATA pilots in the Hamble mess. *(Courtesy of Diana Barnato Walker)*

20. Ann Wood Kelly delivers a cargo of fresh strawberries to the ATA. *(Courtesy Ann Wood Kelly)*

21. The ATA mess at Thame. *(Courtesy the ATA Association)*

22. The ATA on parade. *(Courtesy Michael Fahie)*

23. The King and Queen with pilots of the ATA. *(Courtesy Ann Wood Kelly)*

24. Eleanor Roosevelt meets the women pilots of the ATA. *(Courtesy Michael Fahie)*

25. Joan Hughes at the controls of a four-engine heavy bomber. *(Courtesy Maidenhead Heritage Centre)*

26. Joan Hughes is seen dwarfed below a Short Stirling, one of the many types she often flew. *(Courtesy Maidenhead Heritage Centre)*

27. This Luftwaffe Junkers Ju 88 attacked Hatfield aerodrome on 3 October 1940. It was hit by the ground defences but dropped its bombs before crashing, causing considerable damage and loss of life. *(Courtesy Michael Fahie)*

28. *Above:* Pilots of the ATA pose with the Soviet Army. *(Courtesy the ATA Association)*

29. *Top right:* Gerard d'Erlanger. *(Courtesy the ATA Association)*

30. *Right:* ATA's call-sign. Ferdinand and the Bull. *(Courtesy the ATA Association)*

31. *Below:* Pauline Gower and Jacqueline Cochran. *(Courtesy Maidenhead Heritage Centre)*

32. *bottom:* Jacqueline Cochrane and General Arnold.
(Courtesy of the National Archives Washington. No 342-FH-4A05627)

33. American WASP recruits arriving at Avenger Field in Sweetwater.
(Courtesy of the National Archives Washington. No 342-FH-4A05348)

34. WASP barracks at Avenger.

(Courtesy of the National Archives Washington. No 342-FH-4A05430)

35. The cafeteria at Avenger Field.

(Courtesy of the National Archives Washington. No 342-FH-4A05402)

36. Daily physical training at Avenger.

(Courtesy of the National Archives Washington. No 342-FH-4A05397)

37. WASP at ground school at Avenger Field.

(Courtesy of the National Archives Washington. No 342-FH-4A05362)

38. WASP undergoing training on the Norton bombsight. *(Courtesy of the National Archives Washington. No 342-FH-4A05675)*

39. WASP are tested in the altitude chamber. *(Courtesy of the National Archives Washington. No 342-FH-4A05355)*

40. Cochran and trainees at Avenger Field.
(Courtesy of the National Archives Washington. No 342-FH-4A05401)

41. WASP climb aboard their taxi.
(Courtesy of the National Archives Washington. No 342-FH-4A05548)

42. *bottom:* WASP trainees in the cockpit of a Harvard training aircraft.
(Courtesy of the National Archives Washington. No 342-FH-4A05397)

43. A WASP consults with her instructor.
(Courtesy of the National Archives Washington. No 342-FH-4A05519)

44. *Left:* Sunbathing between the barracks at Avenger Field. *(Courtesy of the National Archives Washington. No 342-FH-4A05396)*

45. *Right*: The WASP recreation room. *(Courtesy of the National Archives, Washington. No 342-FH-4A05391)*

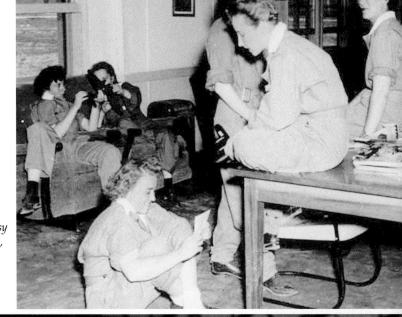

46. *Below*: A cheery wave from a WASP. *(Courtesy of the National Archives, Washington. No 342-FH-4A05410)*

47. After their first solo flight, WASP trainees were thrown in the wishing well. *(Courtesy of the National Archives Washington. No 342-FH-4A05359)*

48. WASP on the flight line. *(Courtesy of the National Archives Washington. No 342-FH-4A05352)*

49. WASP graduation parade. (*Courtesy of the National Archives Washington. No 342-FH-4A05418*)

50. The WASP birthday cake at Avenger in November 1943. (*Courtesy of the National Archives Washington. No 342-FH-4A05624*)

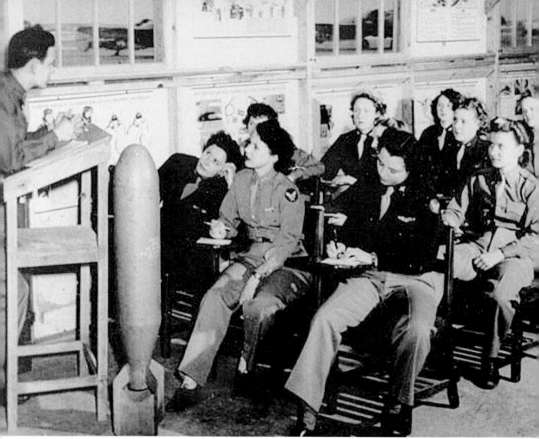

51. WASP in the briefing room before a flight. (*Courtesy of the National Archives, Washington. No 342-FH-4A05376*)

52. WASP march past the control tower at Avenger Field. (*Courtesy of the National Archives Washington. No 342-FH-4A05676*)

53. Three WASP wait in the snow by their aircraft. *(Courtesy of the National Archives Washington. No 342-FH-4A05356)*

54. Flight planning. *(Courtesy of the National Archives Washington. No 342-FH-4A05350)*

55. *Above:* WASP at B-17 Flight School at Lockburne AAF base. *(Courtesy of the National Archives Washington. No 342-FH-4A05344)*

56. *Right:* A WASP pilot in the cockpit of B-17. *(Courtesy of the National Archives, Washington. No 342-FH-4A05339)*

57. *Below:* Pilot and co-pilot in a B-17 Flying Fortress. *(Courtesy of the National Archives Washington. No 342-FH-4A05519)*

lavished praise on the ATA in his opening speech, but personally presented a cheque for GBP 5,000 to the Benevolent Fund. More impressive still, the ATA attracted a crowd of over 12,000 spectators and 'the greatest difficulty was experienced in getting them out at the end of the day . . . .'[44] The ATA was thus given a very festive and public farewell, comparable to a gala dinner with speeches and gifts for a retiring executive, rather than being sent home like an unwanted servant as the WASP had been.

Surprisingly, the improvised ATA also left a lasting legacy to aviation in the form of its Pilot's and Ground Handling Notes and its Ground Engineer School. The Pilot's Handling Notes became institutionalised and were produced in the Ministry of Supply after the war. Ground Handling Notes, similar to the Pilot's Notes, had also been evolved by the ATA because all too frequently ATA aircraft were forced down by weather or technical difficulties at airfields where there were no ground crews familiar with that particular type of aircraft. The ATA Technical Department had therefore developed concise notes for ground crews to help them deal with unfamiliar aircraft. As with the Pilot's Notes, the ATA's concept proved so practical, that the MAP took over the production of these notes on the basis of the ATA's specifications and 'in due course Ground Handling Notes were issued generally as an authoritative document to all RAF and MAP airfields'.[45] In addition, the school for ground engineering, which the ATA had established at White Waltham in 1943, was at the end of the war 'taken over intact for training engineers of the British Overseas Airways Corporation'.[46]

Equally or even more important, the ATA's Director of Operations, Philip Wills, goes so far as to claim that through the 'evolution of methods of Accident Investigation and Prevention, ATA made one of its greatest, if not its greatest, contributions to subsequent aviation history, for it is not too much to say that on our methods have been based all subsequent procedures throughout the world'.[47]

As for the women pilots, they seem to have found it easier to obtain flying jobs after the war than their American colleagues. Diana Barnato Walker was active in the Women's Junior Air Corps and went on to break the sound barrier in a Lightning in August 1963; she was clocked at 1,262 mph, breaking the record previously set by Jacqueline Cochran.[48] Freydis Sharland became the first woman to become British Air Racing Champion in 1954. Ann Welsh became a leading glider pilot and Team Captain of the British Gliding Team in 1956. Lettice Curtis was an air flight test pilot for military aircraft. Other women worked in aerial survey photography, flew as a 'targets' for training radar crews, or earned their living as flight instructors or corporate pilots.

Ironically, although the women of the ATA had never been promised commissions or submitted to de-facto military discipline as had the WASP, the RAF opened up the *flying branch* of the Volunteer Reserve to qualified women pilots in 1947. Many ex-ATA women pilots took advantage of the offer and thereafter enjoyed the privilege of again 'being paid to fly instead of having to pay for it!'[49] What was more, via the RAFVR, the women were able to gain training in areas that had been intentionally neglected in their ATA training, such as night and instrument flying, aerobatics and formation flying.

In America, a dedicated programme had been launched to prove that women could fly military planes as well as men. With great fanfare it had been proclaimed a success – at the very moment when it was discontinued, classified and forgotten. For more than thirty years American women continued to be excluded from Air Force cockpits. In Britain no one had viewed the role of women as 'experimental', no one had found it necessary to establish expensive and exclusive establishments to train the women separately, and no one made any claims of proving something earthshaking. Instead, without any fuss, women simply started to fly military aircraft in 1940 and continued to do so for a number of years after the war via the RAFVR.

Notes:
1   Quoted in Keil, 329.
2   Phelps, 8.
3   Verges, 68.
4   Verges,100.
5   Cochran, Jacqueline & Maryann Bucknum Brinley, Jackie Cochran: An Autobiography, 1987, 213.
6   Merryman, 40.
7   Merryman, 41.
8   Keil, 286.
9   Merryman, 77.
10   New York Herald Tribune, quote in Merryman, 77.
11   Keil, 293.
12   Merryman, 54.
13   Merryman, 54.
14   Merryman, 84.
15   Verges, 217.
16   Merryman, 86–7.
17   Verges, 202.
18   Granger, 284, 332, 341. See also Verges, 203.

19 Granger, 341.
20 Merryman, 87. See also Verges, 207.
21 Cochran, quoted in Merryman, 111.
22 Cochran, quoted in Merryman, 110.
23 Cochran, quoted in Merryman, 111–12.
24 Merryman, 112.
25 Major Elliot, quoted in Merryman, 113.
26 Merryman, 115.
27 Granger, 432.
28 Verges, 227.
29 Granger, 433.
30 Verges, 219.
31 Keil, 326.
32 Tunner, 39.
33 Keil, 330.
34 Keil, 330.
35 Keil, 330.
36 Keil, 331.
37 Keil, 326.
38 Granger, 476, A-108/S.
39 Merryman, 129.
40 Verges, 252.
41 Curtis, 237.
42 Cheeseman, 206.
43 Cheeseman, 208.
44 Cheeseman, 207.
45 Curtis, 77. See also Cheeseman, 69.
46 Cheeseman, 57.
47 Wills quoted in Bergel, 98.
48 Walker, 214.
49 Lucas, 117.

CHAPTER SEVEN

Handmaidens and Guinea Pigs

MILITARY TRADITIONS AND THE WOMEN PILOTS IN THE SECOND WORLD WAR

The importance of military traditions to a nation's morale in wartime should never be underestimated. Tradition alone, however, cannot win wars. The dismal performance of the French Armed Forces in 1940 alone is evidence of that. But there can be equally little doubt that the tradition of Drake and Nelson played an important role in strengthening British resolve to fight on alone against Nazi Germany after the surrender of France. Curiously, it is recorded that many ordinary Englishmen openly expressed relief to be fighting alone, without the 'burden' of allies. Inexplicable as it was to the German government and American journalists at the time, the role of underdog was one in which the British felt remarkably comfortable. Likewise, the response to women pilots – in both Britain and America – had a great deal to do with the tradition – or lack of it – of women in the military.

There had, to be sure, been intrepid aviatrixes ever since man first took to the air, but not within the male bastion of the armed services. The acceptance of women as pilots for the military was, therefore, neither automatic nor self-evident. What is more, unlike the women in other auxiliary services, these women fliers weren't doing a job men did not *want* – like cleaning, cooking and clerking. On the contrary, because flying was at the time considered particularly 'daring' and 'exciting', women pilots were seeking one of the most coveted of all military jobs. Indeed, the competition among young men for the privilege of flying for the military was intense. Those that succeeded at qualifying as military pilots tended to think of themselves as an elite.

It is hardly surprising under the circumstances that there was considerable reluctance to admit women into the club.

It must be remembered that since the institutionalisation of the military in conjunction with the rise of the nation state, women had been strictly excluded from the fighting forces of modern nations. In fact, despite occasional prominent exceptions such as Joan of Arc, bearing arms was a male profession as far back as antiquity. By the 18th and 19th centuries, the role of women in the military, even in support and medical roles, had largely been marginalised, despite a counter-movement in nursing led by Florence Nightingale. By the early 20th century, society in general and military organisations more specifically viewed the participation of women in hostilities as uncivilised and unnatural.

Then came the First World War. Within months, the opposing European powers found themselves deadlocked in a struggle that drained away manpower resources at an alarming rate and, without any apparent impact on the outcome of the war. Unwilling to come to terms diplomatically and unable to achieve a decisive victory on the battle-field, the European countries found themselves condemned to a war of attrition. Sheer desperation forced the War Office to face the previously unthinkable prospect of employing women. Out of necessity, an experiment was made and a precedent was set that hardened in the crucible of conflict into a tradition. On the other side of the Atlantic, however, there was not the necessity, the precedent or the tradition. And it is here, in the dramatically different ways the First World War impacted on British and American military traditions with respect to women, that the roots of the different response to women pilots in the two countries during the Second World War can be found.

WOMEN IN THE BRITISH ARMED FORCES DURING THE FIRST WORLD WAR

In December 1916, even before the United States had been drawn into the conflagration, the War Office in Britain was faced with such an acute manpower shortage that the principle of employing women in support capacities within the Army was reluctantly accepted. By this point, two-and-a-half years into the gruesome conflict, a number of women's volunteer organisations, notably the VAD* and FANY**, had already given dramatic evidence of the ability of women to withstand appalling

* Voluntary Aid Detachments
** First Aid Nursing Yeomanry

conditions and deliver reliable and valuable service, predominantly in the context of medical support services. Thus, in early 1917, in an effort to release more men for front-line service, the military identified a number of trades that it felt could be performed by women. Logically, the Army planned to put women first and foremost into jobs that were already being performed by women in a civilian context, e.g. cooks, waitresses, laundresses, servants, telephone operators and clerks.

The Woman's Auxiliary Army Corps (WAAC) was formed to recruit and organise the women who would fill these posts, thereby freeing men for the front. The members of the WAAC were provided with uniforms modelled on that of the Army (khaki coat frocks for other ranks and khaki jackets and peaked caps for officers), although they technically remained civilian volunteers.

The Royal Navy, whose losses were significantly lower, took almost another year before it followed the Army's example by creating in February 1918 its own women's auxiliary corps, the Women's Royal Naval Service (WRNS – the women were commonly known as Wrens). This too was a voluntary civilian but uniformed service. Again, the duties assigned the women were those that society already accepted as compatible with 'women's' roles, and the women were strictly confined to shore. Their job was to 'free a man for the fleet' – not man the fleet itself.

The last of the women's services to be formed was the Women's Royal Air Force (WRAF), which was established simultaneously with the RAF on 1 April 1918. In addition to being formed at the same time as the male service it supported, the WRAF from its inception opened up trades to women that were not traditionally 'women's work'. Thus, in addition to the usual jobs such as cooks, typists, telephone operators and wait-resses, women in the WRAF were offered training as fitters, riggers, welders and electricians. Some of the women were also offered flying instruction.

Meanwhile, by early 1918 or roughly one year after its founding, the WAAC already numbered nearly 22,500 women, of which 5,000 were deployed in France. Furthermore, in this first year of service, the women, particularly those in France, had already demonstrated their worth to the War Office. Not only had they proved reliable and hard working, they had suffered hardships and casualties and the first commendations had been earned.

This did not spare them from slander and gossip at home, however. On the 'Home Front' women in military uniform had become the objects of malicious jokes and rumours, which imputed widespread immorality to them. It was even suggested that their real function was to supply

Army brothels. The situation was so grave that the Ministry of Labour felt compelled to establish an Official Commission of Inquiry to investigate the rumours. The results of the investigation were, however, a conclusive refutation of all the sordid gossip. In light of this fact and to boost the morale and image of the WAAC, Queen Mary personally assumed the role of Commander-in-Chief of the women's army corps, lending it her own name, so that it was henceforth officially known as Queen Mary's Army Auxiliary Corps.

Thereafter, the respectability of the women's organisations as a whole was not seriously questioned, although the images between the three forces still varied. 'Somehow, the British class system wormed its way into the image of the services – the WRAF women were considered 'nice', just as the Wrens were 'perfect ladies', the WAACs, on the other hand, were just women.'[1]

But class differences were a feature of society and did not alter the fact that by the end of the First World War, roughly 100,000 women had served with the British Armed Forces as uniformed auxiliaries and these women had by then earned the respect of the men with whom they served. The women killed on active service were buried with full military honours, while the women who distinguished themselves were eligible for decorations and were mentioned in dispatches. More important than individual acts of courage, the objective record of the women was so consistently positive that none of the services had any regrets about employing women.

On the contrary, in the critical post-war period when Russia was in the grips of the Bolshevik Revolution and mutinies in the German armed forces had sparked a simmering civil war, the mood in the British Army grew dangerously radical. Not only was there growing political unrest such as strikes, demonstrations and riots, but there were increasing indications that some British troops were tempted to follow the German and Russian examples and turn their weapons against their 'oppressions' from the Ruling Class, i.e. their officers. The Government noticed, however, that women in the auxiliary services were notably immune to these sentiments, and 'since they had already shown that they could occupy men's jobs and trades, the Government decided . . . to expand the Women's Services and use them . . . at home and abroad, so that men could be released from the forces'.[2]

The Government never had reason to regret this decision either. Senior officers observed that the mere presence of WRAF, for example, 'acted beneficially on other ranks RAF, in that the general tone and appearance of the men have most distinctly improved'.[3] They also did the job – whatever it was – as well as the men they were replacing, even in such fields, such as signals, which did not belong to 'traditional' female roles. The Air Officer Commanding RAF on the Rhine went on record saying: 'The discipline of the [WRAF] was at once an example to all, of what a well-organised, well-trained women's force can do. Their work was strenuous and in many cases long, yet, wherever they went, they astonished everyone by their willingness, capability and by their efficiency.'[4] This was the image of women's auxiliaries that the British Armed Forces and their senior officers took with them from the First World War.

WOMEN IN THE AMERICAN FORCES DURING THE FIRST WORLD WAR

The US military by contrast never faced a manpower shortage that made it necessary to consider employing women on a widespread, systematic basis. Curiously, the US Navy was the first of the American armed forces to employ a limited number of women on a voluntary basis, accepting young, unmarried women with education and/or clerical training for duties ranging from clerks to radio-operators, pharmacists and photographers ashore. Significantly, these women served not in an auxiliary organisation but directly as 'yeomanettes' and later received all Navy bonuses and veterans' benefits. The US Marine Corps likewise employed a limited number of women (roughly 300) in clerical positions.

The record of the US Army, however, is a touch of *déjà vu* for the WASP. Having resisted the recruitment of women, the US Army discovered after it had already deployed to France that it had an acute need for French-speaking telephone operators. The demand could most rapidly be met by hiring women, who already had the necessary qualifications, rather than training men. So the US Army hastily recruited qualified women in the US. These women were sworn in as members of the US Army Signal Corps and subjected not only to all Army regulations, but also to additional rules designed to assure their 'moral character'. The women were then sent to France, where they worked long hours under difficult conditions and often close enough behind the front lines to be subject to artillery barrages. When the war was over, however, the Army abruptly decided that 'they could not have been sworn into the army because regulations stated that "males were sworn in and said nothing about persons"'.[5] The women were thus sent home without honourable discharges and enjoyed none of the benefits of veteran status.

Likewise, the US Army recruited physical therapists to deal with soldiers whose nervous condition deteriorated during the long trip home across the Atlantic. These trained women were taken to France and helped establish a unit for treating shell-shock cases close behind the front lines in France – a very innovative medical advancement at the time. But the women involved were treated exactly like their colleagues the telephone operators. When after the war the Army no longer needed them, they were released without veteran status or benefits.[6]

Thus, US Army could be said to have established a precedent of using women in a quasi-military capacity when need arose and denying them all benefits as soon as their services were superfluous. At all events, the numbers of women employed by the US military in the First World War were so small that their admirable record of service was completely omitted from the institutional record and memory.

British Women in the Second World War

When the next world conflict loomed on the horizon, the British military, in contrast, remembered the positive experience with women during and in the aftermath of the First World War, and women's auxiliary organisations were all called into being before the Second World War broke out. Furthermore, at the urging of women's activists, it was soon agreed that women serving with the Armed Forces should be commissioned or enlisted as officers or members of the Armed Forces, rather than 'enrolled' as civilian auxiliaries as had been the case in the First World War. The necessary legislation was passed in early 1941, at a time when all the women with the Services were still volunteers.

By late 1941 the combined demands of the military and war economy had grown so great, however, that for the first time in British history the decision was taken to conscript women. Initially only unmarried, childless women between the ages of twenty and thirty were called up and the women were given a choice between an industrial or military placement. Nevertheless, the precedent was set: henceforth women too could be 'drafted' into military service. In February 1942, all women aged eighteen to sixty, married or unmarried, with or without children, were required to register with the Ministry of Labour. There followed an interview, in which their suitability for various kinds of war work was determined, and again an effort was made to place the women in work that best suited their individual situation, aptitude and wishes. In addition to service with the armed forces, there was a range of other duties from Civil Defence, Land Army, NAAFI and Fire Service, to work in munitions factories, shipyards and the like, all of which qualified as national service. The fundamental principle was simply that everyone in Britain, regardless of sex, class, education or marital status, had to make a contribution to winning the war.

The Armed Forces themselves much preferred volunteers to conscripts, however, and throughout the war made efforts to attract women to their respective services. It is notable that by this time the recruiting campaigns stressed the responsibility of the jobs, rather than their familiarity. While in the First World War, women had been appealed to as women – stressing that in the Army they would be doing the things they did 'best' such as cooking and cleaning, the emphasis in the Second World War was on opportunity, responsibility and contribution. The Wrens, for example, sought to attract volunteers by stressing that WRNS officers were replacing 'naval officers in shore jobs, in convoy rooms, plotting rooms, naval control service offices'.[7] The ATS stressed 'energy and initiative', and 'doing a man-size job, with all a man's opportunities'.[8]

The WRAF tradition of offering women exceptional opportunities was even stronger. Although redesignated Women's Auxiliary Air Force or WAAF during the Second World War, the women who served alongside the RAF continued to enjoy a degree of equality of opportunity exceptional even in wartime Britain. They had support in high places. 'Dowding and Watson-Watt led the way in advocating the employment of WAAF in new signals techniques. Both the Commander-in-Chief of Fighter Command and the Deputy Director of Scientific Research at the Air Ministry . . . were convinced that WAAF would be more useful than any men . . . .' for radar duties.[9] Watson-Watt trained the first airwomen as filterers and plotters as well, while Dowding personally ensured that his 'special duties' WAAF Sergeants received commissions 'as from the day' some civilians were given direct commissions.[10]

The trades open to airwomen expanded from five at the start of the war to over eighty-nine by the end, while WAAF officers' branches grew from one to twenty-two over the same period. In addition to the radar-related duties for which Watson-Watt and Dowding had paved the way in 1939–40, women were by the end of the war involved in a variety of other highly technical trades, from photographic interpretation to meteorology, all aspects of R/T, wireless, signals and flight engineering (fitters, riggers, flight mechanics).[11] It has even been argued that the large number of women recruited for SOE (Special Operations Executive) from the WAAF was a function of the fact that they 'came from a service that had a better record of employing the best person for the job, irrespective of sex'.[12]

The WAAF certainly enjoyed a degree of popularity right from the start. Initial recruitment proved so unexpectedly successful that it had to be discontinued just one month after the start of the war because it was impossible to absorb the sudden influx of recruits. The Battle of Britain and the high-profile role WAAF had played in the Battle boosted the image of the service even further. By now, the WAAF's image was so high, that 'joining up involved a certain amount of string-tugging, much to the wonder of the Labour MP Dr Edith Summerskill'.[13] In response to a question in the House of Commons, it was admitted that 'family connections take precedence, and having a fiancé in the RAF makes a girl more acceptable'.[14] At the end of 1940, roughly 21,000 women were serving in the WAAF. One year later it was almost 100,000. Wartime strength peaked in late-1943 at 181,835. Of the women who served in the WAAF during the entire war, only 33,932, or roughly 15 per cent, were conscripts; the rest were volunteers. At its peak in October 1943, the WAAF made up 15 per cent of total RAF strength and 22 per cent of the RAF in Britain.[15]

The degree of integration of the women into the RAF was also note-worthy. As early as 1930, the 'Father of the Air Force', Lord Trenchard, remarked: 'I do not look on the "W" in WRAF as anything more than an unnecessary initial put at the beginning of it. It was all part of the RAF and I'm sure it will be again.'[16] In the Second World War, WAAF sub-stituted for men with very few exceptions on the basis of one-for-one, and the women served under the same conditions and were issued the same equipment. The RAF and WAAF trained together for the various trades, and had to pass the same exams. Uniforms were as similar to RAF as was practical for clothing designed for women; i.e. for dress occasions wear skirts and stockings were obviously purely women's attire, but for duties in maintenance hangars or handling barrage balloons the women wore trousers and battle-dress, overalls and/or sheep-lined jackets and boots, just like their male colleagues. Perhaps more important, rank and speciality badges were identical to those of the RAF, and – very significantly WAAF officers and NCOs could and did have command authority over men of the RAF.

In one trade, in fact, women were commissioned/enlisted directly into the RAF rather than the WAAF, and that was the medical service. It was to seven RAF nursing orderlies that the honour of becoming the first women to set foot on the Continent after the D-Day fell. With fighting still taking place a few miles farther inland, these women aboard an air-ambulance flew directly to the beaches to collect severely wounded personnel.

The WAAF followed closely in the wake of the RAF nurses. WAAF serving with the 2nd Tactical Air Force advanced on the heels of the retreating Wehrmacht, and by the end of the war nearly 1900 WAAF were stationed in Europe. Many others were stationed in other overseas posts from Egypt to Ceylon so that on 1 September 1945 more than 7,500 WAAF were serving outside Britain.[17]

Being so closely integrated into the work of the RAF had its price. Some 191 WAAF were killed and 420 were wounded while on active service. Nor did the courage of the women go unnoticed. Five WAAF were awarded Military MBEs, three BEMs for Gallantry. Altogether, WAAF received two GCs, two DBEs, three CBEs, twenty OBEs, ninety-two Civil MBEs, six MMs, ninety BEMs, eight Commendations and 2,497 Mentions in Dispatches.

In only one trade did the RAF show a curious reluctance to recognise the capabilities of women, and that was with regard to flying. The Air Ministry opposed a Flying Branch of the WAAF from the very start, and it was not until after the war that the RAF opened flying to women – the RAFVR long before the active RAF. There was, of course, a general prohibition against women engaging in combat (which was why mixed Anti-Aircraft batteries throughout the war only allowed women to man search-lights and fire control instruments but not to *fire* the guns). This prohibition would have justified stopping WAAF from flying as aircrew on aircraft engaged on combat operations. After all, Wrens were not allowed to serve on fighting ships either. (Although the Civil Lord of the Admiralty admitted during a debate in the House of Commons that he had 'no doubt that if you gave the WRNS half a chance they would be perfectly prepared to sail a battleship'.[18]) The RAF logic for not letting women fly in non-combat capacities is, however, abstruse. After all, WAAF *did* fly RAF service aircraft in non-combat capacities during the war – but only after they had been seconded to the ATA!

Finally, a note on pay. WAAF pay was set at two-thirds that of RAF personnel of equivalent rank, while all allowances were identical. Initially, rations were set at four-fifths of men, but with the increasing appearance of joint messes this became impractical and was discontinued before the end of the war. Since pay and allowances were determined by rank and length of service, members of the WAAF could expect to gradually increase their income as they were promoted.

AMERICAN WOMEN AND THE SECOND WORLD WAR

The American situation in the Second World War was again dramatically different due to the all-important issue of manpower resources. As in the First World War, the United States never faced a manpower shortfall of such dimensions that the entire adult population needed to be registered and conscripted or directed. On the other hand, the United States was fighting a war in two continents, and – more important – it was acting as the 'arsenal of democracy' supplying vital war materials and equipment not only for its own military but for the forces of Great Britain and the Soviet Union as well. In consequence, although the Armed Forces – familiar with British practices – rapidly recognised the advantages of employing women in support capacities, the US Manpower Commission and the Office of War Mobilisation objected to recruiting campaigns aimed at women because it felt women were needed in war industries and agriculture. Public opinion in the United States was also far more conservative with regard to the role of women generally, and a number of Catholic bishops protested publicly against the mere notion of enlisting women in the Armed Forces.

Nevertheless, in the patriotic frenzy that followed the attack on Pearl Harbor, the Armed Forces did develop plans for the use of female volunteers. As in the First World War, the Marines accepted women directly into the Marine Corps without any distinction for sex. The Navy and Coast Guard established women's services that were militarised and fully integrated into their organisation with equal status and rights. The Army, in contrast, opted for a civilian 'Auxiliary'. The result was that the Army suffered significant handicaps in recruiting, and had to go back to Congress requesting the transformation of its WAAC (Women's Army Auxiliary Corps) into the WAC (Women's Army Corps).

The change in name and legal status did little to disguise – much less alter – a fundamental difference in attitude toward women that was apparent to all observers. While the Marine Corps employed women as auto and aircraft mechanics, drivers and parachute riggers as well as in conventional 'women's work', and the Navy bragged that thousands of WAVEs were being transferred to Washington to release Navy officers for sea duty, the US Army employed women almost exclusively in menial tasks. The Congressional legislation authorising the WAC furthermore explicitly excluded the possibility of WAC officers ever giving orders to men. The result was that despite the fact that the women were generally better educated than male conscripts/recruits, the women were consistently under-utilised; women with fluent Japanese were employed as cooks, PhDs remained clerks, and so on. Adding insult to injustice, the women serving in the Pacific Theatre were issued wholly unsuitable uniforms, provided with neither recreation facilities nor leave, and so ended up working 12–16 hour days in 100-degree heat without leave or recreation; the men by contrast had suitable uniforms, leave and recreation facilities. Clearly, regardless of qualifications, the women in the WAC were not considered equal partners, but second-class subordinates.

Given this attitude on the part of senior officers, it is hardly surprising that the image of the WAC was not particularly good. While the

American press focused on the design and colour of the uniforms for the 'gals', rumours soon started to circulate about immorality, pregnancy and VD. As with the British WAAC in the First World War, political action followed. Congressional Hearings were held that proved that the unmarried pregnancy rate was lower in the WAC than among civilians, and that VD was virtually non-existent (although allegedly epidemic among soldiers). Furthermore, the women were eighty-nine times less likely to go AWOL, eighty-five times less likely to get drunk and 150 times less likely to violate the military code than were men.[19] The facts were unambiguous, but the image remained tarnished – perhaps because in America there was no Queen who could put herself at the head of the WAC and so lend them dignity and respectability.

It is interesting to note, however, that the American WAC reportedly received the best treatment in the European Theatre, especially in Eisenhower's command. It is hard to escape the conclusion that it was the pervasive and positive example of British women in the ATS, WRNS and WAAF that influenced Eisenhower, his officers and staff to view and treat women in uniform more fairly than their colleagues in the Pacific and at home.

In summary, it is clear that the greater demands placed on the limited manpower resources of the United Kingdom, and particularly the introduction of female conscription during the Second World War, accounts for the greater role granted women in society at large and in the Services specifically. Furthermore, British women had already established an admirable track record in the First World War, which made senior officers more disposed to accept their services in the Second. American women had also done well in the First World War, but on such a small scale that their contribution was more easily forgotten – at least by the US Army, whose gratitude to the women who served in its ranks did not last long enough to give the women honourable discharges.

When looking for the reasons for the WASP's fate, therefore, the fact that they were dealing with the hidebound US Army cannot be ignored. The ATA, by contrast, had the advantage of working most closely with the most progressive and open-minded of the British Services.

Notes:

1   Adie, 78.
2   Escott, Beryl, *Women in Air Force Blue: The Story of Women in the Royal Air Force from 1918 to the Present Day*, 1989, 49.

3   Beauman, Katherine Bentley, *Partners in Blue: The Story of the Women's Service with the Royal Air Force*, 1971, 49.
4   Beauman, 47.
5   Adie, 250.
6   Page, Christie Tufts, personal experiences as told to the author (her granddaughter) in several interviews.
7   Adie, 163.
8   ATS Recruiting Poster reproduced in Harris, Carol, *Women at War in Uniform 1939 – 1945*, 2003, 34.
9   Beauman, 103–104.
10   Beauman, 121.
11   Beauman, 286–7, Escott, 298–9.
12   Adie, 224.
13   Adie, 168.
14   Adie, 169.
15   Escott, 296, 301.
16   Beauman, 56.
17   Escott, 302.
18   Adie, 163.
19   www.gendergap.com/military

CHAPTER EIGHT

Friends and Foes

THE REACTIONS AND ATTITUDES OF MALE PILOTS TO WOMEN IN THEIR MIDST

Male reactions to the women pilots were as diverse as the men themselves. They ranged from active enthusiasm and encouragement – often for a wife or girlfriend – to disdain and open hostility. On the whole, American women faced a significantly harsher climate from their male colleagues than did the British. And while differing attitudes toward women in their ranks had their roots in the respective military traditions, a deeper explanation must be sought for the vehement antipathy that led some American men to consider murder less offensive than a female in the cockpit of a military aircraft.

The RAF and the ATA

Before turning to an analysis of the attitudes women pilots encountered from their male superiors, colleagues and – where relevant – subordinates, it is worth taking a brief look at the experiences of the male pilots of the ATA in the early months of operation. The ATA had been 'hatched up' in the Air Ministry at the suggestions of a Director of BOAC, and the RAF initially viewed the sudden appearance of a bunch of 'hobby' fliers in their midst with scepticism if not scorn. ATA pilots who flew during the first months of the war, reported feeling that they 'were in everybody's way',[1] while an RAF officer openly admits that the young RAF pilots laughed at the old men of the ATA when they first appeared.[2] A Flight Commander of the ATA described feeling that they were only 'amateur *faits accomplis* angling for recognition'.[3]

In short, RAF personnel initially made it quite obvious that they doubted the ability of these elderly, amateur airman to stand up to the task of ferrying the latest service aircraft, which were, after all, at the pinnacle of technological progress. Hence, the men flying for the ATA in the early months were equally aware that 'one broken aircraft and we're done – even if the undercart won't come down. We can only get on with the job and do our best. After a reasonable period of success, we shall no doubt be treated with less scepticism'.[4]

And that was exactly what happened. A senior ATA officer reported that 'the nearer one got to the operational side of the RAF, the more friendly and less stuffy did everybody seem to be'.[5] By the time the Ferry Pool was established at Aston Down in June 1942, the new Commander there could report:

> No. 9 FP was unique – it was the only Pool stationed on an aero-drome operated by Fighter Command of the RAF. This turned out to be an enormous advantage . . . The Unit at Aston Down was a Fighter OTU largely staffed and run by survivors of 'The Few' – mostly from Nos 1 and 73 Squadrons. These almost legendary men . . . extended to our motley group of amateur pilots a friend-liness that I shall never forget – a friendliness that made a great deal of difference to our enthusiasm and our efficiency. With men of their calibre all round us, we could not fail to go flat out.[6]

It is important to keep the RAF's *initial* mistrust of the ATA's fliers as a whole in mind when reviewing the experiences of the women pilots in Britain. The sense of being on probation was, after all, something the women fliers also sensed, but it was a mistrust that could and was over-come simply by doing a good job – just as their male colleagues had done before them.

Women in the ATA

That women were given a chance to prove they could do a good job is directly attributable to the men who founded and shaped the organis-ation itself. As has been described previously, the Air Minister had from the start indicated a willingness to employ women – on an equal basis except for pay, but only the genuine acceptance of the women by their superiors and colleagues could make a theoretical scheme function in practice. By all accounts, Gerard d'Erlanger was a man without the slightest prejudice against women pilots. Equally important, Chief Instructor MacMillian, who was responsible for making the decision to admit any woman into the organisation, also 'appears to have been entirely unbiased in his approach to women pilots . . . .'[7] To MacMillan, 'pilots were simply pilots, good or bad, not to be thought of in terms of men or women . . . .'[8]

The founders of the ATA formed the core of administrative and supervisory personnel at ATA HQ in White Waltham, and here a pattern of absolute 'no prejudice' was established and consistently maintained. As one woman pilot put it: 'There was never any hostility or prejudice, women pilots were treated as equals to the men – we carried our own parachutes!!'[9] New women recruits were warned that they 'would survive entirely on their own merits'.[10] While the emphasis in the official greeting was that the women should not expect gallantry or favouritism, it was also a promise of fair treatment, which the ATA consistently delivered – as an organisation.

Which is not to say that there was no scepticism, doubts or prejudice on the part of *individuals* within the organisation. The commander of the Ferry Pool at Whitchurch, for example, long resisted the notion of women at his pool, and accepted them only reluctantly. Lettice Curtis described her brief interlude at the Ferry Pool at Ratcliffe, another male-dominated Pool, as the most unhappy period of her entire ATA career because the Pool had 'collected a band of relatively young, tough and self-assured pilots, many of them American, who liked to think of themselves a the dead-end kids who could deliver their aircraft when even the birds were walking'.[11] Such a self-image could only be damaged by having 'helpless females' flying about in Spitfires while they were 'washed out'.

But damaging to the ego or not, fly the women did and with the same rights as male ATA pilots to fly at their own discretion. Furthermore, the reports of helpful colleagues far out-weigh the references to prejudice in any shape or form. Curtis stresses that many of the men were 'vastly experienced pre-war pilots and yet, whatever they may have thought about women flying four-engined aircraft – and some certainly had reservations – they never for one moment showed anything other than absolute friendship and kindness'.[12] Likewise, when the Ferry Pool at Hamble was converted into an all-women Pool, four of the men remained behind under the command of the newly appointed female CO for a transition period. Not only was there no evidence of resentment, 'the "boys" couldn't have been kinder or more helpful. They flew us around in the taxi aircraft . . . they introduced us to new factories and Maintenance Units and what was even more valuable, as well as being thoroughly efficient, they were really good fun'.[13] In retrospect, the women pilots of the ATA all seem to look back on the treatment they received from their colleagues as predominantly co-operative, helpful and encouraging.[14] In return, Alec Matthews, seems to speak on the behalf of many male members of the ATA, when he stresses that 'the contribution those girls made was tremendous. They were ahead of their time. It was unbelievable'.[15]

Perhaps the attitude of the male ATA pilots can best be summarised as scepticism, yes, but hostility or bigotry, no. Furthermore, although no organisation can dictate the attitude or beliefs of individual members, the consistent policy of giving women equal treatment inevitably gave them the opportunity to wear down the prejudices of even the most conservative men. Thus, it is recorded that when women were being given their first opportunity to qualify on heavy bombers, some men shook their heads and told the women 'you'll never be able to hold 'em, dears, if one engine cuts'. Once the women pilots had successfully qualified, however, there were no further comments of this nature. By February 1942, the women of the ATA were being allowed to progress as far as their individual abilities allowed, and from that point on, the women themselves were responsible for proving what they could do; there were no more institutional barriers in their way. Their colleagues by most accounts not only applauded, but actively assisted the women with advice and encouragement.

Aside from their own colleagues, the women pilots of the ATA had daily contact with the RAF. As has been outlined previously, the RAF had an outstanding record of giving women greater equality of opportunity than other Services, but it also had remained firmly opposed to women flying. Interestingly, following the fall of France, when Pauline Gower was trying to get permission to expand the women's section she ran into more bureaucratic resistance from the Civil Branch of the Air Ministry than from the RAF, which instructed her to expand immediately the women's section by an additional ten pilots.[16] While most accounts stress that the RAF were initially sceptical about the ability of women to fly service aircraft – just as they had been sceptical about the ability of ageing, amateurs to do the same thing – they were as willing to be won over by the women as by the 'ancient' men. Cheeseman summarised the attitude of the RAF to the ATA women as follows:

> At first there was naturally a certain amount of scepticism in Service circles as to whether the women would have the endurance and necessary qualities to cope with the ever-growing variety of operational aircraft, but as time went on and they methodically continued to 'deliver the goods' this attitude changed to a more easy comraderie and healthy admiration of their work.[17]

Rosemary du Cros, one of the original eight women hired by ATA, also noted that the fuss made over women pilots declined over time, but she experienced the reception as positive from the start. She claims that:

We created far more of a stir arriving in our little Moths at RAF stations than we ever did again. We were still news, and everyone was very kind and attentive. Once when we were at a remote Scottish airfield and faced with a frightful train journey, the member of the party with the most charming voice was put on to ring up the CO of a fighter station nearby to ask if he could *possibly* arrange air transport to the nearest town with a civilised railway. He said he would be delighted, 'In fact I might come myself.' He did – and kept it up on many subsequent trips. We often got lifts in those days . . . Later, of course, ATA became such a big and efficient organisation that they could fix you up with linking deliveries which took you all over the country and back by night-fall.[18]

Lettice Curtis describes the RAF response to the first women in Hurricanes as follows: 'At Finningley the RAF, recovering from their surprise at the arrival of two females in Hurricanes, were all helpful-ness.'[19] By 1945, she claimed in contrast that 'a state had now been reached, where women flying aeroplanes were so completely accepted, that even arriving in a Liberator raised few eyebrows'.[20] Joy Lofthouse, a latecomer to the ATA, felt more than acceptance, she felt that 'the RAF personnel treated us with the greatest respect and admiration'.[21]

While the above references deal predominantly with the response of the RAF ground crews, there is no evidence of any reluctance on the part of RAF pilots to accept the women of the ATA as equals either. Rosemary du Cros summarised the attitudes of the pilots as follows:

To begin with some of the young and dashing RAF pilots, who liked to think that in order to fly fast, heavy, fighting aeroplanes you had to be something of a superman, felt a little bit deflated when they saw that we could handle them too. The more sensible ones could see, of course, that there was a vast difference between fighting in an aeroplane, as they had to do, and just flying it care-fully from one place to another as we did. So there was no longer any feeling over that, and indeed they were supermen.[22]

There were also many instances of RAF pilots taking an actively positive attitude toward women flying – particularly if they knew the women involved personally. Diana Barnato Walker, for example, describes how two RAF pilots encouraged her to apply to the ATA in the first place, and coached her for her flight test. More amusing if less typical, was the reported eagerness of one RAF pilot to fly as a passenger with an ATA woman pilot – because he wanted to boast he had flown with a grand-mother! RAF pilot husbands and boyfriends were common among the women of the ATA, and this is the best indication that they were viewed positively and fully accepted by the fliers in the RAF.

Admittedly, the FAA had a reputation for being somewhat more stand-offish. An ATA woman pilot making an emergency landing after one of her two engines had gone unserviceable in the air with a great deal of noise and vibration, was greeted by an 'irate naval officer'. He was outraged that she had landed despite receiving a 'red' from the tower, and indignant that she continued to block the runway. Her reply ('You try turning right with only a right engine and see if you can do it!') did, at least, elicit an apology.[23] In another incident, a woman pilot delivering a Priority One Swordfish not only received a cold reception from the CO of the FAA station that required it, but the Navy lodged a formal complaint against her. The Navy objected on the grounds that 'girls should not be allowed to fly aircraft about in weather that was considered completely unsuitable for their most experienced pilots'.[24] Perhaps coincidentally – perhaps not – both these mildly negative encounters with the Navy were reported by WAAF officers serving with the ATA.

The fact that ATA pilots held a 'flight authorisation' card that enabled them to decide for themselves whether or not conditions were fit for flying was a minor point of friction with the Services generally. Male ATA pilots also report that the RAF resented the fact that the 'ancient and tattered airmen' of the ATA could make their own decisions, while the young bloods of the RAF/FAA were strictly under orders. The USAAF was no less happy with the independence of ATA pilots. Diana Barnato Walker relates the following incident:

> The chit handed to me . . . was for a Blenheim IV . . . .It was marked 'NEA', which meant 'Not Essentially Airworthy', or it was fit for one flight only . . . .
>
> When I first caught sight of [it], it was a very sorry mess indeed . . . I did a very thorough walk-round, noting evidence of old leaks from the starboard engine plus sundry patches on the fuselage and tail-plane. I couldn't be certain but I thought the port under-carriage oleo-leg was listing a bit. The wings did not look quite parallel to the ground, but it could have been the angle of the concrete standing at dispersal.
>
> Still, it was a lovely day, and the ground crew was most helpful. The starboard engine took some time to start, then when it finally got going, clouds and clouds of smoke came out of it. I felt a little

more confident after run-up, so I signalled 'chocks away'. As I did so, I thought I saw expressions of relief on the ground crew's faces at the imminent departure of their problem NEA. But perhaps I was a trifle paranoid.

On the way south, all sorts of little things began to happen. The starboard revs suddenly went down to zero on the rev-counter, but as the engine was churning away happily in spite of its earlier smoking, I decided that it was only an unserviceable rev-counter . . .

Next the port engine oil pressure gauge fluctuated alarmingly, then also went down to zero. That worried me no end, so much so that I throttled back until I saw its oil temperature gauge was keeping at normal. So I decided that it was [the] oil pressure gauge which was at fault . . .

It was difficult to keep the engines tuned . . . [because] the throttles kept jamming . . . But the thing that really worried me most of all was the fumes in the cockpit.

It was an extremely slow aircraft . . . and 12 December was nearly the shortest day of the year, so the daylight was now starting to go. The ATA were not supposed to fly at night . . . I obviously wasn't going to reach my destination before darkness set in, so decided to put down en route at Membury . . . .

My decrepit Blenheim and I were waved to a hardstanding by an American airman. He looked a little startled when he saw a girl (gal!) in the cockpit. Then . . . I couldn't stop the starboard engine . . . In the end I just yanked the throttle of that engine back with a jerk, which stopped it easily enough . . . .

I explained to the airman that my aircraft had been signed out for one flight only, but that if he would do a DI [Daily Inspection] in the morning, I would take it on. He looked somewhat dubious.

I was . . . given the usual American dinner of unrationed food: tinned pork chops, sweet corn, sweet potatoes followed by lashings of ice-cream. This seemed to be the ritual laid on for starving British pilots when they dumped themselves on the Yanks – or maybe I was just lucky?

When I got down to the Watch office the following morning, I was told that their CO had said that 'no-one could fly that messed-up dog's dinner again'! I explained that ATA were their own Captains, making their own decisions as to what, when and where they flew. I was taken to the CO again who tried to dissuade me as he ' . . . didn't want his runways blocked by my forthcoming prang!' nor did he ' . . . want the responsibility of my imminent demise'.

In the end I rang Margot ('What, another woman?' said the CO): She confirmed the ATA rules, assuring the American CO that her ATA pilots, such as I, were fully competent to judge the situation . . .

The Blenheim was not in the same place where I had left it. As the Americans were not trained to work on Blenheims, an RAF ground crew had been specially brought in to do the DI on the aircraft, and they reported that the right-hand oleo-leg had gone down in the night, but that they had jacked it up and refilled it with hydraulic oil. I noticed that they had wound a lot of thick black insulating tape around the leaking joint. They suggested that perhaps I could fly the short distance with the wheels down in case the tape jammed up the retracting mechanism. They also said they had moved the aircraft away from its overnight standing because the port engine had leaked a lot of petrol onto the ground, but they had found the leak, fixing that too. I began to wonder if the American CO wasn't right after all.

. . . I got fond of nursing that little Blenheim. It was its last flight, so I didn't need a snag-sheet at all – nobody was going to fix anything that was wrong anymore. But it felt good to let at least someone know what an ATA pilot could fly and deliver.[25]

It is not entirely accidental that two of the mildly negative experiences reported by ATA women involved Americans: the American men at Kirkbride and Ratcliffe Ferry Pools and the American CO in the above incident. The American women who joined the WFTD and WASP encountered consistent and pervasive hostility of a significantly more profound nature than the scepticism the ATA women faced.

WASP

The problems for the American women began right in flight school. The first CO the women encountered at Houston made it clear that he didn't like his assignment, did not believe women could fly, was convinced the entire programme (WFTD) would fail, and in effect wanted nothing whatever to do with his command. The instructors took their cue from the CO; they were allegedly 'under orders to wring the students out, skin 'em alive and learn what makes them tick'.[26] To achieve this, they 'yelled and cussed and in general tried to make [the girls] feel like earthbound worms'.[27] (By comparison, the Americans trained by the ATA recall that being told by their instructor that he took 'a very poor view' of some manoeuvre was the worst abuse encountered.)

When WFTD training moved to Avenger Field, the Army officer

commanding the unit had a more neutral attitude, but the instructing itself remained in the hands of the civilian contractors. These were 'resentful and disconcerted that Avenger Field had switched from male to female cadets . . . .'[28] A woman dispatcher working at Avenger Field was in an excellent position to compare the treatment the women endured versus what their male predecessors had received. She claimed that the instructors were indifferent to the women, made no particular effort to help them and in one case an instructor refused to speak to a woman trainee during the entire training course.

The women trainees, however, had no way of knowing that their treatment compared unfavourably to that meted out to male cadets. Fresh from sheltered family homes, yet eager and excited, they naively accepted the profanity and toughness of the instructors as part of the 'Army' experience – just as they accepted the barracks, the rattlesnakes, the PT and drill.

Yet, while anything that made them feel that they too were participating in the absorbing experience that had turned half the nation into an armed camp was readily accepted, sexual harassment was not. Unfortunately, there was a great deal of this. One WASP reports:

> Among ourselves we discussed how to handle the pawing types. No use reporting it . . . You know, that girl who refused to date her instructor. He told her he would wash her out if she said no – and he did.[29]

This was no isolated incident. Another trainee appealed to a review board, claiming she had been washed out by an instructor who was punishing her for not submitting to his sexual advances. She had entered training with the highest number of flying hours and during the proceedings it became evident that they were dealing with 'the bitterness of a man rebuffed by a pretty trainee'.[30] Not that this insight helped the woman involved; she was sent home nevertheless. Henceforth, however, it was recognised that in future the judgement of no single instructor could be allowed to be decisive. Thereafter, any candidate who was washed out by one instructor, got five hours of instruction with another before a final decision was made.

This rule applied only to the civilian instructors, however, and it was the Army test pilots that the women trainees in the WFTD feared the most. One WASP put it this way:

> We certainly didn't enjoy check rides with the Army pilots . . . . They were very unhappy being associated with a women's field.

They wanted to be out there being gung-ho. I really think they were embarrassed about it.[31]

WASP Joanne Wallace was told by her Army check pilot that he had come to Avenger Field with the sole purpose of seeing how many of the women he could wash out. The situation was so bad that even the Army recognised the problem and set up a review board to investigate complaints from trainees claiming unfair treatment from Army check pilots.

Yet for all this, the experience at Avenger field was still looked back on nostalgically by many WASP. One claimed that 'while in the nurturing atmosphere of a training situation, the WASPs were accepted and amply able to prove their flying ability . . . once they set forth from the training base to duty assignments on operational AAF bases, they were repeatedly met with distrust'.[32] The feeling was not merely subjective paranoia on the part of the WASP. The official Air Inspector, Colonel Outcult, investigating the WASP in October/November 1943, found that resentment against the women at operational bases was widespread and that there were deliberate efforts to keep them grounded or fail them during check rides.

Many WASP tried to explain to themselves the resentment they encountered. They speculated that they were resented because they were taking relatively 'safe' jobs away from men, who in consequence were sent overseas. Others felt the reverse: that men in domestic flying duties were 'tired of arguing with bums and drunks who called them yellow because they weren't overseas flying in combat'.[33] Added to this was all the publicity that the first women had been given; the men felt that their contribution to the war was ignored or even denigrated, while the women doing the same job were made into media stars.

A number of WASP could sympathise with the men. Delphine Bohn, for example, pointed out that when the women started flying 'pursuits' it was hard on the men:

I can easily understand how the young pilots felt. Here they were, just out of flight school and very proud of the fact that they were 'fighter pilots' . . . and now the girls were starting to fly fighters too. One day they were supermen and all of a sudden the next day the girls were doing it.[34]

Whatever the reason, the male response to the WASP could be very hostile indeed. News that women pilots were coming to Camp Davis so incensed the personnel that enlisted men requested transfers *en masse*, while male pilots openly discussed the option of a strike. The Commander of the Tow Targeting Squadron at the base, Major Stevenson, evidently shared the sentiments of his mutinous subordinates. He told the WASP they were welcome to check out on the Dauntless Dive Bomber because, in his words, 'these planes are dispensable . . . and you're dispensable'.[35]

Another WASP reports being greeted at her new assignment with the words: 'We didn't ask for you and we don't want you so just stay out of our way.'[36] At the Air Forces' own prestigious Randolph Field the CO treated the women with open 'disdain', refused them both housing on base and access to the Officers' Club. At the Training Command units where the WASP flew aircraft to help train bombardiers and navigators, the relations between the women pilots and their trainees were particularly strained. 'Navigators and bombardiers were often washouts from AAF flying schools who viewed successful Sweetwater graduates with less than good humour.'[37]

The USAAF itself noted that the resentment of male pilots was most evident 'where the WASPs were flying "heavier" or "faster" ships than the ones the male pilots were flying'.[38] Yet, this situation very often resulted from the fact that male pilots had shown a reluctance to fly a certain type of aircraft (e.g. the P-39, the B-26 or the B-29). The fact that the women were willing to fly these disliked types not only meant that they could fly difficult types, but that they had shamed the men to boot.

The resentment of female success is almost the only explanation for clear instances of 'double standards'. In one case, for example, a WASP cleared for take-off by the tower collided with an aircraft piloted by a male cadet that crossed the runway in front of her. The initial reaction of the Army was to pin the blame for the accident on the WASP, but recordings from the tower were unambiguous: she had been cleared for take-off. The male pilot, who *had* caused the accident, however, faced no disciplinary action whatsoever – although the WASP had nearly been killed and suffered severe injuries and burns as a result of his carelessness.[39]

Yet, it would be inaccurate to imply that all WASP encountered resentment and negative attitudes everywhere. At the 6th Ferrying Division in Long Beach, California, the WAFS were not only made to feel welcome, the CO paid them the ultimate compliment of clamouring for more women pilots. Likewise, the WASP assigned target-towing duties at bases in Dodge City, Kansas and Boise found an atmosphere of comradeship. At Boise, admittedly, the men had been sceptical at first, but then two of the WASP made a one-engine landing in a B-26. One of the other WASP stationed at Boise described what happened:

> Here comes this B-26, limping across the airport . . . one engine out, and they made a turn into the good engine and landed on a closed runway. There were airplanes parked on each side. They landed and didn't damage a thing! I'll tell you, the WASPs were 'in' after that time. Before that the men were always a little scep- tical about what women could do and what they couldn't. In this particular case, the whole Gowen field was out. They were standing on the ramp area watching. The cheer that went up after they landed! It was something to see and we were so proud of them![40]

The women assigned to B-17 training were also pleasantly surprised to find a positive attitude right from the start. Again, there was a degree of scepticism, but one of the women contrasted training at Lockbourne AAB to treatment at Avenger Field, saying: 'At Sweetwater they seemed to dare you to graduate from the program. It helped a lot not to have that terrific mental strain here all the time . . . .'[41]

In short, the nostalgia for Sweetwater was only found among WASP who experienced something still *worse* afterwards, and the experiences of the WASP were varied indeed. The operations officer at Stuttgart, Arkansas AAFB, made the following observation about the attitude of the men in his command toward the women pilots:

> I can almost gauge the intelligence and background of the average officer or enlisted man by the way they treat the WASP. Those who receive them as they should be received – openly and warmly as co-workers in the war effort and with admiration and respect for their ability – are usually in the upper bracket all around. Those who do not, and I have found some who are resentful of their presence to the point of insult, are definitely in the lower classification every time.[42]

The women assigned to FERD naturally faced the same diversity of in- dividual attitudes, but they had two advantages over those WASP sent to other assignments. First, the Commanding General of FERD had been instrumental in giving women pilots a chance to fly and was fully committed to their employment, and, second, the WAFS, as highly skilled pilots, had paved the way for the less skilled graduates of the WFTD. At the swearing in of the first WAFS, a policy of absolute equality had been laid down, which did not fail to have its effect. FERD moved comparatively rapidly to open different aircraft types to the women, and remained committed to the trained pilots to the end.

There was one area, however, in which the treatment of women pilots in FERD was unquestionably discriminatory. The senior officers of the command and particularly at the Ferry Group HQ, showed an almost pathological fear of any kind of sexual scandal and this meant going to extremes to protect the 'reputation' of the women in their employ. For example, the women were prohibited from smoking in public – their male colleagues were not. The women were expected to eat at separate tables in the Mess. No men were allowed into the women's BOQ unless it was 'an officer on inspection'.[43] The greatest indignity, however, was that:

> In the interests of decorum and appearances, the base assigned the WAFS a housemother, an older woman named Mrs Anderson . . . It did not seem to matter that there were many wives and mothers in the group, some in their thirties, and that such a set-up for male civilians would have been unthinkable.[44]

It was paranoia about possible scandal that also led to the absurd orders prohibiting women pilots from hitchhiking rides in military aircraft after deliveries or from acting as co-pilots to male pilots. These orders were allegedly issued to 'protect the WAFS reputation', but one of the early WAFS, Cornelia Fort, felt it had far more to do with placating jealous officers' wives. Fort described the otherwise warm welcome extended to the women at Long Beach (6th Ferrying Group) being marred by the following:

> Today we went perforce to the bi-monthly luncheon at the officers' club of officers' wives. It was the most desperate ordeal I ever saw. Talk about being stared at & appraised & in a decidedly unfriendly fashion. Whew! They are in a frenzy of jealousy that we will co-pilot with their husbands. Of all the damned, stupid, female rot!
>
> Col Spake sent his Deputy to make a speech – which had a dual purpose. Theoretically it was a speech of welcome for us; actually, it was an announcement to the wives that they need not worry, that no 'mixed operations orders' would be issued, i.e. no man & girl as pilot and co-pilot.
>
> And can you believe it, the rude women applauded right in front of us! I was so livid at an exhibition whose equal I had never

seen that I got up & walked out, whereupon the other girls followed me. I hope [the wives] had the grace to be ashamed of their rudeness, if not their feelings.[45]

After Cornelia Fort was killed in a mid-air collision with a male pilot, women were even prohibited (briefly) from flying in mixed *formations*. Theoretically, men and women were henceforth only to fly to the same destination on alternate days.

In the long run the strict segregation of WASP was simply not practical; it inhibited vitally important operations too severely. Therefore, gradually the inhibiting regulations were forgotten or ignored, women flew as needed and were allowed into the same cockpits as men, first only on training flights, and later – without any fuss – on operational flights or when hitching rides home as well.

Meanwhile, however, the Army Air Forces had become hysterical about the idea of women flying and menstruating at the same time. Suddenly, in March 1943, the Air Transport Command ordered all women pilots grounded for the week of their period. Again, the order proved impractical. 'In a matter of weeks, the Ferrying Division realised that the order was neither obeyed, nor enforced. As none of the men in high command was particularly willing to try monitoring women pilots in this regard, the regulation was formally dropped.'[46]

Yet all the irritations, insults or inhospitality encountered by the WASP fade into insignificance beside the indications that some men resented the women pilots so intently that they were prepared to sabotage the aircraft the women flew. WASP Mary Ellen Keil described an incident where all the flight controls came loose from the side of the plane shortly after take-off. She concludes:

> I don't think that could have been anything but sabotage. Nobody could be so careless as to leave the whole throttle quadrant unscrewed from the airplane, and it could not have been unscrewed all the way when I took off because I checked the plane. Several others had bad experiences too.[47]

A second WASP described the following incident:

> I had taken off, and apparently there were some bolts that had been removed and they were rolling back and forth in the plane. I came down and cracked up on landing . . . . They thought it was sabotage because base personnel found other items loose in the plane as well.[48]

A far more unambiguous incident was reported by WASP Lorraine Zillner. She crashed in a B-13 during training and the investigation showed that the rudder cables had been cut. She explains: 'You know, they were cut through just part way, so I took off and went up and then, just when I was doing some manoeuvre, they snapped, and that was it. No rudders.'[49] In each of these incidents, an aircraft was lost and the WASP could have been killed. At least one WASP *was* killed by sabotage.

> ... there was one case of sabotage, where a man who didn't really feel that women had any business in a cockpit put sugar in a gas tank, and it didn't run very well, and she crashed.[50]

Verges describes the incident as follows:

> Betty Taylor Wood died when she overshot a landing and as she tried to go around, the engine failed. Her aircraft cartwheeled off the end of the runway.
>
> Jackie [Cochran] was shaken to discover evidence of sabotage – traces of sugar in the gasoline tank of Wood's plane. 'Enough to stop an engine in no time at all,' she said privately . . . .[51]

None of these alleged cases of sabotage was ever formally proved, but for the purposes of this study it is not relevant whether the sabotage was real or imagined. Important is merely the fact that the WASP *believed* they were working together with men so hostile to the idea of women in the cockpits of military aircraft that they would not stop short of attempted murder.

Notes:
1   Cheeseman, 18.
2   Phelps, 15.
3   Cheeseman, 18.
4   Cheeseman, 20.
5   Bergel, 107.
6   Bergel, 107.
7   Curtis, 170.
8   Curtis, 189.
9   Wilkins, Mary, Letter to the Author, 20 June 2004.
10   Lucas, 25.
11   Curtis, 114.
12   Curtis, 198.
13   Curtis, 110.

14 Letters to the Author from Joy Lofthouse, Freydis Sharland, Mary Wilkins, Margaret Frost, Diana Barnato Walker.

15 Mathews, Alec, Letter to the Author, 21 June 2004.

16 Fahie, 148.

17 Cheeseman, 74.

18 Du Cros, Rosemary, ATA Girl: Memoirs of a Wartime Ferry Pilot, 1983, 39.

19 Curtis, 100.

20 Curtis, 271.

21 Lofthouse, Letter to Author, 14 July 2004.

22 Du Cros, 58.

23 Lucas, 110.

24 Lucas, 84–5.

25 Walker, 134–7.

26 Granger 244.

27 Granger, 78.

28 Keil, 163.

29 Granger, 240.

30 Keil, 165.

31 Cole, 52.

32 Keil, 270

33 Verges, 59.

34 Rickman, 178.

35 Keil, 216.

36 Cole, 108.

37 Keil, 272.

38 Merryman, 22.

39 Cole, 127.

40 Cole, 86.

41 Granger, 273.

42 Granger, 471.

43 Bartels, 186.

44 Simbeck, 145.

45 Simbeck, 214.

46 Keil, 129.

47 Cole, 45.

48 Cole, 113.

49 Cole, 41.

50 Merryman, 27.

51 Verges, 139.

CHAPTER NINE

Separate but Not Equal

ORGANISATIONAL STRUCTURE

The success of the ATA compared with the WASP was not exclusively a function of the environment in which the two organisations respectively operated. Key organisational differences likewise impacted upon the experiences of the women involved.

For example, Evelyn Sharp was the adopted and only child of a very poor couple in Nebraska, but she fell in love with flying at an early age. She took her first flying lessons at fourteen – in exchange for the instructor boarding free with her parents. She soloed at sixteen and earned her commercial licence at eighteen. Local businessmen pooled resources to loan her the money to buy an aircraft so she could make a living giving joy-rides, but the business model failed in Depression America. Evelyn lost her aircraft and had to get a job as an instructor, now supporting both her parents as well. She worked hard and well, winning the respect of her students and employers, even though she was still hardly more than a girl. When in late 1942 Nancy Love's cable arrived inviting her to join the WAFS, she was just twenty-two years old, but she had nearly 3,000 flying hours and so was the most experienced pilot among that select group of pilots invited to join the WAFS. She was also an exotic small-town, poor girl among the sophisticated socialites that made up the bulk of the squadron. Evelyn Sharp epitomised the American dream of the honest, hard-working, self-made man/woman.

Less than two years later she was dead. The left engine of a USAAF P-38 Lightning failed on take-off. All the flying experience in the world could not help her. Although she managed to put the aircraft down in one piece, she was killed on impact. And although she was killed in the service of her country under Army orders in an Army aircraft, the Army did not so much as pay to send her body home to Nebraska. There was no insurance for her dependent and grieving parents, and when her hometown turned out to honour her, there was no representative of the USAAF, no band, no honour guard, no salute, not even a flag. That was donated by an ordinary citizen and placed over the coffin in defiance of regulations. Evelyn Sharp might have spent the best years of her life under Army discipline, orders and sanctions, but she was not part of it.

The injustice of such treatment rankled with the survivors until they finally won recognition of their status by Act of Congress more than thirty years later, but in all the noise about 'militarisation', the essential point is often obscured. The issue was not so much one of militarisation as of integration – as a comparison with the ATA makes clear.

Integration of the Women Pilots within their Respective Organisation

The issue of integration versus segregation carries with it all the usual arguments about 'separate but equal' that have dominated the discussions on racial and sexual integration for the last century. There are always a number of good arguments for segregating, for example, pubescent schoolgirls from boys of the same age in the classroom. Many American black colleges had admirable academic programmes and produced graduates of substantially higher quality than mediocre integrated educational establishments. Yet, the bottom line that the historical record draws under all the various experiments in providing 'separate but equal' facilities is that in the long run they don't function as well for the disadvantaged. Again and again, in different contexts, integration has proved the best means of providing individuals with equality of opportunity. The history of the ATA and the WASP is, in a sense, simply another of many examples of this phenomenon.

The women pilots of the ATA were employees of the same organisation as their male colleagues, and as such it proved impossible in the long run to deny them the same terms of service, benefits and opportunities as their male colleagues. In fact, from the start they were hired on the same basis with the exception of pay rates and – initially – aircraft type. Both restrictions were broken down, so that complete equality of opportunity and remuneration was established more than two-and-a-half years prior to deactivation. Precisely because they were employees of the same organisation and doing the same job as their male colleagues, it proved organisationally impossible to retain artificial barriers or discriminatory practices.

Nor did the organisation find it practical to retain separate facilities for men and women on a wide scale. Although there were three all-women Ferry Pools (Hatfield, Hamble and Cosford) and two Pools (Lossiemouth and Belfast) where no women served, most of the Pools were eventually 'mixed'. That is, women pilots could be and were assigned to them as needed. Thus, the predominant experience for women flying with the ATA was to spend at least some of their time in a mixed Pool. Certainly during training, whether at Luton/Thame or White Waltham, the women were living and working alongside their male colleagues on an equal basis.

Admittedly, even where official, organisational obstacles have been removed, personal and attitudinal obstacles often remain. Many women pilots felt there was initial resistance on the part of some male Pool Commanders to the posting of women pilots to their Pools. This was allegedly true of Kirkbride, Prestwick, Sherburn, and Ratcliffe, for example. But ATA Headquarters continued to post women to Pools as they were needed or for personal reasons, such as being married to a male pilot or staff member working at a certain Pool. In effect, official policy and Headquarters forced individual Pool Commanders to overcome any lingering prejudices they harboured against women pilots.

Once the women were posted, it was a matter of individual personality whether they made a place for themselves at that particular Pool or not. Lettice Curtis, for example, reports that she 'did not seem to fit in at Ratcliffe . . . . Gaby was unhappy too but Ruth and Ursula were both settling in having decided that any "mixed" pool was better than the cloistered life of either Hatfield or Hamble'.[1] On the other hand, at White Waltham, also a mixed Pool, Curtis found 'some of the happiest and most fulfilling months' of her life.[2] Similarly, Mary de Bunsen was posted to Sherburn at a time when resistance to women pilots there was supposed to be strong. In fact, there was only one other woman at Sherburn at the time – the wife of the adjutant. Yet, she found it to be 'a happy pool, with a strong local element like a territorial regiment';[3] and not only fitted in but seemed to find her stride here as well. Rosemary du Cros and Freydis Sharland, on the other hand, were most contented at the all-women pool at Hamble, where neither Curtis nor de Bunsen had been completely contented. Joy Gough summed up her experience saying: 'As a young woman I probably preferred mixed pools, but that was a frivolous choice. I can't recall any disadvantages either way'.[4]

In short, like a good pub or a squadron, each Pool had its own character and the individual members assigned to it had to fit in to be happy. Almost all pilots, male and female, remember being assigned to one Pool or another where they were not quite happy. The factors for dissatisfaction included available housing, proximity to family, friends and spouses, weather, the type of aircraft predominantly flown – and of course the atmosphere at the Pool itself. But wherever they were, the women pilots had the same job as their male colleagues, reported to the same Mess, were assigned their aircraft by the same Operations Officer and flew according to the same rules. Furthermore, the women of the ATA reported to the same commanders and, if there was a problem, there was a clear, well defined and common chain of command by which they could take their complaints to the same central headquarters. This meant that while the atmosphere and group dynamics of each Pool might vary, ultimately:

> It was accepted that all pilots from the CO to the humblest single-engine pilots had the same basic responsibilities when it came to ferrying and amongst all, there was such a wealth of kindness and mature good nature that not one single person could have felt out of place.[5]

The women flying in the United States were, in contrast, always disadvantaged by the fact that they were not members of the organisation that controlled their activities, assignments, assessments, living quarters and terms of service. With the possible exception of training at Avenger Field, the women were operating within a world to which they technically and legally did not belong. Because they did not belong, they faced ambivalence and confusion with regard to their status and rights wherever they went.

The women sometimes were welcomed into Officers' Clubs and sometimes excluded. They were sometimes allowed into military hospitals and sometimes turned away. They were certainly not given the same ranks, uniforms, pay or benefits as the men around them doing the same jobs. They did not even enjoy a clear chain of command, because the responsibilities of their respective Base Commanders, the Army Command in which they served, Nancy Love and Jacqueline Cochran all to a certain extent over-lapped. The ATC frequently complained of interference from Cochran, but was unable to curb it. In consequence, when WASP encountered a hostile environment or were assigned tasks for which they had not volunteered and did not want, there was no organisational mechanism to enable them to seek redress. WASP, for example, seeking to reverse a compulsory and allegedly temporary transfer from FERD to Training Command, were summarily dismissed by Cochran – despite the explicit efforts by FERD to retain and employ the women.

It was the fact that the WASP were 'alien bodies' within the homogeneous Army organisation in which they lived and worked that made militarisation seem such a logical solution to the problem. The long political battle for the militarisation of the WASP has been described previously, but organisational realities of the WASP deserve a little closer scrutiny.

First and foremost, the women were told to anticipate militarisation and (just as the telephone operators and physical therapists of the First World War) subjected to military discipline. They were on twenty-four-hour call, required permission to be off their home base, were subjected to drill and inspections, and required to respect military courtesy. They had, in effect, all the negative aspects of military life without the pay, benefits or status.

The situation of the ATA was the exact reverse. As the *Picture Post* worded it in its 16 September 1944 issue:

> The ATA are civilians in uniform, enjoying both civil and military privileges. Their only military obligations consist of observing certain rules of dress. But they can come and go as they wish on airfields, in the messes of the RAF or the American Army Air Force on the same footing as officers.[6]

Furthermore, although the women of the ATA, averaging 16 per cent of total pilot strength, might at individual mixed Pools represent a slightly smaller proportion of the pilots than this organisational average, they were generally not isolated. After all, the ATA itself never employed more than 3,555 people altogether, and ground personnel also included a number of women, including women Operations Officers, aircraft mechanics, motor transport drivers, clerks, nurses etc.

The situation of the WASP by contrast was aggravated by the fact that they were generally just a handful of girls amidst literally tens-of-thousands of men. At the Ferry Squadrons and some of the Target Towing Bases there might be a score of women pilots or more assigned at any one time, but there were also instances of a single WASP being the only woman assigned to a particular post. Most WASP served on bases where there were fewer than twenty women pilots among thousands of men. There were not always WAC or nurses on these bases, and so the WASP often found themselves to be the only women – and civilians – whatsoever.

To Be or Not to Be an Officer

Under the circumstances, it is understandable that the USAAF thought militarisation of the WASP, in one form or another, made sense. It is interesting to note, furthermore, that in 1939 the British too had seriously considered militarising the ATA pilots – and rapidly decided against it.

In the early months of its existence, the ATA pilots – like the WASP later – did not operate from their own Pools under their own administration but were simply 'loaned' out to the RAF. Like the WASP later, they operated from RAF bases, getting their assignments from RAF officers and flying alongside RAF ferry pilots. The situation – even in the absence of sexual differences (since all the ATA pilots at this time were men) – proved unsatisfactory. The different rates of pay, the absence of Mess privileges, and above all the lack of military manners, so-to-speak, created enough tensions for the Air Ministry to conclude that the mixing of military and civilian pilots would not work in the long run.

The Air Ministry – like the USAAF with regard to the WASP later – therefore considered commissioning the civilian volunteers. The idea was rapidly rejected, however. For a start, there was serious doubt about whether the independent-minded hobby fliers would accept the King's Commission. Another factor militating against the absorption of the civilians into the RAF was the fact that the employment of women was already contemplated, and it was clear that they would pose even greater difficulties for the RAF. Yet a third factor was that in a civilian organisation, foreign pilots – notably those from neutral countries, i.e. the Americans and Irish – would not face sanctions from their own governments for serving in a foreign military. Thus it was the need for pilots, whether female or foreign, that made the establishment of a separate, civilian organisation the most practical solution in the British context.

Once the decision had been made to keep the ATA civilian, the ATA evolved its own, distinct – and distinctly civilian – character and ethos. It established its own Headquarters at White Waltham in December 1939, and an organisational structure as suitable to an airline as a military organisation gradually evolved. In addition to the pilots, who had been the origins of the organisation in 1939, an entire organisation grew up, which at its peak numbered 3,555 people, of which just 764 were aircrew (including 127 flight engineers).[7]

The ground staff was divided between ground crews and administrative staff. The ground crews, like the pilots themselves, had to be exceptionally versatile and flexible. They, too, had to be prepared to handle any kind of aircraft the RAF or FAA flew. RAF ground crews, in contrast, could specialise in the aircraft flown by the unit to which they were assigned. Notably, the ATA here too showed no discrimination against women and an increasing number of women were employed in aircraft maintenance, including highly technical work such as electrical repairs and less skilled jobs such as refuelling. The organisation, recruitment, training and administration of the ground crews were in the capable hands of experienced maintenance engineers seconded from British Airways.

A Technical Department was also formed for the purpose of developing the vital Handling and Pilot's Notes. To this purpose ATA test pilots were employed to test each type of aircraft flown by the ATA and lay down recommended ATA speeds, flap, rpm, mixture settings etc. and to record any particular quirks and dangers. This Department was also headed by a former airline executive.

The Administrative Departments that made up the rest of the ground staff included Recruitment and Training, Establishment, Supplies, Operations, Finance, and Medical Services. Each Ferry Pool had its own Meteorology Officer, its own Intelligence (aka Maps and Signals) and Operations Officer(s). The Meteorology Officers were predominantly WAAF meteorologists seconded to ATA. The Intelligence Officers were ATA personnel responsible for keeping up-to-date with regard to defences such as barrage balloons, restricted areas, the state of all aerodromes, and the like.

The Operations Officer and his or her assistants were responsible for working out the ferrying schedule for all the aircraft that needed to be ferried by the Pool on any given day. They were also responsible for 'routeing' the aircraft if they were to be flying through a 'Defended Area', that is, informing Fighter Command of any aircraft movements that might cross a Defended Area in order to reduce the risk of these being mistaken for 'bandits' – i.e. enemy aircraft – and possibly shot down. Because weather and technical difficulties could interfere with plans at any time, the Operations Officer was furthermore required to improvise constantly, putting on extra taxi trips and organising lifts and new links as best as possible as the day went on. At the end of the day the Operations Officer had to report to No. 41 Group just what had been moved where.

Ferry Pools also had their own Motor Transport Pool (often with a fair number of women drivers). These collected pilots and ground crews from their billets or from the train station if returning by ground transportation from a delivery, and took them back to their respective quarters at the end of the day. The ATA also maintained its own police, fire, ambulance and catering staff serving the separate Messes for engineers, clerical and flying staff. Bergel, CO of the Ferry Pool at Aston Down, writes that the 'typical Ferry Pool' consisted of roughly fifty pilots, thirty engineers, and sixteen to eighteen other staff from Meterology and Operations Officers to canteen waitress and drivers, making for a staff of roughly one hundred per Pool.[8] In short, the ATA evolved into a completely independent, self-sufficient organisation.

Long before it had reached its peak organisational expansion, however, it had already established a reputation for efficiency. It was rapidly recognised that any efforts to bind ATA more closely to the RAF would be disadvantageous since its effectiveness was 'to a large extent due to the informality and flexibility with which the organisation' was run.[9]

Curiously, even in the United States there was a minority opinion that opposed the militarisation of the WASP on the grounds that their employment as civilians permitted 'greater flexibility for experimentation than would any military organisation'.[10] While the case is made in terms of flexibility for experimentation, there is another aspect that has received far too little attention in the literature about the WASP.

Throughout the Second World War hundreds of American men flew for the ATC and FERD *without* ever receiving commissions. In fact, the hiring of the first WAFS took place on the basis of the legislation already in place for the employment of these men. The women were from the start treated differently. They were paid much less, they were put into barracks and given a chaperone, for example. But when the legislation for the militarisation of the WASP failed in Congress, the Commanding General of FERD advocated the retention of the most qualified women pilots on the same basis as these civilian men. He had good reason to advocate it – not just because he wanted to keep the trained women pilots, but because ATC's experience with these civilians had been very positive.

One of the male civilian pilots flying with ATC described the situation as follows: 'we were almost totally independent. The army told us where the cargo was destined. How and when it arrived, became our individual responsibility.'[11] He goes on to comment:

> None of us believed this pleasant and relaxed situation could endure for long. But we under-estimated both the perception of our military masters and also the formidable task to be done. It did not occur to us that the Army Air Force, pre-occupied with training for actual combat, lacked experienced men for such an

endeavour or that they recognised the value of a tight professional group which would be operating free of elephantine
officialdom. Using us without danger of interference or superior
restriction, a general could accomplish far more than he could
with his own personnel. The last thing they wanted us to do was
join the army.[12]

The most intriguing aspect of this account is the uncanny way it
almost perfectly describes the ultimate relationship between the ATA
and the RAF. By the end of the war, when the RAF was a calling on the
ATA help them out at Arnhem or to get photo-reconnaissance
Spitfires across the Channel in a hurry, the last thing the RAF would
have wanted was for the ATA to be bound by 'elephantine officialdom' or subject to RAF regulations. It was by then all too obvious that
the ATA worked best precisely because it was a small, flexible,
civilian organisation.

Whether the women of the WAFS and WASP might have been
effectively integrated into the ATC's close-knit body of male civilians
is another question altogether. The men flying with ATC came predominantly from the civilian airlines – where no women were allowed
to fly before or for many years after the war. Because they tended to be
deployed in groups based on their former airline affiliation, they also
had an *esprit de corps* that pre-dated their service with the USAAF. That
esprit often had decidedly 'macho' overtones. There was no separate
organisation with accompanying procedures and guidelines that
formalised equality of opportunity for women as in the ATA. In such
an environment, it seems highly unlikely that the women would have
been accepted as equal partners, but it is not entirely inconceivable.
After all, the women that FERD wanted to retain were all qualified on
pursuits and had accumulated significant flying time as ferry pilots. It
is sad that General Arnold was not willing to give them this last chance
to continue to serve their country in a different organisational environment.

Regarding the organisations themselves, however, it is fair to say
that the independent – and self-sufficient ATA – proved to be the
organisationally better vehicle both in terms of fulfilling its mission and
in terms of providing equality of opportunity. The 'separate but equal'
status of the WASP in an organisation that had no real independence
was clearly a major disadvantage.

Notes:

1   Curtis, 117.
2   Curtis, 155.
3   De Bunsen, 125.
4   Joy Lofthouse (neé Gough), Letter to the Author, 14 July 2004.
5   Curtis, 179–80.
6   Picture Post, 16 Sept. 1944.
7   Cheeseman, 246.
8   Bergel, 105.
9   Curtis, 32.
10   Granger, 154.
11   Gann, Ernest K., *Fate is the Hunter*, 1961, 164.
12   Gann, 164.

CHAPTER TEN

Sum of the Parts

ORGANISATIONAL COMPOSITION

An organisation is not defined by its formal structure and function alone, but by the individuals that comprise it as well. The composition of the ATA and WASP therefore had a profound impact upon the character of each organisation. As one observer put it: 'People who were keen on flying . . . were almost by definition slightly mad. It is my experience that the nicest people are all slightly mad, so it was pretty well inevitable that ATA was full of the nicest people.'[1] The same, of course, could be said for the WASP. Yet there was a profound difference between the two organisations: while the WASP was extremely uniform, the ATA was exceptionally diverse.

The difference was not just a function of the fact that the WASP was an all-female organisation, while the ATA was mixed. The WASP was also strictly American and white, while the ATA took pilots from twenty-eight different countries, including non-whites. The age limits for WASP were more restrictive than in the ATA, namely eighteen to thirty-five, while the ATA employed both male and female pilots who were over fifty years old by the end of the war. Last but not least, whereas Cochran bragged that her girls had to pass the same physical requirements as male cadets of the USAAF, the the ATA was proud that it employed the rejects of the RAF and FAA.

The women of the WAFS were even more homogeneous than the WASP as a whole. Because of the high number of flying hours required, the WAFS tended to come from well-off families. The first women to arrive included two heiresses to industrial fortunes and the others were predominantly former debutantes who had married into wealth and now had children. The second in-take of WAFS were younger and single, but they were still wealthy, sophisticated, well-travelled professionals for the most part. One of them had operated her own flying school, another had run an airport. One of the women had driven an ambulance in France, and another had won two gold medals in swimming at the Berlin Olympics 1936. The majority of the WAFS, twenty-one out of twenty-five, had worked as flying instructors and held instructor's licences.

The WASP, in contrast to the WAFS, were rarely professional fliers. They tended to be young, single, and less financially secure. They had worked as teachers, secretaries, journalists and models, and they came from all over the country. The WASP themselves always felt they were part of a 'terribly diverse' group – apparently blind to the absence of blacks and foreigners, but this was an age when being Catholic – much less Jewish – was not entirely acceptable in many circles and certainly viewed as 'different'. Many WASP had never lived away from home before, and some were shocked to discover that 'nice' girls drank alcohol or smoked. Ultimately, it was the very limitations of their own previous experience that made many WASP view a girl from a different state or a different social background as frightfully exotic.

By contrast, the ATA's members really were diverse and that diversity was as much a defining feature of the organisation as its civilian status. It encompassed the 'Ancient and Tattered' – from the one-armed and one-eyed to one pilot reportedly too fat to fit in a single-seated-fighter. But it also employed young American pilots fit enough to meet the USAAF's tough physical standards when the time came. It gave women a chance to fly, and gave refugees from the Continent, who had found their way to England only after dangerous adventures, a chance to continue the fight against the occupiers of their homelands. Perhaps most touching of all, was that it gave 'invalids' who had been told they would never fly again, the chance to do just that. An RAF fighter pilot, who had been so severely wounded in the Battle of Britain as to be invalided out, applied to the ATA as an air-gunner, 'praying that even though I was considered unfit to pilot any aeroplane I might thus be given the chance to work off some spite on those responsible'.[2] The story continues:

> Interviewed by the Officer in charge of Defence, a charming ex-major, I diffidently put forward my qualifications. I realise now that in reality he was an angel in disguise, for after examining my papers he looked up.
> 'But wouldn't you rather join us as a pilot?' he said.
> For a moment I was speechless with joy, and then my heart sank as I explained the circumstances. He looked at my papers again.
> 'That's all right,' he said. 'As long as your medical standard is "A" licence you are good enough.'

He whisked me into a private office, where, still in a golden dream, I answered more questions. Someone thrust a flying helmet and goggles at me, and without even waking up I found myself walking out to a Tiger Moth for a flight test.[3]

Given this open-minded attitude toward applicants, it is hardly surprising that the former occupations of ATA pilots also ranged across the board. There were former RAF and commercial pilots, and even famous, record-breaking pilots, such as Amy Johnson and Jim Mollison. Yet, 'perhaps 90% had never in any sense earned their living in flying, or expected to do so. They were men and women who had learned to fly at their own expense as members of light aeroplane clubs because flying was the one thing they passionately wanted to do'.[4] Thus there were stockbrokers and artists, lawyers and conjurers, doctors and salesmen, journalists and innkeepers, manufacturers and farmers, antique dealers and racing drivers.

Inevitably, under the circumstances, the flying skills of the pilots varied enormously too. Initially, of course, they were expected to have logged considerable flying time, but *how* those hours had been obtained could vary from First World War experience, barnstorming and circuses, to flying for airlines, instructing or simply flying for fun. Some of the pilots of the ATA were, in fact, immensely experienced.

The largest contingent of foreign pilots in the ATA came from the United States. The first four American men arrived shortly before 12 August 1940, that is prior to the hottest phase of the Battle of Britain. These men together had nearly 9,000 hours of flying experience, and represented just the vanguard. By June 1941, Americans accounted for 30 per cent of ATA strength, but experience levels now averaged 'just' 350 hours' flying, and the proportion of ATA flying staff from the United States soon declined. Nevertheless, altogether, over two hundred American men and twenty-five American women signed contracts with the ATA during its six-year existence. A small number of American pilots who signed up failed to pass their flight tests, and no fewer than fourteen American recruits lost their lives while crossing the Atlantic by sea (i.e. to U-boat attacks). Others proved unsuitable to the business of ferrying; having joined the ATA out of a sense of adventure or to help the war effort, they found the tedious business of flying from A to B by visual contact on a small island insufficiently exciting. The single most important factor in the sharp decline in the United States contingent of ATA was, however, America's entry into the war. When the United States joined the war following Pearl Harbor, no fewer than 160 of the American men returned to America with the intention of joining the USAAF, and several of the American women followed their example as their contracts also expired. At least two of these former ATA women pilots joined the WASP after returning home.

The second largest contingent of foreigners in the ATA came from Poland. Although younger Polish pilots found a welcome reception in the RAF where they distinguished themselves very early in the war, the older and female pilots found a home – and an opportunity to fight the common enemy – by joining the ATA. Many other countries from Occupied Europe were also represented in the ATA: Belgium, France, Denmark, Holland, Norway, Czechoslovakia and Estonia.

Perhaps more surprising was the number of pilots from technically neutral countries. The Americans have already been mentioned, but there were also roughly a half-dozen Irish pilots as well as Swiss, Spanish, Siamese, Cuban, Chilean and Argentine pilots. In addition to the usual 'Colonials' (New Zealand, Australia, South Africa, India and Canada), pilots also came to ATA from more unusual parts of the Empire such as Ceylon, Malaya and Mauritius. Last but not least, one 'enemy' national also flew for the ATA, an Austrian pilot.

The women of the ATA in the first four years of the war were a microcosm of the whole. There were young unmarried girls and grandmothers. Several of the women had disabilities such as poor eyesight, withered legs (the result of polio as a child) or heart conditions that would have prohibited their service with WAFS or WASP. The professions the women had pursued prior to joining the ATA included architecture, farming, dancing, typing, acting, and, of course, doing nothing at all, as was quite common among young ladies from the upper class. Some of the women had been involved in commercial aviation, running flying clubs or aerodromes or working as flying instructors. Amy Johnson, another famous flier and record holder, also joined the ATA in 1940 – and died in service in early 1941.

When the ATA was opened up to women with no experience, the need to reduce the number of applications to a manageable number dictated the introduction of more rigorous requirements. This had the effect of making the intake more homogeneous. Suddenly, the women had to have school-leaving certificates, had to be single, young and healthy and not too short or too short-sighted. Preference was clearly given to girls with ATA/RAF/WAAF connections.

The very few WAAF who made it through the lengthy selection process tried to guess what the common denominator was that had given them an edge over the thousands of other applicants. It appeared that the majority of the WAAF selected came from certain RAF trades, particularly those involving intelligence, reliability and discretion, trades that 'needed calmness and speed – and to be "unflappable" as the expression went – under extreme pressure . . . All involved qualities likely to help make a good pilot . . . .'[5] Comparing notes, the former WAAF also noted that they had all been questioned about sport. All the WAAF in the ATA had been active in sports that entailed risk on the one hand and required judgement on the other – such as hunting, skiing and dinghy sailing. Many also had ATA/RAF connections – brothers, husbands, fiancés or boyfriends who were pilots.

Rosemary du Cros sums up the change that came about with this move toward an almost WASP-like selection of only educated, healthy, single, young women.

> At our peak period of work, about two years before the end of the War, ATA decided to take in some people who had never flown and train them from scratch. A few men were trained, but as always with men they had to be unsuitable for use in the Services. But the women! There were thousands of applications – from the WAAF and from enormous numbers of girls in other jobs. ATA could afford to be choosy and they were.
>
> Successful applicants had to be in a certain age group, of a certain height, perfect in vision and in health, and of course quick and well adapted when learning to fly. Anyone who made the grade could feel quite pleased with herself . . . but we original ones used to say, 'If the war lasts long enough ATA will be nothing but these beautiful Amazons and we shall be 'Oh her, she only got in because she could fly'.[6]

Notes:

1   Bergel, 75.
2   Phelps,11–12.
3   Phelps, 12.
4   Bergel, 74.
5   Lucas, 18.
6   Du Cros, 84.

CHAPTER ELEVEN

Age Before Beauty

THE ORGANISATIONAL ETHOS OF THE ATA AND WASP

When Marion Toevs killed herself trying to roll an aircraft at 300 ft, her CO was – understandably – appalled. However, her CO had more reason to be distressed than normal. He was a returned combat pilot, and he had flown with the 8th Air Force in England. 'He [knew] American women serving in England with the ATA. They [were] safe pilots, all of them. They would never [have] buzz[ed], much less [tried] a slow roll at 300'.'[1] The difference in behaviour between the women of the ATA and the WASP was not a result of nationality but organisational ethos.

As the President of a cosmetics firm, Cochran appears to have had a genuine concern about the 'image' of her 'girls'. She hand-picked them to fit her subjective criteria of what a WASP should be. She designed their uniforms to make them chic and distinct. She advised her girls to 'act like ladies' and 'let the men carry their parachutes'. But in the end she always flew back to Washington. From her distant office in the Pentagon, Cochran singularly failed to give the WASP what we would today call a 'corporate culture'. Thus, while the ATA was compared to a 'crack Squadron', the WASP on active duty were left to face their various problems without the benefit of an organisational ethos capable of giving them psychological support and motivation.

The Ancient and Tattered Airmen

Given the fact that the ATA was a completely new organisation composed of a diverse group of individuals as outlined in the previous chapter, it is surprising how rapidly it developed its own organisational ethos. Within a year of its founding, the ATA had evolved such a distinct character that new-comers to the organisation instantly recognised it. Anthony Phelps, coming from the RAF, felt that:

Every man and every woman of the ATA has had to operate as an
individual and not as one of a formation, and yet each one has
been upheld by a sense of duty and an *esprit de corps* as high as
that in any crack Squadron in the RAF.[2]

It was an *esprit*, however, heavily based on tolerance for the eccentricity
of its members. There was no pressure to conform in the ATA, rather
the non-conformists set the tone, and the ATA prided itself on being a
collection of individualists.

From the start, this entailed an outright aversion to any kind of red
tape, military drill or rigid structures. Discipline was consciously
informal. There was no officially drawn up code of discipline, tellingly
'because there was no need of one – the almost unspoken hint that
misbehaviour or dangerous flying might mean exclusion from the
privilege of being in ATA was quite enough'.[3] Even rank and promotion held less appeal than is normally the case in an organisation,
'because everyone knew what everyone else was earning and because
it was clear that the more promotion you got the less flying you would
get'.[4]

There was certainly never any military drill in the ATA, and when in
April 1943 a Daily Routine Order announced that the ATA would
henceforth be required to salute Senior Officers, the impact was nil. As
Lettice Curtis put it: 'I do not recall this order making any noticeable
difference to ATA's informal non-saluting habits.'[5] Even had they
wanted to salute (as was the case when the King and Queen visited, for
example), no one had bothered to teach the pilots of the ATA how.
Curtis reports: 'I very self-consciously put in some practice, tilting my
hand at every conceivable angle and trying to work out which was the
correct one.'[6]

In general, orders seem to have been obeyed only if the recipients
found them sensible – which in most cases they apparently did. But the
incidents of ignoring ATA 'minimum flight requirements' are legion.
There can be just as little doubt that the standing order against aerobatics was observed mostly in the breach. Another example of the
attitude toward orders is provided by Douglas Fairweather:

He knew his way round England and Scotland so well that he
never carried maps. One day he was ticked off for this; soon after,
he was seen peering anxiously at the landscape below him and at
a map in front of him. A worried passenger went up to see if he
could help – and found that the map was a map of Roman Britain.[7]

Likewise:

> ... ATA Standing Orders had not thought it necessary to forbid the carrying of livestock in His Majesty's aircraft, so [one ATA pilot] bundled his young daughter's pet goat into an Anson and delivered it to her.[8]

Also, while smoking was strictly forbidden in aircraft, this rule clearly failed to stop the truly addicted from doing as they pleased. As one of the early flight commanders put it: 'There are great disadvantages in having a gang of people, each of whom has done a thousand or more hours. Because I'm their Flight Commander, they listen politely but do nothing about it.'[9]

This attitude of conforming to rules only to the degree each individual found sensible, included a degree of rebelliousness against uniforms. The women pilots were notorious for taking liberties with their uniforms, whether it was in preferring headscarves to helmets, trousers to skirts (or vice versa), or natural-coloured hose to black. The latter misled the Adjutant of a mixed Pool into posting the unfortunate notice: 'Women pilots will wear black stockings ONLY!' Reportedly, there was an exceptionally large number of male pilots waiting in the Mess the next morning in the hope that at least one of the women would take the order literally.[10] As for helmets and goggles, Rosemary du Cros explains the situation simply: '. . . some of the young girls did not consider them becoming. They much preferred to arrive among the fighter boys, when bringing them a new aeroplane, with their hair fetchingly confined by a beautiful silk scarf.'[11]

The women, however, were not alone in their insistence on personal style. Cheeseman reminisces (rather fondly one suspects):

> Even after they were fitted out in the regulation manner, some of those boys had the most colourful ideas on the subject of uniform. Many seemed to have a rooted objection to wearing the Field Service cap on the right side of the head. Socks were also a sore point; rather than wear black they appeared in all colours, but the favourite seemed to be rather a bright shade of green.
>
> Wings were worn in all sorts of places, and one pilot even went so far as to wear them on his overcoat. He eventually removed them, but not until his English colleagues had discovered his overcoat hanging in the rest-room and had adorned it with every emblem and medal they could lay their hands on.[12]

The pride in individuality was well suited to a job where every pilot worked predominantly alone and independently of both his fellows and other authorities. Only the very large, heavy aircraft required a second crewmember in the form of a flight engineer. Pilots of the ATA flew the medium bombers, such as Wellingtons and Hampdens, solo. Even the most junior ATA pilots made their own flight plans, flew independently of one another, and were authorised to make their own decisions with regard to flying itself – something that only RAF officers with the rank of Squadron Leader and above were allowed to do.[13] This meant that the RAF and FAA could *advise* them – but had no authority either to stop or order a flight. The pilots of the ATA could literally take off and land whenever they felt like it.

This exceptional degree of freedom and self-reliance would have been disastrous in an organisation without an exceptionally high standard of dedication. Given the *carte blanche* issued to the pilots, the opportunities for abuse were almost infinite, but the record of the ATA as a whole was admirable. Pilots who took inappropriate advantage of their privileges were soon weeded out.

Equally dangerous, of course, was that this freedom to fly when others were grounded could lead to excessive zeal or even a deadly kind of competition to prove one's skill or fearlessness. A certain tendency in this direction was noted at certain Pools dominated by younger fliers. But on the whole, ATA pilots demonstrated a remarkable maturity in flying as rapidly and directly to their destinations *as was prudent* – that is, without taking either too many liberties or too many risks.

One suspects that maturity is the operative word here; the ATA's 'corporate culture' was created to a great extent by the early pilots. These, it will be remembered, had been not barnstormers and circus pilots, but mature, dependable and conscientious men. Many came to the ATA from positions of significant authority and responsibility in civilian life, such as bank directors and businessmen. They were by no means the usual kind of hard-drinking, reckless, vagabond pilot one often found in the aviation community – although a fair number of the American male recruits fit this description. By the time the Americans arrived, however, the tone had already been set by the 'Ancient and Tattered Airmen' who had initially been recruited from among the most experienced private fliers in Britain. These elderly civilian fliers brought with them to the ATA a sense of self-reliance and quiet self-confidence that scorned the bravado and 'line-shooting' of the 'sky-jockey' kind of pilot and so discouraged these characteristics in the organisation as a whole.

It is largely to the credit of these Ancient and Tattered Airmen that the ATA was – in the words of one of the women pilots – 'a very civilised organisation. You were never, ever criticised for turning back – no matter how inconvenient for the taxi pilot or anyone else'.[14] That is, rather than nurturing competition between pilots for the most deliveries, the ATA strictly respected *every* pilot's right to make his or her own decision. This too has a great deal to do with maturity – and respect for one's colleagues.

Obviously, the purpose of the ATA was to deliver aircraft safely. Consequently, 'all accidents were viewed with the utmost seriousness, and any pilot held responsible could be heavily disciplined'.[15] On the other hand, as one of the pilots stationed at the Ferry Pool at Kirkbride pointed out, if they had followed ATA guidelines about minimum flying conditions and visual contact too strictly, then as much as 30 per cent of the deliveries would never have been made.[16] So it all boiled down to a subjective assessment of risk and utility. There is a very fine line between courage and foolhardiness, and the point at which discretion is the better part of valour is not always clear. At what point the risk of an accident superseded the importance of a delivery was something each pilot had to decide for his/herself based on a cocktail of factors from the priority of the delivery and the weather to the pilot's own level of experience. The latter factor was what made it so important that no pilot be criticised for aborting a flight when others carried on.

Because skill levels varied dramatically, it is not so much the fact that some pilots flew in conditions where others stayed on the ground that is remarkable, but that the ATA ethos did not allow those who were more timid to be pressured into flying against their better judgement. At the same time, the more than 150 casualties, most caused by weather, document the spirit of dedication that induced pilots to fly at – and sometimes beyond – their limits.

In fairness, it is in the nature of flying that many unexpected situations arise – usually suddenly and at great speed – for which even the best and most experienced pilot is not necessarily prepared. In the worst cases, these end fatally; in the best cases the pilot gets off with only a fright. These 'near-misses' were such a fact of life that the ATA evolved it own rituals for dealing with them. For example:

> The undertaker with whom I was billeted made us a beautiful miniature padded coffin with a slot into which we dropped money when we had given ourselves a fright, and the Red Cross made about three pounds a month out of this. I frightened myself up to half a crown's worth now and then, but one day another pilot came home and quietly put in a pound note.[17]

When accidents did occur in the ATA, they were very thoroughly investigated. This is so self-evident today that it is easy to forget that flying safety regulations and the systematic investigation of air crashes were still in their infancy in the Second World War. General Tunner, for example, points out that the USAAF had absolutely *no* procedures for dealing with, investigating and attempting to prevent accidents until the Flying Safety Programme was introduced in Ferrying Command at his instigation in early 1942.[18] The ATA with its commercial airline antecedents and ties was more attuned to the necessity for accident investigation, and a mechanism for the systematic handling of all accidents, large and small, was formed simultaneously with the Headquarters in early 1940. These procedures took the form of the Accidents Committee, which met weekly, and not only attempted to identify the cause of any accident, but also kept statistical records and circulated monthly summaries of proceedings. The Committee was composed of the Director of Operations, the Chief Operations Officer, the Director of Training, Director of Women Personnel, Chief Medical Officer, Chief Inspection Officer of the AID attached to the ATA, a representative of HQ 41 Group, RAF, a representative of the Ministry of Aircraft Production and two senior pilots.

When an accident occurred, the Committee investigated the circumstances, taking into account physical evidence from the aircraft involved, the written record with regard to maintenance reports, weather reports and flight plans and the verbal testimony of the people involved. Accidents were then classified into five categories: 1) pilot not responsible and commended, 2) pilot not responsible, 3) pilot responsible, 4) pilot to blame, and 5) insufficient evidence to determine responsibility. The distinction between blame and responsibility was that 'blame' meant the accident was 'entirely due to an error or bad airmanship on the part of the pilot'.[19] Responsible, on the other hand, meant that although the accident was not entirely the pilot's fault, it could have been prevented if the pilot had responded differently to the circumstances.

One or more accidents where the pilot was to 'blame' were grounds for dismissal from the ATA, but this was rare; the ATA as a whole was held responsible for less than half of 1 per cent of all accidents that occurred. The pilots themselves felt that the system was 'very fair and sensible and the result of experience and much understanding'[20] – which is not to say they did not fear the Accidents Committee. In fact, more than one pilot reported being more afraid of the Committee than of actually crashing!

Here again, the ATA had an unofficial as well as an official way of dealing with the unavoidable phenomenon of accidents:

Any pilot who was held responsible for an accident at the Sherburn pool was awarded an imaginary decoration called the Distinguished Pranging Cross. The names of the holders were painted on a carved oak shield with the motto of the Order (If Ever a Man Suffered . . .) inscribed in Latin on the top.[21]

While competition with regard to flying in poor weather was discouraged, another kind of 'competition' was widespread – the competition for flying different types of aircraft. Lettice Curtis remarks that it was invariably deemed 'lucky' to get a new type, while Cheeseman reports there was 'generally a scramble to be the first to fly a strange machine'.[22] Even the Pool Commander at Aston Down, Hugh Bergel, admitted:

> Some of us, I'm afraid, became avid, scheming type-collectors. We would hear that such and such a Pool was getting Whirlwinds, or Mark 12 Spitfires, or Gladiators, or Grumman Martlets, or Avro Manchesters, and the hunt was on.[23]

Rosemary du Cros puts it like this:

> We all got extremely childish about collecting 'types'. You felt very smug if you got a rare American type which other people hadn't flown, and when the first jet aircraft began coming in there was keen competition to fly them.[24]

Such competition did not always end well. Genovese remembers:

> It had been just shortly after my transfer to Kirkbride that the first Airacobras had arrived in England . . . The 'Cobras were terrific-looking planes of radical design, with the motor located behind the pilot and a long bullet-like snout stretching out in front of the cockpit to the hub of the prop. They were the first planes we had seen with the new tricycle landing gear . . . Naturally there was considerable competition among the pilots as to who would take the first one off the ground . . . Captain Hanley, a Britisher, who had quite a reputation before the war as a sportsman pilot . . . put in a strong bid for the privilege of the first flight and he finally got it.
> We all gathered on the field to see Captain Hanley take off on his check flight – normally a couple of circles around the field and then down for a report – and I know I wasn't the only one who was alarmed at the way he gunned the 1200 hp motor as he

shot that Airacobra down the runway. He gave it far more
throttle than he needed for his take-off, but he got the ship off the
ground all right and was in the middle of a slow climb and wide
circle bending around to the left when the ship blew up in mid-
air . . . .[25]

Death was never far away in the ATA – and that was an important
aspect of the ATA-experience and ethos too. Aside from the accidents
associated with flying, the ATA, flying as it did between priority targets
for the *Luftwaffe* throughout the war, was more likely than the population at large to be caught in an air raid. There were also multiple
incidents, as described above, of ATA aircraft being attacked – or at least
fired upon – by the *Luftwaffe* while in the air.

Because the pilots of the ATA were making roughly half their
deliveries to or from operational squadrons, they were confronted
personally with the continuous attrition in aircrews that others – even
in Britain – saw only as statistics in the newspapers. The ATA was
often on hand when the damaged bombers returned home, the 'blood-
wagon' and fire engines waiting on the taxiway. They saw the
wounded removed from the damaged aircraft – and flew shot-up
aircraft back to Maintenance Units. Any night stuck out at a Bomber
Command station usually meant 'one heard the thunder of their take-
off in the dark and the next morning in the Mess there was a dreadful
pall of gloom and sadness for those who had not returned.'[26]

The pilots of the ATA inevitably identified strongly with fellow-
airman facing the risks and horrors of those nightly flights into enemy
airspace for the common goal of victory; but for the women of the ATA
the ties were often closer. Many were widows of RAF or Allied Air
Forces pilots before they even joined the ATA. Others lost their
husbands while on active service with the ATA. Walker lost more than
one of her 'boy-friends' and a fiancé in the air war and her RAF
husband in an accident shortly afterwards. Others lost brothers and
close friends.

The pilots of the ATA could not cope with that reality – any more
than the RAF did – by being gloomy or depressed or sad. De Bunsen
writes:

> We were not ashamed of enjoying ourselves while others got
> killed, because, just occasionally, we got killed too. This, in our
> world, was the biggest joke of all. We saw ourselves as a lot of
> middle-aged men and women and crocks, dug out of safe occu-
> pations to fly intimidating aeroplanes and somehow managing to

get away with it, and the real imminence of death was part of the humorous cartoon we built up about our daily lives.[27]

The Always Terrified Airwomen

While the women of the ATA shared the overall ethos of the ATA – its mature self-reliance, its informal, individualistic tone, its irreverent attitudes toward discipline and death, its pride in diversity and greed for new aircraft types – the women had some unique characteristics as well. First and foremost, the women of the ATA were by all accounts very feminine. Whether in contemporary press accounts or modern remembrances, men encountering the women of the ATA invariably comment on this fact. They sewed, knitted, worried about their appearance, flirted, dated, and generally behaved like normal women of their age.

This included, for example, carrying make-up and lipstick with them when flying, so that they could fix themselves up before disembarking from their aircraft. The anxious pilots of No. 247 Fighter Squadron dubiously awaiting their first Tempest delivery might not have been *quite* so reassured about its docility, if the woman pilot who delivered it had not taken the time 'to powder her nose and put on lipstick' before climbing down from the cockpit. Still, there were hazards to carrying make-up around with one, as Diana Barnato Walker discovered.

> One day I was flying another light, pale-blue PR [Photo-Reconnaissance] Spitfire . . . It was a day when the sky too was a lovely shade of blue, so, feeling very good about things in general, I thought it was about time to see if I could at least do a roll . . . . At about 5,000 ft, while keeping the nose on my chosen delivery course, I put the ailerons over on one side, then the other, but couldn't summon up enough courage at first to turn the thing right over. At last it happened, but I promptly got stuck upside down! In this attitude, while wondering what to do next, from out of my top overall pocket fell my beautifully engraved, round, silver powder compact. It wheeled round and round the bubble canopy like a drunken sailor on a wall of death, opened, then sent all the face powder over absolutely everything.
>
> When I found myself right way up again, the inside of the canopy was like a frosted lavatory window. I smeared a clear view but it made an awful mess . . . It was simply amazing how much powder there seemed to be. It rapidly spread over the whole inside of the cockpit, instruments, windscreen, knobs and switches – just everywhere![28]

One would not have blamed the RAF ground crews that had to clean up the mess for being rather sour toward women pilots for some time after this.

Another drawback of their femininity was that whereas they wanted (and were required) to wear skirts when in an Officers' Mess or otherwise on leave, skirts were simply not practical in a cockpit. Nor was it practical to wear a skirt under the flying overalls. Most of the women therefore wore only their underwear, shirt, tie and jacket under the overalls. This meant they could not remove the overalls until they were in a secluded place – which sometimes proved awkward. More serious, if for some reason (like returning late from or rushing to an important date for which one had worn or wanted to wear a skirt) one might be caught in an emergency – in a skirt. Walker was probably not alone in risking a crash rather than being willing to bale-out while wearing a skirt.

In short, the women of the ATA were not Amazons or lesbians or even feminists particularly. What set them apart from other women of their age was simply that they all loved to fly. One of the women hid the fact that she was pregnant for seven months because she didn't want to have to stop. A Chilean volunteer hung about in hangars and did odd jobs until she had picked up enough English to be allowed to fly. The WAAFs trying to meet the rigorous requirements were not above cheating in any way they could – from padding their stockings to meet the height requirement, to pretending technical interests and qualifications they did not have.

The women's keenness was not only noted by their male colleagues, it made them quite indifferent to the differentials in pay. Walker claims 'this was considered perfectly natural and was accepted at the time'.[29] Curtis felt 'the question of equal pay was to me quite irrelevant, something that never crossed my mind . . . .'[30] Even after the war, after the ATA women had enjoyed equal pay for equal work for more than two years, the women accepted a reduction of pay and status within the RAFVR without the least outrage as the following episode illustrates:

> One day an officer from the legal branch of the RAF, who knew Peggy, saw her and they had a drink together. He asked what she was doing in just an aircraftwoman's uniform. She said, 'That's all I am now.' He said to her 'You are still an officer in the WAAF Reserve, they cannot possibly do this to you.' She replied 'They appear to have done it, and I'm not grumbling. The main thing is that at last they have allowed women into the flying branch of the RAF even if only the reserve.'[31]

The women felt privileged to be allowed to fly at all, and the conditions were not important. (The RAF, incidentally, did rethink the issue of commissioned WAAF in the Flying Branch and re-commissioned them.)

The women were not concerned with equality as such or with compensation, but rather with being given a *chance* to fly and then getting *recognition* of their competence. Gower had from the start pursued a policy of opening opportunities for her women by *demonstrating* competence. Rather than making a great deal of noise or demands, Gower had quietly set about ensuring that her women's section did their job in such an exemplary manner that more and more doors would be opened for them.

While this strategy worked in the long run, in the early years the women pilots did feel considerable pressure to perform better than their male colleagues. This put an extra strain on them. Curtis remembers that she was given her first Hurricane delivery at a time when she'd had no practice on them whatsoever. She was, in consequence, uncomfortable about it but 'saw no alternative to accepting the task, feeling as ever that any excuse I made to get out of it would reflect badly on women pilots generally'.[32] As the first woman to convert to four-engined aircraft, she again felt the pressure that 'any mistakes or failures in the early days even if not of my own making could result in a decision that four-engined aircraft were not for women'.[33] Almost all the women who joined the organisation early, when there was still a degree of open or latent scepticism about their abilities, felt the same pressure. They felt that individual mistakes would reflect poorly on all women. Their response was to try harder, something that undoubtedly contributed to their overall better accident record.

The WASP
The WASP never evolved a distinctive and cohesive ethos comparable to that of the ATA. In some ways, this is hardly surprising. For almost a year there was no single organisation, since the WAFS were separate, and even training for the WFTD was split between Houston and Avenger Field until April 1943. By the time the WFTD and WAFS were merged into the WASP, many of the women had already been assigned to dozens of different bases across the country, where they represented a tiny, often insignificant, feminine and civilian cog in a massive military machine. The different tasks assigned to the women also militated against a common ethos. Target-towing or slow-timing engines required different skills and resulted in different adventures and cultures to that of, say, ferrying.

On the other hand, the homogeneity of the WASP and the very fact that they were so isolated in a man's world, were factors that might have helped create a common identity. Furthermore, unlike the ATA, they were under pressure to conform. WASP Verda-Mae Lowe hadn't been at Williams Army Air Force Base very long before she got a surprise visit from Jacqueline Cochran personally. It seemed the other WASP at the base had complained to Cochran about her. She wasn't 'fitting in'. She didn't drink. She didn't party. And she didn't date the same kind of men. In fact, she was engaged to marry an enlisted man. Cochran told Lowe she couldn't do that. In the WASP there was no tolerance for being even a little different.

But there were few cases like Lowe who needed to be told to conform. The selection process had ensured that the similarities out-weighed the differences from the start. And, like the women in England, all WASP were fanatical about flying and unwilling to risk being dismissed from the WASP for any kind of unacceptable behaviour. After the Civilian Pilot Training Program was closed to women in 1941, the WFTD became the only way girls from poor families could learn to fly at all; paying for private flying instruction again became the privilege of the rich. Even rich girls found the craving for flying was addictive and consuming. Cornelia Fort observed:

> When I got my commercial license, I thought that I would be satis-fied, but this flying is like an awful thirst; one wants to learn more and more and accumulate ratings. The more experience I get the less I seem to know, which is terribly discouraging.[34]

For someone who felt like that, the opportunity to fly the nation's most advanced aircraft was clearly seductive, no matter how many private hours she could afford – and no matter what the cost in conformity.

All the WASP shared that thirst for flight. Many of the WASP gave up more lucrative jobs for the chance to fly with the Army. Like the WAAFs who wanted to fly with the ATA, the American women applying to the WASP were not above cheating to get through the rigorous selection process. Cole reports that 'many of the thirty-four WASPs who spoke with me for this account squeezed in by various methods, not all of which were above board'.[35] There were instances of thick socks, memorised eye-charts, padded log-books and the like. WASP Ruth Woods admitted years later:

> I joined the WASP, but – it seems terrible for me to say this – it wasn't particularly out of patriotism, although that had some-

thing to do with it, at the time. Primarily it was because I could get to fly aircraft that I couldn't get my hands on any other way. No matter how much money I had, I wouldn't have been able to buy time on them, because they were military planes.[36]

Evelyn Sharp is another pilot for whom the love of flying – and earning a living to support herself and her parents – was paramount. She wrote to relatives:

> I meet so many interesting people. I can't think of a better job. I have shelter, food, clothing, money in the bank, get to travel and meet people, have good times and do the job I want to do & at the same time serve my country. No sir, they don't make better jobs.[37]

Yet, the patriotic factor should not be underestimated either. It figures very prominently – particularly in the diaries and letters of WASP, which have not been falsified by subsequent changes in political attitude and the inevitable exhaustion of passion that comes with maturity. Cornelia Fort wired her mother the following message after receiving the cable inviting her to report to the WAFS: 'The heavens have opened up and rained blessings on me. The army has decided to let women ferry ships and I'm going to be one of them.'[38] Fort, who had been caught in the Japanese attack on Pearl Harbor, had earlier told reporters: 'I wish I were a man – just for the duration. I'd give anything to train to be a fighter pilot and then meet up with that Jap again.'[39]

Perhaps Cornelia Fort's patriotism was, in consequence of that direct experience at Pearl Harbor, particularly pronounced and conscious, but many other WASP clearly felt the tug of patriotism too. After the attack on Pearl Harbor all of America was in a war-fever, and young American men were enlisting by the thousands. Many of the women desperately wanted not only 'to do their part', but to be part of the 'heel-clicking, uniform flashing pageant of wartime America'.[40] Phyllis Burchfield described learning about the WAFS as follows:

> I was in the air when the tower called me and told me that the Air Corps had just opened up to women . . . I told my boss I had to do it, I had to go. He tried hard to get me to stay because there weren't enough instructors, and I was making twice as much money in Memphis, but I went to Wilmington anyway. I was like all the others, hopped up on the idea of winning the war.[41]

WASP Teresa James wrote in her diary on 12 October 1942:

The mud doesn't matter. The continuous rain and cold don't matter. I'm just so proud to be here, to be part of this Army. There is something a little difficult to describe about soloing a plane with a big star on it.[42]

For some, service to their country was more than just being part of something, it was a sacred duty. WASP Nadine Nagle explains her position as follows: 'In the summer of 1942, my husband [a B-24 pilot] was killed on a mission in England. I read an article on the women pilots the next month. I got this patriotic feeling that I was to fly in his place.'[43]

World War II was different, it was a situation that welded us together – men, women, and children, from all the different countries – and soon it was such a big thing, and to be part of something that big, that important, that really set the world on course that it latter followed, is pretty important.[44]

Again, the contemporary accounts convey the intensity of feeling at the time better than dry historical accounts. A WASP wrote home:

And then while we were at attention a bomber took off, followed by four pursuit planes. We knew the bomber was headed across the ocean and that the fighters were to escort it part of the way. As they circled over us I could hardly see them for the tears in my eyes. It was striking symbolism, and I think all of us felt it. As long as our planes flew overhead, the skies of America were free and that's what all of us everywhere are fighting for. And that we, in a very small way, are being allowed to help keep that sky free is the most beautiful thing I've ever known.[45]

Like their English colleagues, the WAFS and WASP neither agitated for equal pay nor did they resent their subordinate status. Quite the contrary, the WASP were 'so indoctrinated that their flying duty was of a lower order than the male pilots in the AAF', that when an Air Medal was awarded to WASP Barbara Erickson 'many felt it should have gone to an Air Transport Pilot flying the Hump to China, or ferrying bombers across to England'.[46] Others saw it merely 'as a publicity stunt by WASP headquarters' in support of WASP militarisation efforts in Congress.[47] Cornelia Fort wrote:

We have no hopes of replacing men pilots. Numerically we are too small to have ever conceived of such an idea. But we can each release a man to combat, to faster ships, to overseas work. Naturally we hope to have a chance to fly bigger planes. All pilots do. But the planes we fly, regardless of their size or speed, have to be delivered. Delivering a trainer to Texas may be as important as delivering a bomber to Africa if you take the long view. We want to prove and we are beginning to prove that women can be trusted to deliver airplanes safely and in the doing serve the country which is our country too.[48]

It is striking that in many of these accounts the American women felt the need to *justify* their actions as the women of the ATA never did. Even their patriotism contains a certain defensiveness that was not necessary in Britain – where the conscription of women was necessary before the war was even half over.

The defensiveness was particularly pronounced with regard to proving that they could do the job as well as the men they were replacing. The sentiments of the American women in this regard echo those of Pauline Gower and her first eight women in 1940. Cornelia Fort expressed it as follows: 'All of us realised what a spot we were on. We had to deliver the goods or else. Or else there wouldn't be another chance for women pilots in any part of the service.'[49]

For the Americans, however, the pressure never let up. The pressure was there every time the WASP were assigned to a new base where women had not served before, or took over a new task that women had not performed before. The women in the ATA could, after gradually working up to operational aircraft and then heavy bombers over the first couple of years, to a certain extent rest upon their laurels for the rest of the war. The women in the WASP, in contrast, were constantly facing new challenges and forced over-and-over to convince yet another group of sceptical men to recognise their abilities. Only in FERD did the American women enjoy sufficient continuity of command and assignment to make it possible for them to enjoy their positive track record.

Significantly, and in contrast to the women of the ATA, the WASP were for the most part left to deal with this pressure on their own. Headquarters was very far away, and Cochran much too involved in her big battles for control and militarisation to be of any help to the individual WASP in their daily lives. Recent graduates of Avenger Field were left to deal with a completely unfamiliar situations, jobs and surroundings without any assistance from Headquarters or even fellow WASP. Sent to bases where there had never been women pilots before, young WASP were expected to perform, set a good example, and fit in all at once. Even at those bases and in the Ferrying Squadrons where there were more than a handful of women pilots assigned, the turnover was high. Women came and went; they were transferred or sent off for additional training or resigned. Those engaged in ferrying were often away from their home bases for days or even weeks on end. When they returned, pure chance determined if and which of the other WASP might be there at the same time. Such an environment provided little opportunity for the evolution of *esprit de corps* among the women.

During training and before being dispersed across the country, the first twenty-five WAFS developed – very briefly – a unique team spirit. They were the most homogenous group and being in the spotlight of publicity as they were, they bonded together. 'Being young and vigorous' – and confined to a Spartan barracks in the middle of a desolate Army Base – they evolved their own forms of entertainment. Darts was popular, cocktails were regular, and practical jokes common.

> Sometimes one of the WAFS would come in at night, push her door open, and find herself doused with the contents of a water bucket that had been balanced atop her door. Pulling the string for the light bulb in the middle of the room might lead to a glassful of water emptying onto her head. Someone might spread Limburger cheese on a radiator, tie knots in stockings or pyjamas, short-sheet a bed, or hide oranges between the mattresses.[50]

But the period of training soon gave way to real assignments and then the dispersal across the country to the four different Ferrying Squadrons. The impact upon the WAFS was significant. Sarah Byrn Rickman notes that 'the women known as The Originals never were all together in one place and though individuals retained lifelong friendships, the group has never held regular reunions like their sister pilots, the WASP'.[51]

The WASP bonds were notably not formed on active service, but during training, as Rickman observes 'just as does any group of women – or men – who attend college together and belong to the same sorority or fraternity'.[52] Thus it was at Avenger Field that the WASP came closest to evolving an institutional ethos.

The WASP at Avenger Field had no pilots with thousands of hours of flying time setting the tone – those women were in the WAFS and already flying. They had no Amy Johnson in their ranks; the closest equivalent, Jacqueline Cochran herself, only flew in on rare occasions like a whirlwind in pursuit of her own agenda. The senior woman on the base was not even a pilot, and nor were her assistants. The Army officers were strictly segregated and kept their distance jealousy. The instructors were of very uneven quality and there was a constant turnover so that no continuity came from this source. The women trainees were thus left almost entirely to their own devices. It is hardly surprising, therefore, that the ethos that evolved was decidedly adolescent – a fact undoubtedly aggravated by the fact that the Army insisted on treating the women as if they were eighteen-year-old cadets – regardless of age, education, marital status or civilian profession. At Avenger Field the women trainees were expected to behave like teenage cadets – and they did.

More than that: the girls came to Avenger Field with a strong desire to be 'just like the boys'. They wanted to take part in the national experience, and they wanted to do their part for the war. They wanted uniforms badly enough to 'design' them and pay for them out of their own pockets when their Commander and Director left them in the lurch. For the most part, they wanted to conform – not to stand out in any way. And their role models were the USAAF cadets who had been at Avenger (and other training fields all across the country) before them, rather than experienced civilian fliers. This desire to imitate 'the boys' was so great that it included adopting even the more unpleasant aspects of cadet traditions. Swearing appears to have become increasingly common and accepted. Drinking was glamorous – particularly in a 'dry' state where it had to be 'boot-legged' in or bought from 'moonshiners' on the sly. And when the second class arrived at Avenger Field, they were subjected to the traditional 'hazing' to which all new cadets on Army air bases were subjected.

It is hard to capture the atmosphere of Avenger Field for the modern reader in just a few words. First, there was the harsh Texan climate, the dust and the tumbleweed, intense heat or intense cold and the rattlesnakes. Second, there was the bleak Army Air Force installation with its wooden barracks and admin buildings all lined up in rigid rows. For the young women straight out of protected homes and conventional jobs, it epitomised their great adventure into the new, male world of the USAAF. Whereas there is evidence of bad morale among the first trainees at Houston, the morale at Avenger Field seems to have been consistently high – albeit varying from class to class.

Lieutenant Fleishman, who on his own initiative helped the WFTD by teaching them how to march and drill, claims that 'every good soldier knows that a singing army is a fighting army' and the WASP certainly took singing to heart.[53] The girls wrote their own lyrics to popular tunes and each class learned the songs of their predecessors and added their own variations or additions. To this day, when the surviving

WASP meet for reunions, they remember and sing these songs.

A few examples of the lyrics can, therefore, provide some insight into the spirit at Avenger Field – also known as Cochran's Convent. For example, the women at Avenger sang:

> We are the Yankee Doodle pilots
> Yankee Doodle do or die
> Real live nieces of our Uncle Sam
> Born with a yearning to fly
> Keep in step to all our classes
> March to Flight Line with your pals
> Yankee Doodle come to Texas
> Just to fly the PTs
> We are those Yankee Doodle Gals![54]

Or, to the tune of the 'Caissons Go Rolling Along':

> Over trees, under wires,
> T'hell with landing gear and tires,
> We're the girls of the 319th!
> Over clouds, through the soup,
> We can do inverted loops,
> We're the girls of the 319th![55]

Another well remembered favourite immortalised the hated, over-sized flying overalls the girls at Avenger Field dubbed 'Zoot Suits'.

> Zoot suits and parachutes
> And wings of silver, too,
> He'll ferry planes like
> His Mama used to do![56]

Others immortalised Lieutenant Fleishman himself. For example, to the melody of the 'Battle Hymn of the Republic':

> Mine eyes have seen the glory of my biceps bulging out,
> Mine ears have heard the story of Lieutenant Fleishman's shout
> My teeth have felt the gritty sand that we all gripe about
> The 319th flies on![57]

Allegedly, the text of some of the lyrics the women evolved were too 'earthy" for Cochran's prudish tastes and the girls were strictly prohibited from singing them. Unfortunately these lyrics do not appear to be available in the public domain. The following text sung to the tune of 'Rugged but Right', however, managed to avoid censorship.

> I just called up to tell you that I'm rugged but right!
> A rambling woman, a gambling woman, drunk every night.
> A porterhouse steak three times a day for my board,
> That's more than any decent gal can afford!
> I've got a big electric fan to keep me cool while I eat,
> A tall handsome man to keep me warm while I sleep.
> I'm a rambling woman, a gambling woman and BOY
> am I tight![58]

When one compares the lyrics to the reality of isolation upon a nearly all-women base and the otherwise notably juvenile behaviour of the trainees who can only conclude that these particular lyrics expressed fantasy – or even rather the fantasies of their male role models – more than reality.

The reality at Avenger Field was a Walt Disney mascot, and a newspaper named after it: the *Fifinella Gazette*. It was a wishing well in which the girls were thrown by their classmates after soloing, and the ringing of a disused fire-bell at the end of ground school. Practical jokes similar to those referred to above and pillow fights also figure in the reminiscences of the graduates of Cochran's Convent. The atmosphere was, in short, as much that of a girls' prep school or sorority as a military base.

Nor were the pranks and high spirits confined to the barracks. There are numerous documented incidents of the girls 'buzzing' buildings, roads, trains and even cows. They stripped down and sunned themselves in the cockpits to get suntans in the cooler air. They flew in 'formation' although they had not been taught how and were officially prohibited from doing it. They practised aerobatics rather than concentrating on navigation. Flying about in gaggles together, they got lost – and an Army pilot had to be sent out to find them and lead them home in one instance. (Allegedly, the pilot reported on landing that he had fifty combat missions behind him but had never been so frightened. 'He was sure the girls aimed to bring him down, the way they came at him from every direction, up, down, sideways, front and rear. The skies over Europe were safer.'[59])

At Avenger Field the girls were confronted with a unique situation – the USAAF and its rules and regulations – for the first time in their lives. They were all working toward a common goal: winning their wings.

They were subjected to the same routine, living at very close quarters and virtually imprisoned with one another for the length of their training, on average more than six months. It is hardly surprising that close friendships and bonds of fellowship were formed during this period, but there was not an organisational ethos that went with the graduates when they were assigned to their posts after graduation. On the contrary, the WASP seem to have regarded graduation as 'freedom'. Granger words it as follows:

> Relieved of the lockstep Avenger regimen, the graduates are as frisky as young colts loose in a lush pasture on a bright spring day. Randolph AFB, that stiffly proper 'West Point of the Air' deems them troublesome . . . [Older WASP are] thoroughly irritated by their diddling and giggling, their dawdling at lunch, their doing what they please when they please . . . .[60]

The Commander of 2nd Ferrying Group at New Castle was equally displeased with the attitudes of recent WASP graduates. In sharp contrast to the original WAFS, who had all served at his Group, the graduates of Avenger Field had an '8-hour day mentality' and were constantly complaining about not having free weekends. The experienced WAFS themselves complained that the graduates of Cochran's Convent disregarded Ferrying rules. Equally dangerous, they liked to fly together in 'gaggles' and left all the navigating to the leader; if any of the girls got separated they also got lost. This was what caused the Ferrying Command to refer to the graduates of Avenger Field as 'Airport Pilots' rather than 'Ferry Pilots'.

When they did fly long distances for Ferrying Command, the high morale that had earned Barbara Erickson (one of the original WAFS) her Air Medal by flying far and fast with only minimum down time, appears to have been lacking among graduates of Avenger Field. After several WASP reported how enjoyable their prolonged stopover due to fog in Atlanta had been, 'destinations where the weather was likely to turn sour zoomed to the top of the list for cross-country trips'.[61] Experienced WAFS still driven by the spirit of dedication to get the job done well, were appalled by the bitching and complaining of the women straight out of flight school. Nancy Batson reported the following incident:

> I was on my way to bed when I overheard Sis and Mac grumbling. They said there was no way in you-know-where that they were going to get up at four o'clock in the morning. Well I listened to

them bellyache for a few minutes and I got mad. Betty was putting her reputation on the line and those two were saying they were too good and too tired to get up in the morning and get a move on [to] help get those planes out to Canada on time like Colonel Tunner wanted . . . So I marched into their room and gave them what-for.[62]

These incidents should by no means be blown out of proportion. They are merely illustrative of the fact that in the absence of a firm and pervasive organisational ethos of absolute reliability and dedication, it is easy for individuals to slip into the usual habits of self-interest. It is the presence of an overriding, goal-oriented, keen spirit that distinguishes a crack unit from an ordinary one. The ATA was a first-class, crack unit, but despite their homogeneity and the pressure to conform, the women in the WASP were never given the organisational basis that would have enabled them to become one.

Notes:

1   Granger, 290.
2   Phelps, 8.
3   Bergel, 75.
4   Bergel, 75.
5   Curtis, 199.
6   Curtis, 191.
7   Bergel, 76.
8   Bergel, 76.
9   Cheeseman, 21.
10   King, 81.
11   Du Cros, 77.
12   Cheeseman, 83–4.
13   Bergel, 42.
14   Welch, Talk before the History of Air Navigation Group, Royal Institute of Navigation, 23 Sept. 1998.
15   Fahie, 169.
16   Cheeseman, 157.
17   De Bunsen, 149.
18   Tunner, 42.
19   Lucas, 62.
20   King, 118.
21   De Bunsen, 149.
22   Cheeseman, 68.
23   Bergel, 19.
24   Du Cros, 77.
25   Genovese, 68–9.
26   Du Cros, 53.

27   De Bunsen, 149.
28   Walker, 85—6.
29   Walker, 53.
30   Curtis, 179.
31   Lucas, 120.
32   Curtis, 98.
33   Curtis, 171.
34   Simbeck, 85.
35   Cole, 14.
36   Cole, 18.
37   Bartels, 199.
38   Rickman, 155.
39   Simbeck, 115.
40   Keil, 147.
41   Rickman, 125.
42   Rickman, 67.
43   Merryman, 15.
44   Merryman, 14.
45   Simbeck, 153.
46   Keil, 278.
47   Keil, 278.
48   Simbeck, 185–6.
49   Simbeck, 148.
50   Simbeck, 143.
51   Rickman, 96.
53   Rickman, 96.
54   Granger, 78.
55   Keil, 154.
56   Granger, 78.
57   Keil, 183.
58   Keil, 148.
59   Keil, 279.
60   Granger, 354.
61   Granger, 460–61.
62   Verges, 185.
63   Rickman, 169.

CHAPTER TWELVE

There's a War On – Or is there?

In her *Final Report* on the WASP Jacqueline Cochran claimed that 'the experimental purpose of the program ranked along with but sub-ordinate to the purpose of releasing male pilots from routine and non-combat duties for combat service'.[1] Yet, regardless of the lip-service rendered military needs, Cochran's actions demonstrate that it was the experimental aspects of the programme to which she gave priority and precedence. A review of Cochran's policies and actions will make clear that she was, in fact, obsessed with proving that women could fly as well as men. Everything else – whether it was the requirements of FERD, the needs of Base Commanders, the wishes of the WASP, or the war itself – was only of secondary importance. The consequences of her misguided priorities were fatal for the programme.

In her very first proposal to General Arnold, Cochran argued for a women pilots' programme – not in terms of meeting manpower require-ments, but rather testing to see whether women could be taught to fly as well as men. Cochran's ultimate aim was to prove 'that any healthy, stable young American woman can learn to fly the army way as well as her brothers',[2] and 'determine the capacities, limitations, strength, and weaknesses of women as pilots . . . .'[3]

Just four months after inception, in December 1942, the decision to seek militarisation for the women pilots' programme was postponed because it was felt the 'experiment' had not yet conclusively proved that women had the stamina for military flying. As long as the programme remained 'experimental', it was thought better to keep it informal and civilian in order to facilitate rapid discontinuation.[4]

Cochran greeted the first recruits to her programme by telling them they were 'flying guinea pigs' and the future of women in military aviation depended on them.[5] Six months later, although the programme had now been in existence for nine months – far beyond the ninety-day experimental period given the WAFS – Cochran argued for the merger of the WAFS and WFTD on the grounds that: 'the experimental features of the program could not be properly handled without control over assignments between commands, selection of types of flying duties to be performed, and control over health and welfare according to a centralised plan'. Likewise, Cochran now argued *in favour* of militarisation on the grounds that too many 'elements of the experimental project' were lost due to the civilian status of the women.[6]

More important than what she said about her programme, however, was what Cochran did. This is where it becomes evident that the WASP programme was run with the overriding goal of proving just what women could do and documenting their physical performance while doing so. Thus from the start, Cochran insisted that her women be like the 'Amazons' Rosemary du Cros described entering the ATA in the latter stages of the war.

The carefully selected 'perfect specimens' (the word specimen is Cochran's own[7]) of American womanhood were not only required to pass the Army physical exams, they were required to do physical exercise and drill. Furthermore, they were subjected to systematic monitoring by the Chief Medical Officer at Avenger Field, Dr Mansured, and all subsequent base medical officers.

Dr Mansured's job was not so much providing medical care to the women training at the airfield, but producing 'a formal medical study of women fliers'.[8] Mansured collected data on height and weight, strength, concentration, illness, 'and particularly menstrual cycles'.[9] Likewise, the medical officers of the units to which the women were assigned were required to submit detailed reports on the women's physical and psychological health and how these related to performance of flying duties.

Cochran herself devoted roughly one fifth of her entire Final Report to the medical aspects of the programme, including detailed charts of the women's age, height and weight, their dropout rates by age category and the like. The most peculiar data is a matrix comparing WASP with male cadets with regard to foot-length, chest circumference, arm reach, sitting height, eye height, calf circumference (!) and a battery of other bizarre physical measures from head-breath to face-length.[10] It remains a mystery what these statistics were supposed to prove, but they certainly had no relevance to winning the war.

Still, it is possible to argue that if Army surgeons had nothing better to do with their time than measure the head and calf circumference of WASP and Air Force cadets, then at least the collection of these statistics did not cause direct harm to the war effort or the WASP programme. Unfortunately, the same cannot be said for other measures that Cochran vigorously implemented in the pursuit of her goal of proving women could fly as well as men.

Ten months into the programme, the first women were assigned to duties outside of FERD, namely to Camp Davis, NC, for target-towing. The selected WASP were ceremoniously warned that they were being given a 'top secret' mission and that (again) their performance 'would determine the future of women pilots'.[11] By November of the same year, the 'experiments' had expanded to flying B-25s, B-26s, and B-17s. Cochran explained her motives in her Final Report:

> It was of importance to prove that a whole group of women, without special selection except for physical requirement, could be assigned to the Fortresses or the B-26s or the B-25s, pass through the transition training as successfully as men pilots and thereafter carry on regularly in operations without undue fatigue or higher than normal accident rate.[12]

Unless the USAAF intended to use the women as pilots of these aircraft, one wonders why it was so important to prove women *could*.

The same applies to other experiments as well, such as altitude chamber tests, or training them as instructors. The women trained as flight instructors were never given a single cadet to instruct; they remained 'an experiment to find out if women could pass the course'.[13] Other graduates from Avenger Field were selected to go to operational training schools to test yet other 'capabilities of women pilots'.[14]

One such experiment was conducted at South Plains, where the women were taught how to tow the big boxy gliders, which were to be used in the coming invasion of Europe.[15] There was never the remotest chance that women pilots would be deployed to a combat theatre to perform one of the most dangerous combat missions assigned to the USAAF on D-Day. Not even in a nightmare would General Arnold – who would not let women ferry bombers from Newfoundland to Scotland – imagine letting women tow gliders full of elite Army combat troops over the landing beaches on D-Day. Again, one wonders why it was so important to see how well women could do it.

In the event, they did not do very well at all. The CO of the unit felt they were unsuited to the task, and wanted to send them all back for re-assignment to other duties. Cochran was insistent, as usual, and Central Flying Command explained her position: 'the utilization of women pilots as glider tow pilots is an important part of the experimental program, and every effort should be made to give these women the necessary transition.'[16]

The result of all this experimentation with the women was double frustration. The women themselves were put through lengthy training – only to be told they weren't needed and or wouldn't be allowed to perform the task for which they had trained. Meanwhile, the COs of the units to which the women were nominally assigned had to cope with pilots, who – in contrast to the men assigned to the same duties – were constantly being sent off for special, experimental 'training'.

The officers commanding WASP never knew when, if and for how long the WASP assigned to their units were going to be available for duty. Control of WASP assignments was in the hands of Cochran, not the respective COs. The extent of the problem can be judged by the fact that at any one time as much as 66 per cent of the WASP in any one command might be on temporary duty somewhere else.[17] The objective of proving what women *could* do clearly interfered with what they *did* do.

Furthermore, the situation only reinforced the idea of the women being separate, different and even privileged. The WASP were getting a great deal of special training at the Army's expense *without* putting that training to use for the USAAF or the nation. The WASP were costing the Army money, but rather than freeing men for combat or overseas duties, men had to be on hand and fly extra duties while the WASP enjoyed training for tasks they were never intended to perform. It is hardly surprising that even where – or *especially* where – the WASP had been welcomed, their increasing absence for temporary duty started to create new resentment against them among their colleagues and commanders.

Nothing could have been more fatal for the WASP programme as a whole. Just as Congress was questioning the costs of training and objecting to the militarisation of the WASP, the Commands that had employed the WASP were losing their enthusiasm for the expensive and only sporadically available women. FERD had returned to Training Command over a hundred WASP, who did not want or were unable to convert to 'pursuits'. Training Command had no use for women trained on B-17s as the workhorse bomber became increasing obsolete. Nor did Training Command want to employ female flight instructors. In response to an enquiry from Cochran about the future need for WASP, both the First and Third Air Forces said they don't want any more. The Fourth Air Force was prepared to take a maximum of ten WASP per month. Only the Second Air Force foresaw a substantial need for more WASP, putting their requirements at fifty WASP per month.[18]

Now Cochran's own arguments and strategy came home to roost. If the purpose of the programme had been to prove a point, then its justification ended as soon as the results of the experiment were in. The expensive 'experiment', which had become an embarrassment to the Army as a result of the massive lobbying and press campaign against it, could be closed down in a hurry without loss of face simply by announcing that the experiment was over. Thus, at the graduation ceremonies for the last class of WASP, General Arnold smilingly announced that they could all go home *because* the experiment had 'been a success'. Now that the WASP had 'proved that women could fly as well as men', he argued, there was no need for the programme any more.[19]

The ATA, in contrast, never viewed itself – or the employment of women pilots in its ranks – as an experiment. On the contrary, the decision to employ women was dictated by the overriding need to perform a service in the most effective and efficient manner possible. It simply made sense, from the perspective of the experienced professionals in charge of the ATA, to employ women with thousands of hours of flying experience, before taking in men with far less experience. It likewise made sense to hire women with at least some experience, before training men from scratch. It also made sense to let experienced women ferry pilots fly service aircraft anywhere those aircraft were needed, if it meant getting the job done faster.

The main concern of the ATA was *always* winning the war – even if that meant overriding (or ignoring) Service regulations and standard operating procedures. Thus, there was more than one recorded incident of ATA pilots flying in and out of RAF or FAA airfields that were officially 'closed' to flying. Likewise, the ATA was perfectly willing to disregard the standing orders of Air Chief Marshal Leigh-Mallory and fly to the Continent of Europe if need arose – and to let women do the same, no matter how he felt about it. To the very end, it was the objective of contributing to the war effort that held precedence with the ATA and its members.

What is more, this overriding sense of duty that characterised the ATA from its inception was unique for being almost provocatively informal while at the same time boldly innovative, creative and flexible. The organisation might have been formed to fly light aircraft in liaison or communications capacities after a devastating *Blitzkrieg*, but if the RAF needed hobby fliers to ferry their hottest and heaviest service aircraft then the ATA would make sure that its pilots learned how to do it. If Malta needed Spitfires and the only way to get them to the besieged island in time meant loading them on an American aircraft carrier from a field that was more than 200 yards too short for the Spitfire, then the

ATA would still find a way to do it. (The RAF, incidentally, expected the ATA to wreck at least four of the aircraft in the attempt and so ordered four more Spitfires than could be squeezed aboard the carrier. As a result, four Spitfires had to be returned to stations in England; the ATA had not wrecked a single one.) If the offensive at Arnhem was in trouble for lack of supplies and RAF Transport Command had no excess capacity, then the ATA could turn itself into a freight airline, converting taxi Ansons into transports, literally overnight. Nor was the ATA above flying ambulances or bringing home released POWs or refugees. The ATA was prepared to do *whatever* it could to help the war effort, even – or particularly – when other Services were inhibited by regulations, red tape, or tradition. This overriding sense of duty, which so consistently characterised the ATA, was perhaps best summed up by Hugh Bergel when he wrote: 'it was the ATA's policy that if anyone asked us to ferry a Stirling into Kensington Gardens we would have a go.'[20]

The ATA kept no elaborate medical records on the performance of its pilots, did not require women pilots to report their menstrual cycles, and did not compare the physical features of its members with that of the RAF and FAA. The ATA did not claim to have proved either that 'Ancient and Tattered Airmen' or their women pilots could perform any particular task as well or better than anyone else. It simply set out to do whatever job came its way in the most efficient manner possible. Winning the war, not proving a point, was the overriding goal of the ATA and its leadership.

Notes:
1   Cochran, Final Report.
2   Verges, 69.
3   Cochran, Final Report.
4   Granger, 52.
5   Verges, 73.
6   Granger, 391.
7   Cochran, Jacqueline, and Odlum, Floyd, *The Stars at Noon*, 1954, 127–8.
8   Verges, 168.
9   Verges, 168.
10   Cochran, Final Report.
11   Keil, 211.
12   Cochran, Final Report.
13   Keil, 274.
14   Verges, 151.
15   Granger, 225.
16   Granger, 218.

17   Granger sites Eastern Flying Training Command where ninety-two
     WASP out of 140 were on TDY at one time, 409.
18   Granger, 402.
19   Arnold's speech to the last graduating class of WASP at Avenger
     Field, 7 Dec. 1944, cited in various sources including Keil, 330, Verges,
     234.
20   Bergel, 94.

CHAPTER THIRTEEN

Chasing the Chimera

PRESS RELATIONS AND PRESS RESPONSE

The art of 'spin' and the emergence of professional 'spin doctors' have become hot topics in the media in the last decade. During the Internet boom at the turn of the century, no self-respecting Chief Executive Officer would have been caught dead at a Shareholders' Meeting without first consulting the various public relations and marketing firms responsible for developing the 'corporate message'. In politics as well, candidates and elected officials often appear more interested in the 'spin' to give their words than the content of what they are saying. Even the Pentagon has become very sophisticated in its efforts to control media response to its activities at home and abroad by packaging it in ways designed to make it particularly palatable to the public.

But if public awareness of the degree to which 'messaging' can impact public perceptions has grown dramatically in the last few years, the need for good public and press relations is not really new. A 'good press' has always been an advantage for an organisation or individual, while the dangers of a 'bad press' can hardly be overstated. Bad press can draw attention away from positive achievement to focus only on weakness and flaws. Bad press can completely obliterate realities, obscuring facts with allegations, insinuations and falsehoods. Bad press can destroy a reputation, erode popular support, and ultimately drive a person, business or institution into ruin. This is why it is so important to 'chase the chimera' of the news media in the hope of feeding it with just those delicacies that will tame the beast and make it docile to one's own aims.

Any modern 'spin doctor' looking for a case study to prove his value to a potential employer could hardly do better than by comparing the media coverage of the women pilots in the United Kingdom and the United States during the Second World War. The ferocious media campaign launched against the WASP in 1944 was only the last act of a drama that started much earlier and had its roots in media mismanagement from the start. The women of the ATA by contrast got off to a somewhat difficult start, but profited from professional management of media relations of a quality to leave even jaded modern readers full of admiration.

THE ATA WOMEN AND THE PRESS

While the creation of the ATA in the early months of the war had passed almost unnoticed in the British press, the decision to employ a handful of female aviators produced a 'storm' of publicity. Admittedly, this was not alone attributable to the precedent-setting nature of the decision with regard to women pilots. Rather, the founding of the ATA had coincided with the outbreak of the war and Germany's first terrifying demonstration of *Blitzkrieg*. The headlines coming out of Poland, the organisation of the entire country on a war footing, the dispatch of the British Expeditionary Force to France etc. took the headlines away from the founding of a small, modest and rather specialised auxiliary such as the ATA. By the time the women were taken onboard, however, the *Blitzkrieg* had turned into *Sitzkrieg* or the so-called 'Phoney War'. There was very little news generally, and so the first women to fly 'for the RAF' became newsworthy.

In fact, the press had a field day. 'There were photographs in every paper, cinema newsreel and magazine, and Pauline [Gower] herself spoke over the radio', Lettice Curtis recalls.[1] The press were delighted, of course, because they had a story with pretty faces, titles, connections, fame and fortune. Soon, they discovered they had something even better – they had something controversial. No sooner did the news – mostly positive – about the women pilots break, than a storm of indignation arise.

The objections voiced by the outraged opponents of the women pilots were in part based on completely false assumptions and facts. For example, it was alleged that the women were being paid huge salaries – a story whose source might have been none other than Lord Haw Haw. At all events, the famous commentator for Goebbels' Propaganda Ministry claimed that the women in the ATA were receiving 'enormous salaries', and many angry and ostensibly informed individuals wrote letters to the editors of various publications referring to salaries that were at least twice what the women were in fact being paid.

Even after the real salaries became public knowledge, letters to the editor frequently made an unkind comparison between the women's weekly wage of £6 and that of a Sergeant Pilot of the RAF (always demonstratively 'on active service in France') at £4 7s 6d. The fact that the RAF Sergeant Pilot had his bed, board and uniforms at Government expense was conveniently omitted in most commentary on the subject.

Another false assumption was that there were 'thousands' of better qualified men, who were being denied the chance to fly by the women. In a lengthy editorial in *The Aeroplane*, a male pilot argued indignantly:

> The excuse that the scheme is for the purpose of releasing men for active service is a very poor one, especially when there are men up to 50 years of age with years of experience and perfectly capable of such a job as ferrying light aircraft to destinations required. Women are not seeking this job for the sake of doing something for their country, but for the sake of publicity . . . Women who are anxious to serve their country should take on work more befitting their sex instead of encroaching on a man's occupation. Men have made aviation reach its present perfection. Women have only aped men and have contributed nothing to its development.[2]

In another letter, it was furiously asserted that highly qualified (male) pilots could not be expected to do menial jobs for the Army or in some other civil defence organisation just so these spoilt girl fliers could 'show off'.[3] The fact that the first eight women pilots were predominantly professional fliers who had lost their means of support due to the pro-hibition on civil flying was conveniently forgotten.

In short, as so often in the past, the principal offence of the women was that they were 'poaching' from their betters, i.e. men. There was nothing inherently wrong with what they were doing, but – obviously – men ought always to be given precedence over women when it came to prestigious and coveted jobs.

From the start, however, the women pilots were not without their champions. Interestingly, the editorial staff of *The Aeroplane* – in which many of the lengthy diatribes against the women were published – declared: 'In principle we can see no objection to employing skilled women pilots or to paying the "full market value of service".'[4] Lady Londonderry was another ardent advocate of the women pilots. In several letters to the editors of various newspapers, she drew attention to the fact that: 'If it is only the question of pay that rankles, these women are doing exactly the same work as men, with equal risk of life and limb . . . .'[5] What was more, she drew attention to the fact that they are receiving *less* pay than the men despite higher qualifications, adding, 'would any man with the flying qualifications such as these women possess [accept] the lower grade of pay?'[6] She suggested further: 'it is really ridiculous and almost dishonest to try to stir up trouble about eleven women pilots, most of whom used flying as a means of livelihood before the war.'[7]

Other defenders of the women relied more on irony than argument. *Flight* magazine published a picture of the first eight women and Pauline Gower with the caption: 'Finland Threatens Russia . . . This threat to masculine vanity consists of a first officer and eight second officers.' One of the ATA's male pilots felt compelled to come to the defence of his female colleagues writing under 'FDB' in *The Aeroplane*:

> I heard one young officer commenting on the pinching of his job, and his comrades' jobs, by girls. An older officer inquired: 'why, are you afraid they'll bring down more Huns than you?'[8]

Under assaults like this, even the Conservative MP, who had allegedly wanted to raise a question in Parliament concerning the women pilots, soon backed down and publicly disclaimed any opposition to the women fliers. Within six months the storm had blown over, or rather been lost in the hurricane that the Wehrmacht unleashed on 10 May 1940. From that point forward, any lingering or latent criticism of the women flying with the ATA was overwhelmed by the war news and the desperate situation of Britain fighting on alone after the defeat of France.

At the very height of the Battle of Britain and literally just days after Churchill's speech in Parliament praising the exploits of Fighter Command, the women pilots attained the ultimate accolade of the day: they were explicitly associated with the Fighter Boys. Headlines read: 'Mothers are Flying Fast Planes for RAF: Fighter Pilots Trained in Them.' The article went on to catalogue the aircraft the women were then flying stressing: 'some of the women are now allowed to fly the Miles Master, the monoplane with which the RAF trains their fighter pilots in the last stages before putting them in Hurricanes and Spitfires.'[9] At a point in history when the nation idolised the pilots of Hurricanes and Spitfires, this was heady praise for the 'spoilt girls' who had been accused of wanting only to 'show off' just six months earlier.

A month later, before the Battle of Britain was over but when confidence in victory was rising, an article in *The Star* openly referred to earlier criticism of women flying for the ATA, dismissing it as being based on the 'mistaken belief that they were taking the places of men'.[10] The article went on to praise the women by claiming:

... though these women are in ratio of only one in four to the men they are doing an ever-increasing job in helping the RAF. They fly daily in all weathers. They kept it up even through the winter's great freeze. Every minute they are in the air they must keep a watchful eye for enemy raiders whose greetings would be expressed in bullets. No pleasant thought as they themselves are quite unarmed and even without wireless communication.[11]

The reference to enemy aircraft in September 1940 was not sheer melodrama. The *Luftwaffe* had just launched the largest aerial armadas ever to take to the skies. While the size of these early air assaults would be dwarfed later by the efforts of Bomber Command and the US Eighth Air Force with their thousand-plane raids, the *Luftwaffe* presence in British airspace at this time was almost overwhelming – as Fighter Command knew all too well.

The shift in attitude toward the women was sharply reflected in the fact that now reference to the discrepancy in pay rate seemed to imply *criticism* of the discrimination against women. The *Evening Standard* reported on 26 August 1940 in an article about the ATA generally and focusing more on the men, that: 'The pay for the job is £500 a year. Women who do the same work are paid about £300.'[12]

Two months later the same newspaper also reported that the women of the ATA had 'delivered hundreds of aircraft to the RAF without a serious accident and with only one minor casualty – a cut over one eye'.[13] The fact that they would soon be authorised to fly Hurricanes was reported with enthusiasm rather than approbation. Writing at roughly the same time, the *Daily Sketch* proudly described the women pilots whose photographs it published as 'fine faces'. The article explained that the faces belonged to 'a band of brave, skilled British women who are greatly helping the war effort by ferrying RAF machines from factories to flying fields and so releasing more men for action in our fighters and bombers'.[14]

As the war continued, the news coverage of the women tended to become an integral part of the general news coverage of the ATA as a whole. The tone of the reporting was consistently positive, often stressing the risks in unarmed aircraft, the work in open-cockpits in the cold and rain, and the long hours the pilots worked. One article concluded: 'the glamour which goes with the fighting forces is not for them. But a similar brand of courage is necessary for the job.'[15]

In January 1942 a documentary film about the ATA was released showing a day in the life of a ferry pilot and focusing on two male pilots, one of them American. Both of the pilots who 'starred' in the film were real, active ATA pilots. The film-crew spent a great deal of time with the ATA and recorded the activities of the ATA factually and accurately, albeit within a contrived structure. None of the occurrences were fabricated, but they did not occur spontaneously in the course of the one day's work allegedly filmed either. The women pilots play a very secondary role in the film; in a short sequence the pilots of a women's pool are shown going out to their taxi Ansons, and later two women pilots are shown collecting training aircraft at the same field from which the men collect Spitfires. The role of the women is definitely subordinate to that of the men in this film.

The following month a Royal visit was the source of yet more positive publicity for the ATA, and as text and photos testify 'particular interest was shown by the Queen in the women's section'. The Queen also took a keen interest in the ATS, WRNS and WAAF, but apparently in consequence the press made rather a fuss about the women again for a period afterwards, including printing very flattering eulogies and poems.

In September 1942 the ATA celebrated its third anniversary, and again the occasion was exploited for publicity. (The ATA was not run by former airline executives for nothing!) While the emphasis during the anniversary was on the accomplishments of the ATA as a whole, the visit of Mrs Roosevelt a month later swung attention back to the women's division specifically. By chance, Lettice Curtis was at the review and she was at the time in the midst of training on four-engined aircraft – a fact that consequently became known to the press. At once this became a topic for headlines such as 'Mrs Roosevelt meets Halifax Girl Pilot' and 'Girl Flies Halifax'.[16]

By now a consistent pattern had emerged: the press reported very favourably on the successes of the ATA as a whole, with special – but not undue – reference to the role played by women. A good example of this is a long article in the *Picture Post* in September 1944. The magazine placed a full-page photo of an attractive woman pilot in flying kit combing her fingers through her long hair on its cover – but devoted the bulk of its internal text to the men. The article claimed that 'the organisation now works with almost mathematical precision', and ended by asserting simply it is doing a grand job'.[17]

Admittedly, the members of the ATA remember the press attention lavished on the women somewhat differently. Cheeseman felt that: 'throughout the war there was a distinct tendency on the part of the Press to glamorise the life of the girl pilot.'[18] But then again, wasn't it comparatively glamorous compared with, say, the life of a land girl, factory worker or nurse?

King felt that the 'press seemed to waver between the homely and the bizarre'.[19] She sites article titles such as 'Flying Grandmothers', or 'Mother Knits While Waiting For Her Bomber', and 'Flying Debs', or 'Atta Girls'. One 'tenacious young man, who very much wanted to get the personal touch' particularly stuck in her mind. He described the Hamble Ferry Pool as 'a stronghold of femininity'. King insists that:

> . . . the girl who landed in a Spitfire, who slipped off her helmet, who sipped a cup of tea, who glanced fearlessly up or shyly down, invariably shook out her golden curls. She was slim, beautiful, nonchalant, devil-may-care, yet modest – and none of us had ever met her![20]

In fairness to the press, there were countless other stories of a similar nature being printed at this time about land girls and factory girls, nurses and the women's Services; it was what the reading public appeared to want. Furthermore, the women would no doubt have been even more enraged if they had been described as plain, fat, dull and timid or as crude, loose and forward. The photos prove all too convincingly that a great many of the women in the ATA were indeed young and attractive, and others were in fact mothers and grandmothers, while many of the women *did* knit while waiting for their aircraft. The press was not distorting anything by trying to give their readers a 'human interest' story.

Not that there *never* was any exaggeration. The above mentioned film about the ATA included a sequence in which a German aircraft attacks an ATA Anson. While this did happen more than once, it is not credible that the British possessed captured German film footage, which documented an attack on an ATA taxi Anson from the perspective of the German aircraft involved. The sequence was almost certainly staged, and it is fair to say that the film consciously stretched the truth for the sake of drama.

Du Cros provides another example of distorting the truth slightly. During an interview at Hatfield, the women pilots were asked to pick up their parachutes and run to their aeroplanes. 'We said, "what, scramble? To Tiger Moths?" The press replied in the affirmative, and so – absurd as they knew it to be – the ATA women ran in their new creaking flying suits and their new stiff fur lined flying boots carrying their 30lb parachutes. When they came panting back, the press said: 'We didn't get that very well, please do it again." '[21] Undoubtedly, the women were also allowed to brush out their hair and apply make-up before being photographed too. But these minor alterations to reality were standard practice at the time, and not only accepted but expected by the public.

In summary, the press coverage of the ATA can best be characterised as positive to flattering, with the women receiving perhaps a disproportionate but not an overwhelming portion of the attention. What strikes the modern reader is the consistent focus on the job the ATA was doing, how it was helping the RAF, and how efficiently that job was being done. The ATA managed the extremely difficult task of turning *not* having adventures into a news story, with a rigorous focus on successful deliveries and low accident rates. This is masterful messaging, to say the least, and something very few organisations succeed in doing. It speaks volumes for the professionalism and discipline of the ATA's management in 'speaking with one voice' and in effectively managing the press, which by nature looks for the exotic, sensational or scandalous. It is hard to escape the impression that d'Erlanger and his staff had what can only be called an outstanding understanding of modern public and press relations, and masterminded a publicity campaign that served the interests of their organisation brilliantly.

Press Coverage of the WAFS, WFTD and WASP

In the United States, the USAAF feared a negative reaction to the employment of women and wanted to maintain a low profile.[22] In the event, however, the USAAF both failed in their objective and misjudged the mood in America at the time. The founding of the WAFS was heralded in the press with a flurry of attention quite disproportionate to the importance of the women in the overall war effort.

Furthermore, this wild enthusiasm was not tempered by the kind of critical comment that had been voiced in the United Kingdom when the first women pilots had been employed. The ATC summarised the situation by saying: 'A public relations problem existed from the outset. It was inherent in the fact that these pilots were women, that they were generally young and not unattractive. The danger of over-glamorisation, excessive sentimentality, and also of scandal was ever present.'[23]

And so the WAFS became front-page news overnight. All national media gave prominent coverage to the WAFS, while every hometown newspaper that could claim one of the 'Originals' featured them prominently. 'The WAFS posed endlessly in groups and individually, inspecting parachutes, planning navigation, climbing in and out of planes.'[24] Nancy Love appeared on the front page of *New York Times Magazine,* in *Cosmopolitan,* and in a full-page close-up in *Life.* If WAFS got fogged in somewhere overnight, it was front-page news in the local papers. Within a short period of time, Nancy Love found herself so in-undated with requests for interviews that she hardly had time to get her job done; she started to refuse interviews.

By October, just one month after the WAFS had been announced, the CO of FERD, Colonel William Tunner, had also had enough. He wrote to the War Department's Bureau of PR complaining that:

> Because the disproportionate publicity which the WAFS has received seems inconsistent with the nature, scope and accomplishment of this squadron; and because the publicity is actually interfering with the operations of the squadron, the Ferrying Division believes that it will be advisable to cease all widespread publicity on the WAFS until definite and substantial results of the experiment may be observed.[25]

His plea had little effect. The publicity 'blitz' continued right into April of the next year. Furthermore, although the furore died down gradually as the novelty of the story wore off, this did not occur before a notice-able pattern had been established and much damage had been done. For a start, 'many of the stories written and disseminated were blatantly incorrect, grossly exaggerated, or just plain fabricated'.[26] Equally typical: the February issue of *Look* ran a series of pictures showing the girls not just zipping up their flight-suits but applying make-up and the like. Nancy Love was picked as one of the six American women in public life with 'The Most Beautiful Legs'.[27] Furthermore, Nancy had been requested to give 'cheese-cake shots' showing lots of leg or a bare shoulder.[28] Thus from the start, the women pilots were treated not so much as a war story but as a glamour story. The emphasis was not on what the women were doing to win the war, but on their attractiveness. The facts were only incidental – if they were accurately provided at all.

In February 1943, less than six months after the WAFS had been launched, Hollywood jumped on the bandwagon. A film went into production 'about the WAFS'. This was not to be a documentary, however, or even a docu-drama along the lines of the film *Ferry Pilot* about the ATA described above, but a regular Hollywood film. It had a fictionalised story line (love story) and actors and actresses rather than real ferry pilots starred in it. Not only did this film contain the usual Hollywood travesties of women emerging from their cockpits after alleged adventures and mishaps in perfect coiffeur and make-up, but also managed to make errors that grated on every pilot's nerves – things like standing a P-38 on its nose despite it having tricycle gear.

Most damaging of all, the focus of the film was on the emotional life of the women pilots. One could say the WAFS was only the setting rather than the content of the film. Worse: the film portrayed the women as irresponsible and emotional (not to say hysterical) young things. Their contribution to the war effort was not even a theme. On the contrary, 'their personal problems weigh more than their careers in the air, they live in an atmosphere of petty bickering, [and] things get so bad that their commander resigns in shame'.[29] Thus, the film was not only completely fictional, it also conveyed a negative image of the WAFS even if this was not its intention. If fact, Hollywood appears to have been oblivious to the possibility that it was inappropriate to portray women holding responsible and dangerous jobs in wartime as obsessed with their private lives.

The making of the film, however, fit in with the ongoing 'media-hype' about the women pilots generally. When a WAFS went to California on duty, she was treated like a celebrity. She was booked into 'the swankiest hotel on the West Coast'. The next day she was introduced to one star after another, including Katherine Hepburn and Spencer Tracy, who asked her out to the set of Stormy Weather. Here, she met more celebrities, including Marlene Dietrich, Ginger Rogers, Baron von Rothschild, Ingrid Bergman and Gary Cooper. She was taken to dinner by Bob Hope, and invited to appear on the Philip Morris radio programme as guest star. She was on the air for five minutes – reading from a script.[30]

In the face of this kind of attention, it is hardly surprising that Nancy Love's efforts to emphasise the hard work that the women pilot's were doing were futile. It made little difference what she said, she was just asked for a 'big smile' and 'more leg please'. Under the circumstances, it is perhaps also not surprising that the Army was more than a little annoyed – and increasingly paranoid about the risk of scandal. Certainly, it is to the credit of the WAFS that despite this attention and the craving of the press for a good story, there never was a whiff of scandal, but the image of being America's most glamorous and elite auxiliary service had been firmly and fatally established.

The WFTD, Jacqueline Cochran's training squadron, had been launched at the same time as the WAFS, but Cochran carefully kept her girls out of the limelight at this stage. For a start, it was November before she actually had her recruits together. They were then collected at an improvised school located on a civilian airfield and without any kind of uniform. With the WAFS providing such photogenic material, there was no need for the press to pay any attention to this first class of female flight cadets. To be fair, however, it was also Cochran's policy. She told the first class that 'there would be no publicity, no glory. Just hard work'.[31] She stressed that they were an experiment and that nothing would be announced until they had proved that they could make the grade.

As the time came for the women to graduate (thereby proving that women could successfully be trained to fly the Army way at an Army installation), Cochran launched her publicity campaign. In the interests of ensuring the best press coverage possible, Cochran even delayed the graduation ceremonies by several weeks – disregarding FERD's desperate need for pilots, which had already taken three months longer to train than Cochran had promised. Of what interest were the needs of the USAAF (in the midst of its first air offensive against Nazi Germany and incurring unprecedented losses in daylight raids) when they interfered with efforts to assure that Cochran's 'girls' got as much attention as Love's?

The first WFTD graduation therefore became a huge publicity event. 'Reporters were everywhere. The local papers were nearly smothered by the United Press, Associated Press and Movietone newsreels.'[32] A 'great human interest story' was offered by the fact that one of the graduating women was the daughter of an Admiral; the Admiral was flown in for the event and provided the press with the mouth-watering image of a proud father pinning pilot's wings on his daughter's breast. 'Father-daughter, navy-army: the picture was in every major paper the next morning.'[33] How lucky for Cochran that the graduates had improvised uniforms at their own cost and scrounged up unofficial wings to make those pictures possible; Cochran hadn't bothered about such important details despite her craving for good press.

But Cochran was nothing if not persistent and having got off to a good start (despite her own inadequacies) she kept trying. In July 1943 a cinematography team was sent to Avenger Field to produce both stills and movies of training for the major news services. For the sake of the camera the girls were provided with matching uniforms for doing callisthenics – despite the continuing lack of real uniforms. Again, two particularly pretty girls – 'winsome blonds with pigtails' – were featured, one (Shirley Shade) on the cover of *Life Magazine,* and the other (Leonora Horton) on the cover of *Army-Navy Screen Magazine.*[34]

A few months later, the girls in training were subjected to yet another barrage of press attention. One of the victims described it as follows:

> ... someone decided we needed some publicity. Newsreel camera crews came down to Sweetwater. First they showed us at Physical Education, then they showed us sunbathing. Then they piled us

into the cattle cars [buses] and took us to some lake about fifty miles out of town.[35]

In short, the publicity was focused exclusively on the sexuality of the girls. The photographers were interested in showing as much skin as was possible in prudish America, and if that meant taking the girls swimming to a place otherwise completely off-limits and unknown to them, then that was fine. Their qualifications, their growing competence, and their function were not of particular interest to the press. Their eventual contribution to the war effort appears completely irrelevant, not to say irritating. Who wants to think of pretty, sunbathing young girls possibly getting killed in an air crash?

Very likely, the 'someone' who had launched this latest publicity campaign was again Cochran herself. She had just successfully taken charge of the entire women pilots' programme with the merging of the WAFS and WFTD into the WASP in July 1943. Shortly afterwards she had finally convinced General Arnold to apply to Congress for the militarisation of the women pilots as a separate organisation. Cochran was now working extra hard to drum up even more press coverage for her programme.

In addition to seeking more publicity for the training at Avenger Field, Cochran wanted to be sure the press knew that her pilots did more than 'just' ferry aircraft. (All the attention given to the WAFS had been before Cochran took control of the programme, after all, and had given Mrs Love and not Ms Cochran the prominent billing.) In early October 1943, Cochran therefore invited reporters down to Camp Davis to show off her first target-towing unit. Cochran's intended message might have been that her women pilots were being trained to free men for combat duties, but her unconscious message was that they were 'pretty girls' – she appeared in a flowered print dress with open-toed sandals.[36]

While the newspapers dutifully reported on the fact that women pilots in addition to ferrying aircraft were now performing at least six other 'highly specialised jobs for the Army Air Forces', the reporters also made repeated reference to the physical features of the WASP. The papers seemed incapable of quoting any WASP without describing her as 'pretty', 'attractive', 'blonde', brown-eyed' or whatever. [37]

One month later, in November 1943, Cochran's selection of a uniform for the WASP was occasion for more press coverage. The *New York Times* ran pictures of Cochran herself modelling the uniform (only Cochran, of course, because none of the ordinary WASP had them yet). The article made a point of reporting that 'WASPs averaged four inches narrower in the hips than other selected women's groups because of the exercise and training they get'.[38] The source of this fascinating piece of information could only have been Cochran, with her obsession for measuring every conceivable part of her girls' bodies from head to foot. It remains unclear whether she thought this information would frighten the *Luftwaffe* and Japanese Imperial air forces or assist her girls to get jobs as models if they washed out as pilots.

It is not surprising given this pattern of press coverage, that when just after the New Year in 1944, a WASP who had been training on B-17s married, it was her marriage to a fellow B-17 pilot, not her competence as a pilot that attracted media attention. Photographers swamped the little Ohio town to get pictures of the bride being given away by the base CO – not to get pictures of her at the controls of American's workhorse bomber.[39]

In March 1944, Cochran staged the award of an Air Medal to one of the original WAFS, now one of her WASP, during a graduation ceremony at Avenger Field. The recipient herself felt she was being exploited purely for 'propaganda' purposes. She insisted her own accomplishments had been nothing special (and the record bears her out on this) and stated: 'it was a tool to get our militarization through Congress.'[40]

Cochran needed all the good publicity she could get, because by this time it was evident that the WASP militarisation bill was in trouble. Large portions of the press had already turned against the WASP. This shift in mood was in part the result of a change in the ground swell of public opinion.

At the start of the war, any attempt to assist the war effort – no matter how insignificant or illogical – had been praised. While men were being called to the colours, women were mobilised to support their men by helping 'on the Home Front'. Whether on the farms or in the home, they were portrayed as part of the great national effort – but always in the supportive rather than the leading role. What was more, the more unusual the task the women assumed, the more heroic the woman's 'sacrifice' was presumed to be. The implication was that the greater the deviation from traditional roles, the greater the sacrifice for the nation and victory. Thus, 'women in factories developing war materials were all portrayed as heroines dedicated to the cause of freedom'.[41]

With regard to the women's Services the situation was even more pronounced. They had been created at the height of the national emergency despite deep-seated, conservative opposition. The justification had been that they represented 'exceptional' measures, which testified to America's flexibility, creativity and dedication to winning the war. To emphasise this point and keep criticism to a minimum, the women in these services were consistently portrayed in the US media as women first and soldiers second. A six-page *Life* article about US Army nurses serving in the Pacific, for example, showed them as if they were vacationing in the South Seas. As with the WASP at Avenger, the photographers preferred pictures of the women in bathing suits or at sport rather than showing them doing serious tasks such as assisting in surgery or dealing with casualties in a ward.

Thus, even during the most uncertain period of the war, when the US military was anxious to mobilise all available manpower resources and increasingly willing to *employ* women in new capacities, the media carefully maintained the *image* of women being 'the same as ever'. The press was careful not to 'offend' anyone by depicting women in uniform in roles too removed from the ones with which conservative readers were comfortable. Furthermore, *if* they *were* in unusual roles, then – so the press was careful to imply – it was only out of patriotism and love for their men on the fighting front. The overriding theme in American media portrayals of women during the war was thus that no matter what job they were 'temporarily' doing for the sake of the nation, they retained their essential femininity. The women were depicted as essentially domestic creatures, helping their country only in ways that were compatible with remaining nice, docile, sweet and pretty girls.

By 1944 the situation had changed in as much as victory already seemed certain and so a return to 'normalcy' was on the agenda – preferably sooner rather than later. Americans have never had a long attention span and anything that costs American lives will – sooner or later – be called into question by the American public; the Second World War was no exception. By early 1944 the shock of Pearl Harbor had worn off, and the costs of the war in both dollars and lives increasingly dominated the public debate. Military appropriations bills were no longer being rubber-stamped by Congress. Even the strategy and tactics of America's military, once praised even in humiliating defeat, were now – despite steady success – being subjected to critical analysis. Battle losses were criticised and the war itself was increasingly questioned. There was a growing – though still minority – portion of the population that wanted to 'bring the boys home' *now*. A larger portion of the population wanted to win the war rapidly, and turn its attention to the post-war world as soon as possible. The US media both contributed to and reflected these attitudes.

With regard to women, the message was uniform: it was time for them to return 'home' too – meaning return to domestic work. Women were already being laid off from the factories, and their jobs made available to returning veterans. The press was starting to campaign actively for all women to resume their 'natural' place in society – church, children and cooking. 'Women in all aspects of the war effort, once celebrated, were now attacked by the media as self-serving individuals who jeopardised the abilities of returning male soldiers to survive the post-war economy.'[42]

In this environment, the idea of commissioning women pilots into the USAAF was an anachronism. It was easy for the press to seize upon the unauthorised allocations for the women pilots' training programme as just another example of a wasteful, bloated, arrogant military. The fact that WASP were already attending Officer Training School was another red flag for the press, suggesting outright contempt for Congress. At a time when women everywhere were being urged to return to their 'natural' domestic duties, the press was particularly offended by the prospect of spending vast amounts of tax dollars to train women to fly military aircraft when there were so many men who could already do it.

Evidently, the press was fed enough information from inside sources to know that many WASP failed to meet ATC flying standards at graduation from Avenger Field and had failed to graduate from pursuit training. Those who could fly the 'hotter ships', it was claimed, often didn't want to 'because they're a challenge, particularly on the part of those who have husbands and children'.[43] The reference to husbands and children might have been gratuitous, but there can be no doubt that over a hundred WASP had chosen *not* to transition onto pursuits and were therefore being transferred back to Training Command. The press further more got hold of a number of sources who testified to the fact that many WASP (particularly the original WAFS) did not want militarisation.[44] Cochran's arbitrary leadership style, particularly transferring WASP against their wishes, was cited as one of the reasons why the women resisted militarisation. The press, by one means or another, also knew about Cochran's interference in Command decisions and her refusal to integrate her corps of pilots into the WAC.

Soon, however, these facts had been distorted beyond all recognition. The inadequacies of training at Avenger Field for the very high standards of the FERD were twisted by a hostile press into evidence that despite the expensive training, 'most' of the 'girls' still couldn't fly at all. The entrance requirement of thirty-five hours flying time – in fact more than male cadets – was transformed maliciously into the total qualifications of the WASP, so that they were referred to as 'thirty-five hour wonders'.[45] The long-since-rescinded order grounding WASP during their menstrual period was also turned against them, when the press alleged that the women were regularly grounded on a monthly basis.

But the most serious and persistent argument against the WASP was that they were stealing 'cushy' domestic jobs away from American men.

Again and again, it was the plight of the male pilots, whose places the WASP were allegedly unjustly and unfairly stealing, that aroused the greatest indignation. The headlines screamed: 'Army Passes Up Jobless Pilots to Train Wasps: Prefers Women to Older, Experienced Flyers.'[46] The articles claimed such things as:

> With 5,000 experienced airplane pilots looking for jobs as a result of the liquidation of the civil aeronautic commission's training program, the government is training more than 1,000 young women, at an estimated cost of 6 million dollars, as ferry pilots for the army.[47]

Based on the press reports and lobbying efforts, members of Congress concluded that: 'Experienced male fliers with more than 2,000 hours in the air, may soon be cleaning windshields and servicing planes for glamorous women flyers who only have 35 hours of flying time.'[48]

Cochran herself also came under criticism. The most complimentary descriptions called her such things as 'glamorous, dashing ... ex-beauty shop operator'.[49] The less complimentary comments implied that Cochran routinely seduced high-ranking generals and government officials just to get her own way. The tone of articles was reflected in Congress when Representative Isak went on record saying:

> Of course pretty Jacqueline Cochran wants to be a colonel and have 2,500 girls under her. But how about Mrs Oveta Culp Hobby of the WACS, who is not only a colonel but has 63,000 women in her organisation? It won't help the war effort one bit to put these girls into mannikins' uniforms.[50]

The designer uniforms presented a particularly easy target in the hate campaign against the WASP. They made it obvious that the WASP were something 'special' – i.e. privileged, elitist, expensive, and glamorous. The more glamorous the service in the WASP appeared, the easier it was to portray it as something 'social', rather than something related to the war effort. All previous press coverage of the WASP, of course, only served to support this thesis.

In summary, the women pilots were depicted as a waste of taxpayer's money, unskilled, spoilt, and – most offensive of all – stealing jobs from qualified men. In consequence of all these factors, they were portrayed as an outright detriment to the war effort – devouring resources that could better be spent on more tanks for the upcoming invasion of Europe, while keeping really useful, qualified (male) pilots grounded. Reader reaction was understandably: 'If these girls were patriotic, they'd resign.'[51]

Despite the increasingly vehement and insulting tone of the campaign against the 'powder puff brigade', Cochran retained rigid control of her own public relations. She forbade the WASP and their relatives from responding to the unjust allegations against the WASP. She even denied her subordinates and their relatives the freedom to exercise their democratic rights by contacting their own Congressional representatives. The success of her public relations campaign can be judged by the results. The WASP militarisation bill was not only defeated in Congress, but the hostility aroused against the WASP continued to reverberate through the press despite that defeat.

Now, after the battle in Congress was lost, Cochran tried to mobilise public opinion in favour of her programme through the women pilot's organisation, the Ninety-Nines. More baffling still, now – when it could do no earthly good – she suggested the WASP write to their Congressmen. These efforts only further baited the still active anti-WASP lobby.

Cochran's next public relations coup was the release of her report on the WASP. As described previously, this report released in early August 1944, roughly six weeks after the defeat of the militarisation bill, insisted that the programme must be militarised 'soon' or disbanded. The report was widely interpreted in the press as an ultimatum. As such, it was further ammunition against both Cochran personally as a power-hungry, spoilt brat who could not take 'no' as an answer and as a good excuse for getting rid of the entire wasteful, superfluous and offensive programme. In short, Cochran's public relations effort succeeded in igniting a new campaign in the press, this time calling for the outright disbanding of the entire WASP rather than just the training programme. It was a campaign that was as successful as it was short-lived. Less than two months later the fate of the WASP was sealed.

In retrospect, it is evident just how badly the WAFS/WASP suffered from the absence of professional and centralised public relations-management. The initial press coverage was completely out of control, as the frantic pleas from FERD Commander Tunner to the War Office's Press Department testify. One has images of defence bureaucrats lost in the windowless maze of the Pentagon being completely unprepared for the media furore that greeted the WAFS and then even less capable of controlling or guiding it.

Apparently, the woman in the Pentagon responsible for handling the publicity related to the women's services, Hazel Taylor, was hired at the request of Cochran. What her qualifications were is unclear. Other Cochran appointees such as Mrs Deaton had no qualifications whatsoever for the job to which they were appointed. It is therefore hard to judge just how qualified Ms Taylor was; competent she patently was not.

FERD felt compelled to complain to her about the 'fictional situations and technical inaccuracies' appearing in the press. Major Gordon Rust and Lt William Gaddings of FERD specifically objected to a serial entitled 'Lady with Wings' and articles in *Look, Liberty* and *This Week*.[52] Taylor's response is a testimony to helplessness in the vein of 'free speech is worth battling for' and asking 'what emphasis may we suggest to writers?'[53] Whether Taylor was Cochran's appointee or just the Army's, she obviously didn't have a clue about how to handle a public relations campaign. As a result, the image of the American women pilots was created not by the organisation for which they worked, but by the press itself. The image was one of sexy glamour, even before Cochran started to play a more active personal role.

With Cochran's active involvement in public relations, the image of glamour girls was reinforced. Her emphasis on the 'natty' uniforms, her own personal appearances in furs, accompanied by her French maid, or in flower-print dresses did nothing to convey the work-a-day reality of the WASP or its relevance for the war effort. Nor did she make any effort to curb the press' craving for female flesh.

Equally important, the accounts of the WASP who were subjected to the attentions of camera-crews and reporters indicate that they were given no guidance whatsoever on what they were supposed to do or say – beyond observing the Security Act. In other words, no one from WASP headquarters was present during press interviews. No one was standing by, suggesting to reporters that maybe they should take pictures of the girls in ground school or the Link trainer rather than in shorts or bathing suits doing nothing related to their jobs.

Cochran's management of publicity surrounding the militarisation bill hardly requires comment. The saddest feature of her handling of the campaign is that she appears to have completely misjudged her own competence – so much so that she didn't seem to realise she was in trouble until it was too late. There is no other explanation for her prohibition against writing to Congress before the bill went to the vote and her suggestion that WASP do so afterwards. Cochran appears to have believed right up until the vote was cast, that she still had everything under control.

Her subsequent blunder, the public release of a report on the WASP, in which she 'suggested' the organisation be disbanded entirely if she did not get what she wanted (militarisation) 'soon', is a fitting climax to the story of WASP public relations. This last strategic public relations initiative boomeranged back on the WASP and precipitated their de-activation. Everything that followed was just a swan song.

Notes:

1   Curtis, 19.
2   Letter to the Editor by Harold Collings, The Aeroplane, 5 Jan. 1940.
3   The Aeroplane, 5 Jan. 1940.
4   The Aeroplane, 2 Feb.1940.
5   The Daily Telegraph, 24 Feb. 1940.
6   The Daily Telegraph, 26 Feb. 1940.
7   The Daily Telegraph, 4 March 1940.
8   The Aeroplane, 2 Feb. 1940.
9   Evening Standard, 23 Aug. 1940.
10   The Star, 21 Sept. 1940.
11   The Star, 21 Sept. 1940.
12   Evening Standard, 26 Aug. 1940.
13   Evening Standard, 26 Oct. 1940.
14   Daily Sketch, 9 Oct. 1940.
15   Unidentified news clipping, dated 5 May 1941.
16   Curtis, 173.
17   Picture Post, 16 Sept. 1944.
18   Cheeseman, 71.
19   King, 121.
20   King, 121.
21   Du Cros, 36.
22   Merryman, 56.
23   ATC report quoted in Simbeck, 168.
24   Granger, 57–8.
25   Tunner quoted in Simbeck, 168.
26   Rickman, 80.
27   Verges, 51, Simbeck, 147.
28   Rickman, 79.
29   Merryman, 72.
30   Based on the Teresa James' Diary as published in Rickman, 149–51.
31   Verges, 73.
32   Verges, 86.
33   Verges, 87.
34   Verges, 127.
35   Cole, 32.
36   Granger, 198.
37   Washington Herald Tribune, 25 Oct. 1943.
38   Cole, 44.
39   Verges, 153.

40 Rickman, 213.
41 Merryman, 45.
42 Merryman, 45.
43 Washington DC News, 12 June 1944.
44 Granger, 341.
45 Merryman, 65.
46 Merryman, 63.
47 Merryman, 63–4.
48 Merryman, 68.
49 Granger, 333.
50 Granger, 343.
51 Merryman, 65.
52 Granger, 68.
53 Granger, 68.

CHAPTER FOURTEEN

Captains and Commanders

THE ROLE OF PERSONALITIES IN SHAPING THE FATE OF THE ATA AND THE WASP

For all the importance of organisational structures, missions, composition and ethos, there can be no denying that individuals in key positions have an impact on historical developments. Certainly, individuals are themselves restricted in their field of action by the greater forces around them. No one person alone is really in the position to 'change the course of history'. Still, the timing and pace of developments, as well as the shape and colour of events can be much influenced by the acts and errors of individual players. The story of the ATA and WASP is no exception, whereby one person stands out above all the other actors as the most colourful and most dynamic: Jacqueline Cochran. The story, however, must start with the men who made it all possible.

The Men who Made it Possible

No woman would have flown military aircraft during the Second World War if there had not been men willing to give them the chance to do so. In the United Kingdom there appears to have been a consensus in the Air Ministry – even before the outbreak of the war – that women would have to be employed in whatever capacity practicable. An announcement in the House of Commons that women would be used to ferry aircraft in a 'National Emergency' had been made as early as May 1939. Less than a month after the start of the war, on 25 September 1939, the Director General of Civil Aviation indicated in a letter to the Air Ministry that the use of women pilots was already under consideration. On 14 November Miss Pauline Gower was officially requested to start recruiting the first women pilots for the ATA, and on 1 December 1939 she had been appointed head of the women's section.

Throughout this process, Sir Francis Shelmerdine, the Director General of Civil Aviation, had consistently advocated the use of women in the ATA, and – it appears – so did Gerard d'Erlanger himself. Other key figures enabling women to fly service aircraft in the United Kingdom were BOAC/ATA Chief Instructor MacMillan, and the Ministers of Aircraft Production Lord Beaverbrook, Lt-Col Moore Brabazon and Sir Stafford Cripps, all of whom in one way or another smoothed the way for women in the ATA with regard to opportunities and/or compensation. On the whole, however, it must be said that no single man played an outstanding role, and many contributed to creating the level playing field that enabled the women to prove their capabilities.

The situation was, again, quite different on the other side of the Atlantic. Here, the tradition of women in the military was less convincing, the official resistance to the use of women in the military was far greater, and the cultural opposition to women in uniform much more pervasive. Despite the best lobbying efforts of Eleanor Roosevelt, women would never have flown with/for the USAAF if General Arnold had not been won over to the cause.

General Arnold was not, however, ever an *advocate* of women pilots. He long resisted the idea of using them in the USAAF. He had stated unequivocally in August 1941 that there was no military need for women pilots whatsoever. He deflected Cochran's persistent attempts to get him to approve a women pilot's programme by sending her off to recruit women pilots for the ATA. He continued to reject requests from the Air Transport Command for the employment of women pilots right up until September 1942.

Arnold didn't so much want women in his Air Forces as give into pressure at a time when he was facing a serious shortage of manpower and had many other worries as well. In August 1942 he still seemed to be seeking 'every possible way to avoid using women as ferry pilots'.[1] But in early September 1942, General Arnold apparently decided that opposing the use of women was taking more effort than giving in. He gave in first to the nagging of FERD, and then – after Cochran had thrown a fit in his office about not being informed or involved in the WAFS – gave in with respect to a training programme as well. Having done that, however, he summoned his subordinates, and with evident exasperation ordered them to work out some way to merge the programmes and find some way to work with Cochran.

Arnold, by this time the most powerful man in the Air Forces, had long been considered a 'maverick'. He had chosen aviation at a time when it was not taken seriously. In fact, Arnold learned to fly in 1911 from Orville Wright personally, and was only the second officer in the US Army to become a pilot. He worked long and hard for an independent air force, a dream that was not realised until two years after the end of the Second World War. Before that, however, he often chaffed under Army authority and restrictions, feeling (not without justification) that the potential of the Air Force was inadequately recognised by the senior officers of the Army that had come up through the infantry, artillery and cavalry. Even as Chief of the Army Air Corps (1938), he often had to work hard for the interests of his new branch of service against the traditionalists.

Arnold's style, however, was to avoid confrontation as much as possible. That he largely succeeded in getting what he wanted was in part due to a friendly personality that won him the epitaph 'Smiling' or 'Happy' – shortened to 'Hap' – but it also often entailed using somewhat devious routes. If something was important to him, but he was uncertain of getting the approval he needed, he generally found ways of going ahead with it anyway – without official authorisation. This was the method he applied to the development of the B-29 Superfortress, to the initiation of the CPT programme, and to the WFTD programme. None of these programmes were authorised until after the fact. It has been suggested that 'the chaos in the early days of the war suited Arnold just fine. It gave him every excuse to operate outside channels, which had always been his preferred modus operandi'.[2]

During the entire existence of the WAFS/WFTD/WASP, General Arnold was the most senior officer in the United States with responsibility for the air war. He was responsible for both theatres of operations, recruitment, training, supply, transport and R&D. At no time was the women's pilot programme a significant or critical component of the war effort. Indeed, when one considers how tiny the programme was, it is surprising that Arnold paid it as much attention as he did. This 'attention', however, was confined mostly to public-relations appearances with Cochran at graduation ceremonies or the like – in effect, capitalising on the press attention already being showered on the women for the benefit of his own agenda.

There is little evidence that Arnold took an active role in shaping either the training programme of the WFTD, or the employment of women pilots within the Air Forces. Arnold had issued a directive in the autumn of 1942 that the Army intended to experiment with the use of women pilots, and after that the details of running the programme were delegated to Cochran and those officers in whose command the women were employed. Two years later he closed down the programme as abruptly as he had launched it, apparently without any qualms or regret. Arnold's priorities never wavered: he wanted what was best for the Air Force and the United States. Women pilots were at best a means to an end, and at worst a troublesome experiment.

Although Arnold had the final say over whether women were given a chance to fly for the USAAF or not, given Arnold's own reluctance to employ them it is also fair to say that there would never have been a women pilot's programme in the USAAF without the efforts of Generals Olds, George and Tunner. It was these three senior officers of the ATC and FERD that so persistently demanded the right to employ qualified women pilots in FERD that they wore down Arnold's resistance to the idea. If Arnold had not already given in to General George with regard to the WAFS, it is very unlikely he would have succumbed to Cochran's demands for a women's training programme. For a start, Cochran herself would not have stormed into his office in a rage but rather continued to enjoy life as the honorary head of the American women's branch of the ATA.

It was then-Colonel (later General) Tunner, who proved the most consistent and determined advocate of women pilots throughout the existence of the programme – always provided the women met his high standards for flying. It was Tunner who worked with Nancy Love to develop the concept for the WAFS in the first place, Tunner who put his signature on the proposal, and Tunner who kept the pressure up to get it approved. Once women were employed by FERD, Tunner consistently supported their right to transition to ever more difficult aircraft types. He insisted that every pilot be allowed to progress in accordance with their abilities. It was Tunner who specifically asked Love and her deputy to train on the B-17 and ferry one across the Atlantic. Tunner encouraged Love to qualify on as many types of aircraft as she could, and deliberately trained women on aircraft considered difficult, such as the P-39, to show male pilots that it was just a matter of technique.

Tunner's attitude to women appears to have been very similar to d'Erlanger and MacMillan's: he looked on everyone as a pilot first and a man or woman second. Any pilot who could meet his high standards was welcome in his command – and he didn't care if they were female, one-armed, three-headed or anything else. The chief historian of the ATC described Tunner in the official history as follows:

> . . . somewhat arrogant, brilliant, competent. He was the kind of officer whom a junior officer is well advised to salute when approaching his desk. His loyalty to the organisation he

commanded was notable, and so was his ability to maintain the morale of his men . . . He defended them against all comers, and was every whit as ready as General Olds to stand up against higher echelons when the welfare of his command was threatened.[3]

It is important to note that Tunner went on from FERD to command the airlift operations to China from India over the Himalayas, and was also the chief architect of the Berlin Airlift 1948–9. He was without doubt one of the most brilliant organisational minds in the USAAF and an outstanding officer.

He also had a reputation as a 'non-conformist', and for being prepared to act on his own initiative and authority. In his memoirs he describes the following incident:

> Actually our first passengers as such were wounded paratroopers, whom we returned to the States from the combat zones. At first, the medical department was far from co-operative with our first efforts at air evacuation of the wounded. Finally the ATC just went ahead and loaded some wounded soldiers in a United States-bound plane without specific authorization . . . After we did it the first time, with splendid results, it became easier to get permission to do it . . . but as we went along, the operation became more and more standardized. A flight surgeon would check the patients out as capable of flying, and to each plane a crew of a nurse and a male attendant would be attached.[4]

Tunner was fully aware that the officers of the ATC were referred to as 'Allergic to Combat', 'Army of Terrified Civilians' and 'other unpleasant, sometimes unprintable epithets'.[5] However, Tunner set out to prove 'that air transport is a science in itself; to be carried out at its maximum efficiency air transport must be run by men who know the techniques of air transport and who are dedicated to air transport – professionals'.[6] And he did.

Such a cold-blooded professional was completely unimpressed with either the political connections or the alleged charms of Jacqueline Cochran. Tunner and Cochran clashed frequently in the course of the two years during which they had to work together. Tunner was determined to fulfil his mission efficiently and to maintain his standards. While this opened opportunities to women that they otherwise would not have had, it also meant that he was not prepared to bend rules or lower standards for women either. Tunner protested sharply when women were taken out of his command and sent on other, allegedly 'temporary', duties without his consent. He objected vigorously for having to pay the salary of women assigned to duties outside his Command. He was furious to discover that Cochran had let women pilots go without pay for months on end because she didn't know how – or was too lazy – to transfer her pilots via the correct channels. But nothing infuriated Tunner more than the orders that made him retain in his command graduates from Avenger Field, who, he felt, failed to meet his Command standards. He rightly called this policy a 'discriminatory limitation upon the Command's freedom of action'and pointed out that it set the women pilots apart, creating resentment among male pilots.[7] Tunner was consistent in his non-discrimination policy, and it worked two ways as far as he was concerned.

In retrospect, Tunner was prepared to praise the women pilots for their accomplishments. His memoirs, published in 1964 before the WASP had been recognised as veterans, states that 'the women did a magnificent job at home'. He went on to say:

> They freed many men for overseas deliveries. When several had worked up to the point where they were checked out on the most difficult of all ships, the pursuits, we stationed a detachment at the Republic Company on Long Island to fly the P-47s from the factory to the processing station . . . No men were needed there at all. By the end of September 1944, WASPs were delivering three-fifths of all pursuit ships.[8]

Despite this praise for the women themselves, the organisational battles with Cochran left their mark on Tunner. He summarised the WASP programme by stating it was the 'greatest continuing hassle in the Ferrying Division'.[9]

Pauline Gower: The First Lady

While men made it possible for women to fly with the ATA, it is to Pauline Gower's credit that the women's section was so well accepted, successful and smoothly run. The women under her command remember her without exception as being both competent and fair. This is all the more remarkable when one considers that she had been given command of the women's section of the ATA when she was under thirty years of age, and that she had to command women who were older, married, well-connected and in some cases had more flying experience than she. She was not particularly charismatic, but 'she was accepted most happily' by everyone – even such celebrities as Amy Johnson.[10]

This was in part attributable to her apparent lack of ambition. Her primary concern and enthusiasm was 'the acceptance of women as serious contributors to aviation'.[11] And while she may have been young and held no speed or distance records such as Amy Johnson or Jacqueline Cochran did, she had made her living from aviation for five years, flying roughly 2,000 hours and carrying over 30,000 joy-riding passengers. She had also served as one of two female commissioners of the Civil Air Guard. Tact, diplomacy and a keen appreciation of power-politics she had learned practically from the cradle; her father was a Member of Parliament, and she acted as his hostess after her mother's death.

Her leadership style was low-key, never arbitrary or arrogant, but not informal or 'chummy' either.

> She had the ability suddenly to become warmly human, able to joke with anyone immediately after she had told them they must do better or else. At times too she would come down from her inevitably lonely position to find someone to be companionable with, to talk things over with, to tell a few jokes and listen to theirs. And then she would as suddenly go back to her official sanctum and that was that. She would leave the person, whoever it might be, feeling pleased and sparkling, but never for one moment dreaming of taking advantage of her moment of relaxation. In other words, except for her one or two closest friends, she was always the head, whatever she might choose to do.[12]

Like any good leader, she was able to delegate authority, and 'if she delegated authority, then she gave it completely, with full trust and no interference, yet you knew that in an emergency she was there! Strongly and forcibly with you'.[13]

Equally important, Gower was 'always accessible to her pilots and gave them a sympathetic hearing when they came to see her at White Waltham'.[14] When a woman pilot threatened to resign from the ATA because she was removed from Class II aircraft by the Pool Commander after another woman pilot had a minor accident, Gower sent for her immediately. Lucas describes the encounter as follows:

> I went rather nervously into Miss Gower's office and felt myself being scrutinised by her keen blue eyes. She asked me to explain the situation and listened to my point of view, I thought, with a certain sympathy. I think she had had much tougher fights than this over the same sort of thing during the early days. She made

no comment but sent me to see Gerard d'Erlanger, who tried to persuade me that it was for my own good to fly the easier aircraft during the winter. I replied that on joining ATA we had been told to expect no consideration because we were women and accordingly I saw no reason why my good should be considered more than that of the other RAF pilots on the same course. I said I felt I was being secretly 'victimised' because I was a woman . . . He told me to wait and he would talk to Miss Gower.

A few minutes later I was called back and told that they did not want me to feel that there was any victimisation or unfairness and that if my flying reports from Thame were up to the same standard as those of the men, I could go ahead and ferry Class II aircraft.[15]

Yet the really remarkable thing about Gower was that she consistently got what she wanted without making any apparent fuss. Although du Cros felt that she was also capable of 'browbeating' Ministers and Air Marshals 'in the nicest possible way',[16] she moved very cautiously to obtain greater opportunities for her pilots and to expand the women's section as a whole. Progress was only gradual. King felt that 'for someone so intelligent and highly strung, she was the most patient person I ever knew'.[17]

Rosemary de Bunsen felt that women in the ATA 'owed a great deal to her diplomacy and sense of timing, for she had to know how and when to fight or give ground'.[18] Just once, when she by-passsed d'Erlanger to request an expansion of the women's section in early 1940, did she provoke a rebuke from the Director General of Civil Aviation. Fortunately, she managed to excuse herself graciously enough to avoid further repercussions – and any way the RAF had already approved the expansion. Another example of her tact is the way she convinced the RAF to train women on operational aircraft.

She waited for the right moment, and instead of bludgeoning her way in, she asked the Commanding Officer of the Training Flight if he thought his instructors, who were known to be the best in the world, would take on the challenge of training her women ATA pilots up to the standard? It worked![19]

Her fine appreciation of power-politics and the judicious use of pressure is demonstrated by her approach to obtaining equal pay for her women as well. First she persuaded the Directors of ATA to advocate equal pay for the women now that they were cleared to fly all types of aircraft except flying boats. The ATA Director of Services and Personnel met with Sir Stafford Cripps, the Minister of Aircraft Production, to put the case of equal pay to him.

> Sir Stafford, although generally supportive, decided that it was beyond his power to alter the original Treasury ruling. Pauline then took up the challenge and went to see the Minister. It can be imagined that his position remained the same, however, a way around the problem was formulated. It was arranged that Sir Stafford would approach the Treasury, saying that he was likely to be asked in Parliament if women pilots doing exactly the same job as men were being paid less, and if so why? The ploy worked, and when Irene Ward, on the 18th of May, asked the Minister in the House of Commons about women pilots' conditions of pay, he was able to respond by saying that as from June, their salaries would be brought into line with men.[20]

Sometimes, some of Gower's pilots felt she could have pushed things along faster and were impatient for more opportunities. Maybe they were right and things could have been pushed along more vigorously, but the results seem to justify Gower's methods. If things did not go fast enough, still they did move steadily forward and they never ended in disaster as with the WASP.

To the end, Gower retained the respect not only of her pilots but of her superiors as well. On 26 May 1943, roughly a week after the delicate question concerning women pilots' pay had been raised in the House of Commons, Gower was appointed to the Board of Directors of BOAC. She thereby became the first woman to ever be appointed to the Board of Directors of a major, national airline. 'When news that Pauline was to be part of the new Board was announced in Parliament, the Members responded with claps and cheers.'[21] Admittedly, many MPs knew her personally and very possibly her father started the applause, but it is nevertheless a commentary on her ability to retain the respect of everyone she worked with while still getting what she set out to obtain.

Nancy Harkness Love: The First Pilot

There are many similarities between Nancy Harkness Love and Pauline Gower. When Love took over the WAFS she too was under thirty, had substantial flying time (1,200 hours) and had worked in aviation. Twelve years earlier, Love had been the youngest woman in the United States to get a pilot's licence; two years later, she was again the youngest woman to qualify for a commercial licence. Her professional experience in aviation was more varied than Gower's, having worked as a sales-woman for Beechcraft, as a test pilot for Gwinn Aircar Company and having run both flying classes and charters for her husband's aviation company, Inter City. She had even entered a couple of air-races, being placed fifth and second respectively, but soon recognised that this was not her type of flying.

Love was by nature a 'cautious and deliberate' pilot, not daring and showy. Her daughter recounted: 'Dad was a hot pilot. A bit of a cowboy. Mom was careful, deliberate, exacting. They didn't fly a lot together . . . each preferring their own skills and style in the cockpit'.[22] What was more, Nancy Love started to develop 'her own methodical approach to flying that evolved into a routine of carefully written checklists for her pre-flight checks and close attention to details of flight'.[23]

Such qualities made her an ideal ferry pilot and she got her first ex-perience with the task when delivering private aircraft from the factory to the new owners. Then, in 1940, she ferried aircraft to the Canadian border for the RAF/RCAF. It was at this time that she also made an attempt to arouse official interest in the systematic use of women pilots for ferrying by writing a letter to General Olds. Although Olds, a sincere advocate of women pilots, was receptive to the idea, at this point in time, Arnold still opposed women in the Air Force, and so the idea was shelved.

Like Gower, Love came from a 'good' family without financial worries, and she was known for being a perfect lady. Despite her early initiative with regard to women pilots, in the event she obtained her appointment to the WAFS via family connections rather than personal effort. Her husband, Robert Love, was a Major in the Reserves of the USAAF and when called to active duty served in the ATC. A chance encounter with Tunner led the latter to contact Love with regard to hiring women pilots for FERD. In Tunner's own words this is what happened:

> One of our officers, Major Robert M. Love, later deputy commander of ATC, was catching a drink at the same time as I, and he audibly hoped that his wife had gotten to work all right that morning. Turned out that the Loves were living in Washington, but Mrs Love was commuting to her job in Baltimore *by plane*.
>
> 'Good Lord,' I said, 'I'm combing the woods for pilots, and here's one right under my nose. Are there many more women like your wife?'
>
> 'Why don't you ask her?' he said, and a meeting was arranged right then and there.

> Nancy Harkness Love turned out to be an important individual
> . . . .She was not only an excellent pilot with 1,200 hours of flying
> time, but was also experienced in organization and administra-
> tion. And she proved that a woman could be both attractive and
> efficiently dependable at the same time.[24]

Together with Tunner, Love put together a proposal for the employment
of experienced women pilots in FERD. Although she initially proposed
hiring women on the same basis as men, with the option of commissioning after a probationary period, FERD was advised that commissioning
into the WAC would not work without an amendment to the WAC bill.
Believing that such an amendment could take forever to pass through
Congress, Love and Tunner opted for civilian status for the women. For
both, the priority was helping the war effort by providing vitally needed
qualified pilots to FERD at the earliest possible moment; personal status,
title and compensation were all secondary.

Like Gower, Love soon found herself in command of women who
were older, more experienced and more famous than she was. And,
again like Gower, this never seemed to be a problem for her. The WAFS
particularly had great respect for Love, and she does not appear to have
had any difficulty with discipline or morale to the extent that she could
exercise command authority over a growing and dispersed group of
women. Love was located first in New Castle Army Air Force Base,
Delaware, then at Love Field in Texas, at Long Beach, California, and
then in Cincinnati at FERD Headquarters; her pilots were spread out
across the four main Ferrying Squadron bases in Delaware, Texas,
California and Michigan respectively.

Once the WAFS programme was up and running, Love's role was
more reactive than active. She responded to the needs expressed by her
subordinates rather than attempting to formulate new policies or
expand organisationally. In fact, Love never exhibited any ambition for
her organisation or herself. She was apparently content with the status
quo: working as an integral, albeit civilian, part of FERD.

Nevertheless, Love consistently did her best to represent the interests
of her pilots – whether it was getting them released from jail when local
sheriffs failed to recognise their uniforms, or objecting to silly restrictions on their freedom of moment and assignment imposed by the
USAAF. She moved fast to ensure they had standardised and recognisable attire in lieu of a uniform. She worked to get them adequate
accommodation at their home bases across the country. When necessary
to further the interests of her pilots, she was prepared to risk even
Tunner's wrath, by going around him directly to ATC headquarters.

Love won the respect of the women under her by her dedication and reliability. The WAFS felt that Nancy would not leave them in the lurch, and so they turned to her when they were in trouble – whether with small-town sheriffs or stubborn base commanders. Love was never too busy to help the women entrusted to her. And, perhaps most important of all, she respected them and their wishes. Unlike Cochran, Love did not expect the women under her command to be willing pawns to her own plans. She did not feel that anyone should be compelled to perform duties they disliked. WASP who did not want to fly pursuits (or in one case, twin-engined pursuits) were assigned to other duties rather than being forced to resign. Likewise, when a woman proved unsuitable to command, she was relieved of her command but allowed to continue as a normal pilot – at another Ferry Group. In short, Love tried to utilise each pilot to the best of her abilities without compulsion or prejudice.

Love also won respect because she led by example. Unlike Cochran, she did not give pep talks, did not try to build up her pilots by telling them the fate of women in aviation depended on their performance, nor flatter them that they were being given 'top secret' work of the greatest importance to the nation, she simply qualified on more Army Air Force aircraft than any other woman pilot. (Cochran did not qualify on any.) With the tacit approval of Tunner, Love transitioned herself onto as many aircraft as fast as she could. She did this, as she did most things, 'quietly and with absolutely no fanfare'.[25] Within just four months, Love had checked out on fourteen types of aircraft including the C-47 and the still experimental P-51. This proved that women were in theory capable of flying these aircraft and so *de facto* opened the door to all other WASP.

Love would have been equally pleased to help General Tunner by proving that women could fly the heavy bombers across the Atlantic. Tunner had encountered increasing reluctance among some of his male pilots to fly the long, gruelling transatlantic deliveries, and felt that showing them that women could do it might improve their attitude. Tunner asked Love and her second-in-command, Betty Gillies, to give it a try. Both women were given training on the B-17, qualifying on the four-engined bomber in just five days. Then they did several domestic deliveries to get more familiar with the aircraft before starting for England on 1 September. While literally on the runway in Gander, Newfoundland, awaiting clearance for take-off, orders arrived from General Arnold that the flight was to be aborted. The two women were replaced by male pilots, and never again given a chance to make the transatlantic flight.

Love's dedication to flying was both a strength and a weakness. It enabled her to set a good example, to open doors, to win the respect of the officers of the ATC and FERD, but it also meant that she rapidly become 'fed up' with 'flying a desk'. Nor did she lavish praise on others; she *expected* that every woman would perform at the top of her abilities. Most of all, she disliked paperwork and she hated intrigue. The former inhibited her within a bureaucratic institution such as the USAAF, while the later disadvantaged her severely in the power-struggle with Cochran. She lost the latter – much to the dismay of the women under her command. Even Evelyn Sharp, a woman with a background far more similar to Cochran's than Love's, a woman with almost twice Love's flying time and personal fame as well, wrote in a letter to her parents:

> Jackie Cochran is now the head of the WAFS and Nancy is under her. How about that? Isn't that a dirty deal? But you know money talks and Jackie has it.[26]

Jacqueline Cochran: The Prima Dona

No one, male or female, played a greater role in the history of women in US military aviation during the Second World War than Jacqueline Cochran. Without her, the course of events would have been entirely different. First and foremost, there would never have been a training programme for women pilots and so the number of women employed would have remained very much smaller – possibly around the same level as in the United Kingdom. Secondly, the programme would never have suffered its dramatic fate because there would have been no one pushing for militarisation – and demanding deactivation when it was not granted. A history of the WASP is therefore incomplete without a closer look at this very dominant and fascinating personality.

Jacqueline 'Cochran' – the name was her own invention – was in many ways the epitome of the 'self-made' woman – in more ways then one. She rose from bitter poverty to extreme wealth, from nameless obscurity to fame, from utter helplessness to power. She also invented and reinvented herself as she went along. She chose her own birthday and date, her own name, and wrote and rewrote her auto-biography as it suited her ends. Inventing qualifications she did not have, claiming achievements she had not attained, and asserting 'facts' that were not true were so routine for her that she never looked on such things as 'lies'. Even her admiring biographer, Maryann Bucknum Brinley, calls Cochran 'a self-named, self-created phenomenon'.[27]

Based on her own account, Cochran was a foundling who never discovered the names of her genetic parents nor the date or year of her birth. She was raised by a family of itinerant workers, living in abject poverty in the sawmill towns of northern Florida. She attended school so irregularly that her highest level of education was third grade – which according to her own account she did not finish.

Very early – since the date she gave for her birth varied by four years it is impossible to say exactly how old she was – she started to work in the mills herself. She preferred this to school because she could make money. In her autobiography she candidly admits: 'The working conditions were despicable; the pay was delightful. That's why I was happy: money.'[28] She soon had supervisory authority over other children. She describes it as: 'I talked. They listened.'[29] She openly admits she loved that too.

The pattern was set. Cochran loved two things throughout her life: wealth and control over others. Driven by ambition, but lacking enough education to be comfortable writing, she spent her life avoiding written exams. She climbed and scratched her way up the ladder without formal qualifications. She found her way into society by 'the back door' and shamelessly exploited friendships and favours all her life.

She got her first job as a beautician by talking herself into a job as maid and baby-sitter for a woman who ran three beauty shops. Soon, she started helping out in the shops too, mixing shampoos, dyes etc. until she was given a chance to help out with the customers. When she proved adept at perming and styling hair, she did more and more work as a beautician – without formal training or the pay it would have commanded.

When a benefactor, who met her at the beauty shop, offered her a chance at nursing training, she accepted, seeing it as a step up. It was arranged that the formal entry requirements would be waived, and Cochran studied for three years. But she admits her grades were terrible (as was only to be expected) so when the time came, she decided not to sit the State Board Examination; she knew she would fail. Instead, she started work for a doctor in the same dismal towns where she had grown up – a place where no one put much emphasis on formal qualifications anyway.

But this life of helping the poor was not for her; there was no money in it and no authority either. So she went back to work as a beautician, where she at least had daily contact with the 'beautiful people'. It was at this point that Jackie leafed through the phone book until she found a name she liked. She henceforth called herself Jacqueline Cochran – a name she retained even after her marriage. It was also at this time that she had her first indirect exposure to flying. She took a job in Pensacola, Florida, and she became instantly enamoured of the young aviation cadets. They were 'a new kind of man: tanned and handsome, in navy summer whites, living on the edge of danger, facing a new challenge every day'.[30] Perhaps Cochran's craving for military rank dates from this time too.

Getting into a cockpit of an aircraft took a bit longer, and the route was devious. Cochran soon realised that Pensacola was too small for her ambition. She moved to New York and walked into the Ritz demanding a job from the most famous beautician of the times, 'Charles of the Ritz'. Although only in her early twenties and still without any formal training as a beautician, she told the most famous hairdresser in the best salon in New York that she was 'an expert at everything' and further- more, 'probably better than he was'.[31] Her cheek paid off and she was offered a job, but was – in her own words – 'too stubborn' to accept and went to work for the competition at Saks Fifth Avenue instead. In con- sequence, she now had among her customers some of the richest and most powerful women in New York. Through her customers she met Floyd Odlum, a successful financier from a humble background. He was also married with several children.

Cochran confided to him her desire to get away from the beauty salon, set up her own cosmetics company and sell the products across the country. Odlum not only financed her venture, he suggested that she would have to learn to fly in order to manage it. Thus began a relationship that lasted to the end of their respective lives, although it was four years before Odlum divorced his first wife and married Cochran secretly. For the rest of her life, to the extent that the things Cochran wanted could be purchased with cash, Odlum bankrolled her.

Meanwhile, Jackie had taken to the idea of flight like a duck to water. She earned her licence in three weeks and passed the exams verbally – knowing that she would not be able to pass any written exam. Just two years later she entered her first race, the 10,000-mile race from England to Melbourne. Amy Johnson was the only other female contender. Johnson had already flown this route alone two years earlier, the first woman to do so. Cochran did not get beyond Romania. The next year Cochran entered the Bendix Race, a roughly 2,000-mile race from Los Angeles, California, to Cleveland, Ohio, but again failed to finish. In 1937 she was placed for the first time, third, and in 1938 at last won the Bendix Race in a prototype for the P-47. The same year she was awarded the first of many Harmon Trophies she would win; the award was for setting three women's speed records the previous year. Eleanor Roosevelt presented the trophy personally.

The connection to the Roosevelts was critical. Floyd Odlum was a major contributor to Franklin Roosevelt's political campaigns, and so Jackie and he were included in White House circles. It appears that Cochran first met General Arnold at a Washington reception in the spring of 1941. She at once accosted him with the idea of establishing a women's branch of the USAAF. Arnold evaded by suggesting that Cochran fly an American-made bomber across the Atlantic in a goodwill gesture to draw attention to Lend-Lease. Cochran apparently jumped at the idea. Being the first woman to fly a bomber across the Atlantic was the kind of feat that she knew would attract publicity. The fact that she had never flown an aircraft with more than one engine, much less have a twin-engine rating, did not phase her in the least.

Odlum at once rented a Lockheed Lodestar and hired Northeast Airlines pilots to coach Jackie for her flight check. Cochran admits in her autobiography that her 'familiarity with heavy airplanes was nil', but after twenty-five hours she was convinced she 'knew as much as a Northeast Airlines pilot'.[32]

The check pilots for the Atlantic Ferry Organisation did not agree. But, as noted above, Odlum was a major contributor to President Roosevelt's campaign and Roosevelt, or possibly Mrs Roosevelt, favoured the flight. The right words passed between Washington and the Ministry of Aircraft Production in London and orders were issued to the Atlantic Ferry Organisation to let Cochran fly. The pilots threatened to strike. This threat had nothing to do with Cochran's sex – much as she liked to interpret it that way and portray herself as a feminist heroine. The fact was simply that the bulk of the pilots in Atlantic Ferry Organisation were former airline pilots, many from Imperial Airways, with tens of thousands of flying hours. They had worked for years and flown thousands of miles before they were allowed in the Captain's seat. They had no intention of letting a pilot (male or female) with twenty-five hours on twins to be put in command – and they didn't care how much money her husband had contributed to President Roosevelt's campaigns. So a compromise was found: Cochran went aboard a Hudson bomber as co-pilot, a male pilot did both take-off and landing, while Cochran 'flew across the Atlantic'.

Thus, Cochran got off on the wrong foot with the British aviation community right from the start. Lettice Curtis politely suggests that she 'had entirely misjudged the wartime mood of the British people – deeply suspicious of anything resembling a stunt – in thinking that publicity would help either her cause over here or that of women pilots'.[33] It is doubtful if, at this stage, Cochran was interested in any cause but her own. Certainly, her understanding of political and military events was severely limited. Arriving in Britain in June 1941,

Cochran believed she had landed in the 'middle' of the Battle of Britain. She claims furthermore that she was in London 'the night [sic] the East End burned'.[34]

But while her flight to England did not go down well with the British, it impressed at home. Immediately upon her return to the United States in July 1941, President Roosevelt tasked her to investigate the possibility of establishing an organisation of women pilots to serve with the USAAF. She was told to work closely with then Colonel Olds, who had only months earlier been appointed CO of the fledgling ATC. Cochran combed through the lists of licensed pilots from the Civil Air Administration, trying to identify how many women pilots there were in the United States with substantial flying experience. Olds was sympathetic to the use of women in the Air Forces, and authorised Cochran to send out a questionnaire to all women with more than 300 hours flying – i.e. to those women who held the same qualifications as the men then being hired by ATC. Cochran, however, wilfully ignored his directive and sent out the questionnaire to *all* women pilots – she already had her eye on a larger programme.

In doing so, Cochran had made her first, powerful enemy in the USAAF. Her deliberate disregard for what he had authorised infuriated Olds. He told Cochran that if she had been an officer he would have put her before a court martial. Furthermore, her efforts led nowhere. Arnold still insisted there was not the slightest need for women pilots in the US military, and again deflected Cochran from hounding him by suggesting she recruit American women pilots for the ATA. Convinced that she had no prospects in the United States in the foreseeable future, Cochran turned her energies to this new task.

Then came Pearl Harbor. The USAAF sustained significant pilot as well as aircraft losses in the attack, and the perceived continued threat led to virtually all experienced military pilots being posted to combat units. The ATC lost half its pilots overnight and had rapidly to replace them with civilians. Many civilian male pilots were volunteering for the Services, others were employed as instructors to meet the Air Forces' expanded demands for basic training, and so Olds decided the time had come to hire women – as both Love and Cochran had already suggested to him at separate times. Olds was in the comfortable position of already employing hundreds of civilian pilots and had the Congressional authorisation to do so; the Congressional authorisation applied to 'pilots' with no restriction on sex. Olds' intention was to hire women pilots on exactly the same basis as the civilian men he already employed.

Unfortunately for the history of women in US military aviation, the ATC and the Allied war effort, Cochran got wind of Olds' plans. The way Olds was planning to employ the women, without a separate women's organisation, left no room for a female commander; the women would have been employees of FERD and so under the direct command of the respective Ferrying Squadrons. Seeing no place for her own ambitions, Cochran was outraged and determined to put an end to Olds' plans. She wrote an angry letter to General Arnold, arguing that Olds' efforts impaired her ability to recruit women for the ATA and hence harmed inter-Allied relations. General Arnold gave in to Cochran's protests – further evidence of his own ambivalence toward women pilots and his continued resistance to the idea of employing them within his own organisation.

Cochran's intervention was unquestionably detrimental to the war effort. Aside from the fact that she vastly over-estimated the importance of her own efforts for the ATA, she demonstrated absolute indifference to the needs of the USAAF. Even assuming that any woman pilot hired by ATC was lost to ATA, it is still arguable that the RAF would not have minded. In the end the only thing that mattered was that the aircraft got from their factories in America to squadrons in Britain as rapidly as possible. It was just as harmful for them to be languishing at US factories for lack of US ferry pilots as for aircraft to pile up at ports because the ATA could not keep up with deliveries. Furthermore, there was no absolute correlation between the pilots willing to go into ATA and those willing to fly for ATC; many American women were not prepared to cross the Atlantic for any reason. Given the enthusiastic response to the WAFS and WFTD when they were launched some nine months later, there is every reason to believe that recruits could have been found for both the ATA and the ATC simultaneously. Cochran's protest effectively delayed the employment of women in the US and damaged the efficiency of FERD by denying it qualified pilots it desperately needed in the short term. Cochran was prepared to deny her nation's defences the services of scores of qualified women pilots simply because she would not have been their commander.

The act of recruiting twenty-five experienced American women pilots for the ATA is certainly to Cochran's credit. Her record once she was in England is a different story altogether. She was quite simply super-fluous. By the time Cochran arrived on the scene, the ATA had been in existence nearly three years – the women's section two-and-a-half. The ATA was a well run, professional and highly efficient organisation. It had no particular need for an uneducated, American woman, who had never worked in the aviation industry – much less in ferrying – either as an administrator, instructor or pilot.

Furthermore, all pilots joining the ATA were required to go through training; RAF Group Captains and Admirals submitted to being cadets for the period of this training just like everyone else – except Jacqueline Cochran. Cochran insisted that she 'didn't need to prove she could fly', apparently unable to accept that ferrying a variety of different aircraft in wartime Britain *might* just be different than racing from California to Ohio or flying about in her own personal aircraft. One suspects she was secretly afraid of failing – at least the ground-school portion of training for which she would have been required to read and write. Furthermore, she claimed she had 'something more important' to prove, namely 'that women could make a real contribution in wartime'.[35] The argument was ill chosen to sway the opinion of the ATA, whose women had proved that point years earlier. As Curtis put it:

> The ATA had been running for over two years, during which it had evolved standard procedures and training for anyone who joined, regardless of previous flying experience. Jackie . . . immediately set about short-circuiting these procedures. As a race the British are – or were in those days – perhaps particularly averse to anyone who set out to by-pass the 'system'. And ATA did its best to enforce its own rules. But Jackie and her husband . . . moved in the highest political and military circles in the United States and at the time . . . it was of the utmost importance to Britain that good relations be maintained. Government pressures were therefore put on ATA to smooth Jackie's path.[36]

The ATA, with its characteristic irreverent attitude toward higher authority, was unimpressed. It remained steadfast; Cochran never flew a single aircraft in the United Kingdom.

Instead – and much to the evident disgust of some of the women she had herself recruited – she was 'commissioned' Flight Captain and withdrew to London, allegedly to study the administration of the organisation. It is hard to imagine Cochran 'studying' anything, and Curtis writes:

> Our main memories of her are of someone who lived at the Savoy Hotel, wore a lush fur coat and arrived at White Waltham in a Rolls-Royce, both noticeable because by now we had clothes as well as petrol and food rationing.[37]

Cochran liked to play the 'big-spender' for 'her girls' as well, and she welcomed the recruits by inviting them to her hotel and wining and dining them at her expense – for the first night. She bragged too that 'nothing was too good for them' and insisted they would get the 'best medical attention in England'.[38] But she baulked at letting the women undergo a standard physical exam that, in Britain, required them to strip naked. One of the American recruits, Ann Wood, felt:

she'd moan and groan and spend hours fighting our battles, battles that weren't really so important in the long run. But that was Jackie. She felt inferior to the British and she'd pick fights that were silly sometimes.[39]

In her own memoirs, Cochran describes her role in England as advisor to the Eighth Air Force – far removed from the petty business of the ATA:

Because of my knowledge of military channels [sic], I was even invited by the Eighth Air Force to spend several weeks in the organization. The whole air effort and the American role in the English battle were being argued. General Arnold, Admiral John Towers, and Air Marshal Arthur Harris used my little apartment at the Savoy Hotel one night to debate the question of nighttime versus daylight bombing. The Americans wanted a round-the-clock effort, but the British, who were badly in need of more planes, didn't even want to envision how costly the light of day might prove to their men and machines. The upshot was a compromise where the Americans took the daytime bombing raids and the English stuck with the night.[40]

It is hardly surprising, given her history of restless ambition, that Cochran soon bored of her social life in a country where she found the food 'awful', was not allowed to fly and had only nominal command. According to Cochran's own account, her husband informed her about the creation of the WAFS and she reluctantly flew back at Arnold's insistence. No other account of the incident corresponds to this invention. Rather, it is universally recorded that Cochran returned in a rage and furiously demanded of Arnold that he keep an alleged promise to appoint her head of any women pilots' organisation in the USAAF.

September 1942 was not a very rosy time for the Allied war effort. Of particular significance for Arnold, American bombers had taken part in their first raids in Europe in July; the casualties were mounting. The WAFS had already been announced and been well received by the press. Arnold found it easier at this point to give in to Cochran than to continue to resist her. Cochran was appointed head of the 'experimental' Women's Flying Training Detachment (WFTD) and asked to recruit women pilots for training with the USAAF.

Cochran at once called a press conference and announced that she had been 'called back' by General Arnold to head the 'women's air corps'. She said the goal was to train 1,500 women, adding that she would accept girls with lower qualifications as time went on because 'I've had such success with my girls in England'.[41] The problem with this public statement – quite aside from the fact that it implied she had set up the entire ATA training and so bore no resemblance whatsoever to her actual role with the ATA – was that it aroused the immediate ire of General Tunner. Tunner was allergic to any suggestions that pilots with *less* flying experience would be suitable for his Command. With her very first official act, Cochran had offended another powerful officer.

Meanwhile, the USAAF had two women heading two separate and distinct women pilot's programmes: Nancy Love at the WAFS and Jacqueline Cochran at the WFTD. The two women were virtual opposites. Love came from old wealth; Cochran's money was very new. Love was an educated, sophisticated, modest and understated lady. Cochran was a pushy, flamboyant, uneducated upstart. Love was 'not interested in wielding vast administrative power', and was content to be part of FERD, while Cochran 'insisted on founding an entirely new military program over which she would have top authority'.[42] While Love was soft-spoken and low-key, Cochran was from the start 'missionizing'. She sought a high profile, and she was determined – in or own words – to be the 'top dog'. While Love delivered substance – she really qualified on the B-17 before attempting to fly it across the Atlantic, Cochran preferred show, attention and publicity, even if it had little to do with reality.

Love and Cochran's understanding of command responsibilities was also diametrically opposed. While Love disliked the paperwork that went with her job, she never neglected it. Love also attended Officer Training. In contrast, Cochran had no formal military training, not even the OTC course that over 400 other WASPs attended. Furthermore, her obsession with nominal titles – her famed refusal to be a 'mere' major to Hobby's colonel – had nothing to do with a desire to do the work that went with them. Although Cochran had bullied her way into being appointed head of the women pilots' training programme, she showed not the slightest interest in the curriculum, showed no concern about the quality of the instructors, and immediately delegated all the work to do with the actual trainees to her subordinates. Cochran spent on average just four days in any month at her command in Sweetwater, Texas. She much preferred her office in the Pentagon near 'the seat of power' (General Arnold and the White House) to the hard work of actually running a command in the Texan outback.

It has been said that powerful men liked Cochran. Allegedly, they liked the fact that she was 'gutsy'. Certainly, she was attractive and obviously she had the ear of President and his wife. But Cochran had been in her post less than a month before Arnold, returning to Washington from the Pacific, learned that Cochran had already made 'a number of influential enemies'.[43] Not only that, she had made so *many* important enemies, that the entire women's training programme was going nowhere. She had no facility for her school, no equipment and no staff. This was a pattern that would repeat itself throughout the existence of the WFTD/WASP: Cochran alienated almost everyone she had to work with, thereby creating resistance that slowed down progress.

The rivalry between Love and Cochran was also 'legendary' – that is, the press made much of it. In fact, it was one-sided. Love never aspired to the position Cochran carved out for herself, and would have been quite happy if she had simply been left alone to run the WAFS. Cochran, however, was bitterly jealous of Love from the start. She was furious that she had been given any kind of command whatsoever – and responded by demanding a bigger and better command for herself. For a woman used to press attention (even for things she didn't really do, like fly across the Atlantic or train women pilots with the ATA), it infuriated her that Love's women received so much positive press attention. (No doubt it particularly rankled with the beautician and cosmetics queen that Love's legs rather than her own were voted so beautiful.) Her response was to seize control of all press coverage with regard to women pilots – with the success noted previously.

Next, Cochran set to work undermining Love's prerogatives. She first restricted her right to hire women directly into FERD. She then tried to set up a rival Ferrying Squadron in Texas, directly under her command, and proposed that all graduates of her programme be assigned to future squadrons under her command rather than the WAFS; Love was to be demoted to the Squadron Leader at New Castle. While these latter efforts shattered on Tunner's iron control over his own command, she was apparently able to use her growing influence on General Arnold to ensure that Love did not fly a bomber across the Atlantic. And, of course, she won the key battle to have the two women's organisations merged under her command.

By the time she got her way, she had made such an enemy of Nancy Love that the blue-blooded, understated Love had to be reminded by her husband that showing her emotions with regards to 'that bitch' only played into the hands of a gossip-mongering press. He also assured her that her opinion of Cochran was *shared by the entire staff of Air Transport Command* – not an insignificant statement coming from the Deputy Commander, although perhaps not entirely objective.[44]

As the Director of Women Pilots, as her new title went, Cochran rapidly set about treading on everyone else's toes as hard as possible. She used her headquarters staff function to try to interfere with or circumvent decisions that traditionally lay at command level. She ordered her women pilots about between commands, bases and squadrons, without the least regard for the USAAF standard operating procedures. What this meant was that women pilots received telegrams from Cochran ordering them to report to one place or another, but the COs of the bases they were leaving and to which they were not necessarily informed. The women, thinking Cochran was their commander, obeyed orders, but they were neither well received at their destinations nor cherished by the commands that had lost them so abruptly and without being informed, much less consulted. Furthermore, because Cochran did not follow Standard Operating Procedures (SOPs) for transfers, the women did not receive pay for months on end until the bureaucratic confusion had been cleared up.

Meanwhile, however, the bill for all costs associated with travel and accommodation associated with the transfers, not to mention salaries, were sent to the commands from which the WASP had been removed. Needless to say, COs baulked. They were being asked to pay for expenditures they had not authorised and did not want. Tunner not only refused to continue paying the salaries of women taken out of his command at the whim of Cochran, he pointed out it was illegal to pay them for duties they were not performing – and suggested the Ramspeck Civil Service Committee ought to look into the matter. Cochran did not seem to grasp the significance of either her actions or Tunner's threat.

Instead, she continued to alienate large portions of the USAAF establishment by dropping in unannounced at air bases where WASP were stationed. She then 'ignored normal military courtesy by going directly to the WASP alert room, taking care of her business, and leaving without informing the proper chain of command'.[45] While the commanders, executive officers and other personnel thus slighted and angered were not individually powerful enough to protest, Cochran was making scores if not hundreds of enemies, all of whom would be more than happy to talk to the press 'anonymously' when the militarisation bill came up before Congress. Her track record of arrogant disregard for the courtesy owed to others ensured that she had few friends when the issue of deactivation was raised. No matter how good the individual women pilots were, by September 1944 there were very many officers in the USAAF who were more than happy to see *Cochran* get her 'comeuppance'.

Meanwhile, Cochran continued to goad General Tunner particularly. She insisted that he accept graduates of her WFTD regardless of whether he felt they were qualified or not. Tunner objected strenuously, but was forced to accept the graduates. The situation was aggravated by the fact that at the same time, Cochran personally dismissed two women pilots who FERD wished to retain. This amounted to Cochran making personnel decisions over-the-head of the Commanding General.

By November 1943, she thought her position strong enough to issue a 'directive' that henceforth *all* WASP squadron leaders would be appointed by herself rather than the command in which they served. She also announced her intention of appointing a representative from her headquarters to each base where WASP were deployed. This non-flying 'executive officer' was to act rather like a political commissar, reporting directly to Cochran rather than the base commander. She required, furthermore, that all accident reports involving WASP be sent directly to her office.

This time Cochran's craving for control had gone too far. Tunner again objected strenuously to this new attempt to interfere in command prerogatives and treat the women pilots differently from the men of the command. He was backed vigorously by the Commanding General of ATC, and for the first time in more than a year, Arnold came down hard on the side of his generals and against Cochran. USAAF Headquarters overrode Cochran's 'directive', re-establishing unified control over personnel at any base to the base commander.

While Cochran's insensitive and unprofessional treatment of her fellow commanding officers in the USAAF was foolish and undoubtedly helped lead to her eventual downfall, her treatment of subordinates was not only unprofessional but unpardonable. While Cochran paid lip-service to the fact that not every woman was suited to every task, in fact she tolerated no one who objected to the arbitrary assignments she made. The first women sent to do target-towing duties were not even told what they were being asked to do; they were certainly given no chance to opt out. When one wrote a letter of resignation following a fatal accident, Cochran flatly refused to accept it because she felt it would damage her own efforts to extend WASP assignments beyond Ferrying Command. Two women who requested a transfer back to FERD from Camp Davis on the other hand were discharged 'with prejudice' from the programme entirely, although FERD not only wanted the services of these women, but insisted their behaviour had not justified a dismissal on *any* grounds.

Likewise, Cochran encouraged her 'girls' to be open with her and speak up, but those that dared were immediately labelled 'trouble-makers'. Cochran made sure any 'trouble-makers' were forced to resign or were dismissed. A WASP who did no more than remind Cochran of her own words at an earlier meeting was at once threatened: she was told that 'if she wasn't careful she'd be on her way to Camp Davis'.[46] The incident is particularly revealing because it entailed first lying (denying something that was a well recorded fact), then threatening a subordinate in public, and third indicated that Cochran's precious prestige object, target-towing at Camp Davis, was widely understood to be a form of punishment.

There were good reasons why Camp Davis had such a bad reputation. The attitude of the base commander toward the women was poor and that of the other pilots insulting; the machines the women were asked to fly were in a scandalous state of disrepair, while the work was extremely dangerous because this was one base where the gunners used live ammunition. In short, the living conditions were unpleasant, morale terrible and the risks exceptionally high. None of this mattered to the Director of Women Pilots.

Even when a WASP engaged in target-towing at Camp Davis was trapped in her cockpit after a crash and burned to death, Cochran showed no understanding for the shock, anger and outrage of her subordinates. The WASP were shocked because they had heard the victim screaming in her cockpit as she died. They were angered and outraged because the aircraft they were being asked to fly had severe maintenance deficiencies. No fewer than eleven pilots had been forced to make emergency landings during just a month of operations. Tyres were in poor condition and blow-outs during landing and take-off frequent. The mechanics were over-worked and sloppy, admitting that they didn't bother to note down all the things wrong with the aircraft because they couldn't get the necessary spare parts anyway. The instructors were incompetent, and often had less flying time than the WASP they were allegedly training.

Cochran's own investigation indicated that all the allegations made by the WASP were correct, but rather than take any action, she demonstratively sided with the base commander. Cochran was far more concerned about the success of her 'experiment' than the lives of the women in her command.

Because the entire incident had just been covered up and ignored, the maintenance problems continued, which meant the engine failures, fires and crash-landings did as well. Just one month later, another WASP had a fatal accident. Again, Cochran flew down to investigate. This time she discovered evidence of sabotage. Cochran's reaction was identical to learning that her pilots were being asked to fly aircraft hundreds of hours overdue for maintenance overhauls and lacking vital parts: she ordered a 'cover up'. The mechanics who had given evidence to her were told to keep quiet, and no official report was made. Cochran feared an insurrection on the part of the WASP and – most important – that there might have been negative repercussions for her precious experimental programme. She consciously chose to neglect a CO's most sacred duty, the safety of his/her subordinates, for the sake of keeping up appearances.

It is hardly surprising under the circumstances that Cochran's subordinates often felt less than enthusiastic about her. Many WASP felt 'betrayed' by Cochran, while the bulk of the original WAFS dreaded the thought of being brought more completely under her control. They resisted militarisation and said so to both Congressional investigators and the press, precisely because they did not want to be even more at the mercy of Cochran's arbitrary and authoritarian command style. Even the admirers among Cochran's subordinates admit that 'Jackie would walk all over you',[48] or 'she could be ruthless when she wanted to pursue something . . . People got stepped on en route'.[49] Another WASP described Cochran as 'a steel railroad going right down the track. She had a great sense of her own worth and she knew she was good. She bathed in the recognition'.[50]

There can be no doubt that Cochran bathed in the recognition, but was Cochran good? And if so, at what? She was a good racing pilot, although her accomplishments are far more modest than Cochran's dogged, self publicity would lead one to believe. The 'prestigious' Bendix Race was a mere 2,000 miles, completely over the Continental United States with all the accompanying navigational aids and options for aborting at fully operational airports. Amy Johnson's or Amelia Earhart's flying took them across oceans and uncharted continents without ground navigation support.

In fact, although Cochran bills herself as the 'Greatest Woman Pilot in Aviation History'[51] her accomplishments do anything but justify such a claim. Cochran was not qualified to fly on twin- let alone multi-engine aircraft and she never did – except for her spurious transatlantic flight. Cochran did not even have an instructor's rating. She never flew transcontinental flights. She never operated from water. There are surely many other women with a better claim to Cochran's self-awarded accolade.

Amelia Earhart comes immediately to mind, and Amy Johnson. But – just for the sake of argument – Elly Beinhorn could also be a contender for the title. She flew solo to Africa, a flight of over 4,000 miles. She flew from Germany via Calcutta, the Himalayas, Bangkok, and Bali to Port Darwin in Australia. She resumed her flight in Panama and flew to Buenos Aires, surviving three emergency landings on the way.

A pilot of a different kind but certainly one with as much right to call herself the 'greatest woman pilot in aviation history' as Cochran does – even if she would never have been so immodest – was Melitta Gräfin Schenk von Stauffenberg. Countess Stauffenberg earned a degree in aeronautical engineering and was employed by the German Institute for Aviation Testing (*Deutsche Versuchsanstalt für Luftfahrt*). While working as an engineer she earned her pilot's licence. She was instrumental in developing an auto-pilot for German flying boats, particularly for long-distance flying on these exceptionally awkward aircraft. She became the only woman in Germany to obtain pilot licences for all classes of aircraft, powered and unpowered. During the war she was conscripted to the *Luftwaffe*, where she was responsible for improving the bombsight for the Ju 87 ('Stuka') and Ju 88 dive-bombers. To perform her duties she personally made more than 2,500 test dives from 4,000 to 1,000 metres. She sometimes flew as many as fifteen test flights in one day, an extremely demanding physical achievement, which to this day has never been equalled. She was also, from 1942 onward, frequently at risk from Allied aircraft, but continued to fly. She was shot down and killed by an American fighter in the closing days of the war.[52] No ideological bigotry should deny Countess Stauffenberg recognition as an outstanding pilot; both her brothers-in-law gave their lives in the coup-attempt against Hitler on 20 July 1944; one of them, Claus, laid the bomb in Hitler's headquarters.

Last but not least, Cochran's claim to be 'the greatest' must at least be compared to the accomplishments of the Russian women who flew combat missions in the Second World War. Many of these women came from backgrounds as humble as Cochran's own. They, too, often had to fight prejudice, discrimination and even political persecution to obtain their goals. They flew in largely obsolete equipment, from improvised airfields, in appalling weather against an Army equipped with the best anti-aircraft defences of the age, the Wehrmacht's feared 8.8 flak batteries. Many Russian women pilots were killed. Many more suffered serious injuries. They flew both bombers and fighters, mostly as members of three women's regiments, but some as isolated women in otherwise male regiments. One of the women's regiments, the 46th Guards Bomber Regiment, completed a total of 24,000 combat sorties, and supposedly all the pilots in this unit made more than 800 combat sorties each.[53]

Surely pioneering flight across great, uncharted distances, being influential in the technical evolution of flying instruments and test-flying, or consistently out-manoeuvring death in years of combat flying against a technically superior enemy are greater achievements than Cochran's handful of speed records and a grossly mismanaged women pilot's programme?

The picture of Cochran that emerges is one of a woman who consistently over-estimated her own abilities and accomplishments. Whether it was telling New York's best beautician that she was better than he, or claiming to have as much knowledge as an airline captain after just twenty-five hours of lessons, Cochran's faith in her own abilities was boundless.

Describing her first cross-country flight at a time when she – by her own account – did not even know how to read a compass let alone any other instrument in the cockpit, Cochran admits: 'I didn't know anything. I didn't even know what I didn't know.'[54] While some of this hubris may be excusable on the grounds that as a young woman Cochran really *was* ignorant of how much there was to know, it is hard to excuse her persistent insistence on her superiority at a time when, from experience alone, she should have known better. It is hard to escape the conclusion that Cochran truly lacked any perspective when it came to herself and her abilities, a function of the fact that she evidently consistently lied to herself.

Cochran lied so readily and so inconsistently that she probably did not herself know what was fact and what was fiction. Just as she varied the date of her birth, she changed her stories to suit the circumstances. She could go on record saying one thing one day, the opposite a short time later, and would then respond to anyone who challenged her on it by calling *them* a liar. Her autobiography is filled with fictionalised conversations and claims that simply do not square with the historical record from other sources. She brashly claims she was in England to 'show her administrative skills' to the ATA. What administrative skills? She portrays herself as giving advice to the poor, benighted, helpless officials of the ATA who were (apparently) just bungling through until she arrived to help them hash out 'organisational issues'. She finds nothing ironic about claiming she is a military expert without having served one day in any armed force or received so much as girl-scout training. Nor does she have the least compunction about taking sole personal credit for giving the WASP uniforms to 'provide them with identity', while ignoring the fact that she had personally neglected the problem for over a year and blocked other efforts to solve the identity problem earlier. Cochran's autobiography is the most misleading account ever published about the WASP and possibly the most dangerous as well because, coming as it does from the founder, it is attributed a historical credibility that it does not have.

However, it also contains an almost charming admission of the author's inability to separate fact from fiction. Cochran tells of getting her first job by reeling off a list of accomplishments in which she 'added and subtracted information at will, as it suited me'. She adds significantly: 'I didn't see it as lying so much as surviving.'[55] That might be, but lying it was nevertheless. And the pattern was set. Cochran went on to lie about her qualifications as a beautician for getting the job in New York. She lied about her accomplishments with the ATA. She lied about being 'summoned back' by Arnold. She lied with confusing inconsistency about prospects for militarisation. She lied to the women assigned target-towing duties in Camp Davis, saying they would be 'flying bigger and better aircraft than women had ever flown' when on the one hand they were given junk and on the other WAFS were flying brand new P-47s, P-38s and P-39s. She lied again when she told the women they were only being sent to Camp Davis on a 'two-week' temporary duty – when in fact they were sent there permanently and without any chance to transfer out except in a coffin.

Cochran lied so compulsively that it is impossible to catalogue all the lies and tedious to try. The issue is rather one of trying to come to an understanding of what purpose these various lies were meant to serve. While it is understandable, even justifiable, for an unemployed, teenage mill worker to lie about qualifications to get a menial job, it is hard to accept that the winner of the Harmon and various other trophies found it necessary to take credit for things she did not do – whether it was being an advisor to the Eighth Air Force or running the ATA training programme. Even more incomprehensible – or just plain petty – is a Director of Women Pilots who consciously denied credit to her subordinates. Cochran announced in a press conference that some recent WASP graduates were the first women to qualify on the B-17 – though she knew perfectly well that Nancy Love and Betty Gillies had long since held that qualification. In this case Tunner called her bluff, firing off a memo in which he 'requested' that she 'check the accuracy of her statements' before making further press releases.[56] Far too many of Cochran's claims, however, have been guilelessly accepted, and repeated.

Looking for a reason for Cochran's compulsive self-aggrandisement, it is hard to escape the suspicion that at some level Cochran was scared

– scared that someone might prove better than she or simply discover that she was a fake. To avoid facing that possibility, she surrounded herself with evidence of her own success – such as displaying all her trophies in the entrance hall of her apartment. She never tired of complimenting and praising herself. Modesty was a word she literally did not understand, as the following incident described by WASP Margaret Boylan illustrates:

> I remember one time when she landed out near the Grand Canyon, and once on the ground Jackie walked back from the cockpit into the cabin of the plane and said to me, 'Margaret, wasn't that the smoothest landing you've ever experienced? Wasn't it great?'
>
> I said, 'Jackie, you're supposed to wait until other people compliment you. You're not supposed to brag about your own landings when you're the pilot.'
>
> 'Well, I don't know why not,' she said to me. Then she got mad.[57]

The story further illustrates that even as Director of Women Pilots Cochran demanded adulation from her subordinates, and anyone who denied it to her risked being 'trampled on'. It illustrates, too, her insatiable need for praise. One would truly have thought that by this point in her life, with all those 'prestigious' trophies collected in her house, she did not need to have a newly graduated pilot compliment her on a routine landing.

Perhaps Major General Fred Ascani assessed Cochran correctly when he claimed she was 'a prima donna' adding, 'they are like children of five, six or seven'.[58] Whatever the psychological analysis, the bottom line is that the WASP programme was conceived, initiated and managed by a woman with a second-grade education, who had never in her life held a comparably responsible position and who vastly and consistently over-estimated her own abilities. Cochran had turned the German General Staff motto 'be more than you appear to be', on its head. Jacqueline Cochran appeared to be much more than she ever was.

Notes:

1 Rickman, 43.
2 Verges, 35
3 La Farge, Oliver, *The Eagle in the Egg*, quoted by Tunner in *Over the Hump*, 26.
4 Tunner, 40.

5   Tunner, 28.
6   Tunner, 41.
7   Granger, 186.
8   Tunner, 38–9.
9   Tunner, 34.
10   King, 18–19.
11   Fahie, 137.
12   King, 17–18.
13   King, 19.
14   De Bunsen, 103.
15   Lucas, 58–9.
16   Du Cros, 35
17   King, 18.
18   De Bunsen, 103.
19   Fahie, 149.
20   Fahie, 178.
21   Fahie, 183.
22   Rickman, 20–21.
23   Rickman, 21.
24   Tunner, 34–5.
25   Rickman, 135.
26   Bartels, 220.
27   Brinley, x.
28   Cochran in Brinley, 34.
29   Cochran in Brinley, 36.
30   Verges, 11.
31   Cochran in Brinley, 57
32   Cochran in Brinley, 175–6.
33   Curtis, 142.
34   Cochran in Brinley, 187.
35   Verges, 31.
36   Curtis, 142–3.
37   Curtis, 143.
38   Keil, 82.
39   Wood, quoted in Brinley, 198.
40   Cochran in Brinley, 200–201.
41   Rickman, 59.
42   Keil, 119.
43   Verges, 66.
44   Verges, 141–2.
45   Verges, 142.
46   Verges, 150.
47   Keil, 224–5, See also Granger, 170.
48   Beverly Hanson Sfingi quoted in Brinley, 178.
49   Margaret Boylan quoted in Brinley, 195.

50 Boylan in Brinley, 209.
51 This is the subtitle on her Autobiography written with Brinley.
52 Probst, Ernst, *Königinnen der Lüfte: Biographien berühmter Fliegerinnen*, 2002, 69–73.
53 Noggle, Anne, *A Dance with Death: Soviet Airwomen in World War II*, 1994, 18–31.
54 Cochran in Brinley, 80.
55 Cochran in Brinley, 38.
56 Verges, 153.
57 Boylan, quoted in Brinley, 195.
58 Ascani, quoted in Brinley, 21.

Conclusions

Whether flying as ferry pilots with the ATA or performing any of a variety of tasks with the WASP, the women pilots flying in the United States and the United Kingdom during the Second World War did an outstanding job. They demonstrated consistent competence at least equal to that of their male colleagues, and in some regards – such as reliability and patience – were deemed better than male pilots by their contemporaries. They demonstrated without doubt that women could fly the most modern service aircraft of their age. They proved that women could perform a variety of non-combat flying missions, and in both countries their safety record was above average. In short, the women pilots in the United States and the United Kingdom during the Second World War were notably and equally successful.

The same, however, cannot be said about their respective organisations. While the ATA was an exceptionally successful organisation both with respect to fulfilling its objectives and providing its members with superb support and opportunities, the WASP was a dismal failure. While the ATA made itself indispensable to the RAF within just six months of its founding, the WASP was discontinued prematurely – not because its members weren't doing their jobs, but because the organisation had become a liability to the USAAF.

The ATA rapidly established itself as the sole ferrying organisation of the British armed forces, and thereafter it grew steadily in size and function. It responded readily and flexibly to new demands and demonstrated remarkable creativity in doing so. The ATA not only made a significant contribution to the war effort, but also left a legacy to military and civil aviation. The WASP grew much faster, soon attaining a size nearly twice the entire pilot strength (male and female) of the ATA. The variety of tasks assumed likewise far exceeded those ever even contemplated for the ATA. But it singularly failed to make itself indispensable to the USAAF or otherwise make a significant contribution to the war effort.

The ATA was particularly outstanding for the development and implementation of a unique training programme. This turned out pilots trained precisely for the tasks required in a minimum of time. Because the training programme alternated practical experience with short periods of training, it enabled pilots to be productively employed from a very early stage. By allowing pilots to progress at their own pace, it also ensured that they gained confidence before going on to more difficult aircraft, thereby reducing both accident and washout rates to a minimum. During the early stages, ATA training was in the hands of some of the world's most experienced and highly qualified instructors, while in the later phases it was managed by experienced ferry pilots who had helped evolve and effectively practised the kind of flying they were teaching. The result of their efforts was to turn pilots deemed 'unfit' for military service into pilots on whom the RAF and FAA relied – and whom they respected.

The WASP in contrast dramatically failed to develop a satisfactory training programme, although this was the largest and most prominent of its many functions. Although two official USAAF inspections testified to and catalogued the inadequacies of the training programme, no corrective actions were taken. The cumbersome training operations continued to subject trainees to substandard instructors and a rigid training programme weighed down with superfluous subjects such as maths and physical education. At great expense to the American taxpayer, the WASP training arbitrarily washed-out promising pilots and graduated women in need of still more training. Because WASP required additional training and were sent to various other courses and experiments after graduation, it is fair to say that very few repaid the investment made in them.

The ATA was not only remarkably effective in meeting its organisational goal of supporting the war effort, it also pioneered in the field of equality of opportunity for women and the physically handicapped. Furthermore, it enabled women to fly virtually every kind of aircraft including jets. It allowed women to advance to positions of authority over men. It also granted equal pay for equal work at a time when this was against government policy generally.

The WASP, in contrast, failed both to fulfil its organisational objectives and to provide its employees with adequate compensation, terms of service or benefits. With respect to its mission of helping the war effort, the WASP's impact was insignificant. Only a minority of the women who passed through the programme went on active service. The majority of the WASP were still in flight training when the decision was taken to discontinue the programme. Many more were in other kinds of post-flight-school training, whether on service aircraft or at Officer's or Instructor's schools or on one experiment or another. Even in the one command where the WASP served longest and most success-fully, the Ferrying Division of Air Transport Command, the impact of the WASP was marginal. The maximum number of WASP employed in FERD was 303 compared with over 8,000 male pilots.

With respect to its mission of proving women could be taught to fly as well as men, the WASP was even less successful. While it is true that many individual WASP did prove to be competent pilots, the most prominent of these women, the original WAFS, were in fact not pro-ducts of the WASP training program; all were highly competent and experienced pilots at the time of their hiring. The graduates of the WFTD, in contrast, frequently failed to live up to expectations, and needed further training. Eventually, the women did prove competent at many different tasks, but this was not the accomplishment of the WFTD.

While failing to achieve its objectives, the WASP organisation also failed to provide its members with adequate compensation, medical care, insurance or chances of promotion. No WASP was ever given equal compensation for equal work, and no WASP was given the oppor-tunity to exercise command authority over men. For most of its existence, the WASP did not even provide its members with a recog-nisable uniform. When uniforms finally did get issued, they served to undermine identification with the USAAF, thereby contributing more to alienation than integration.

Even more objectionable, because of the incompetence of the WASP management, employees were sometimes left without any pay for months on end. In addition, members were often arbitrarily shifted about from one assignment to another, preventing the women from gaining competence at any one job. There was also no adequate mech-anism for complaints or transfers within the organisation as a whole. Finally, and most damaging in the long run, the appalling mismanage-ment of the organisation's public and press relations resulted in a distorted image of the women pilots and the job they were doing, which proved disastrous for the fate of the organisation.

The incompetent handling of the militarisation issue on the part of the WASP leadership in particular provided an excuse for the elimina-tion of an organisation that was by then widely perceived to be more trouble than it was worth. The very real contributions of competent women pilots were over-shadowed by the memory of in-fighting, Congressional disapproval and a hostile press and public. The USAAF was in a hurry not only to discontinue the programme but to forget about it as well. This as much as anything explains why so few WASP received any kind of official recognition for their services and why it took them more than thirty years even to gain acknowledgement of the feat that they had in fact served – whether with distinction or not – with the armed forces.

In contrast, the ATA managed its publicity masterfully, ensuring a consistently positive image in the press and with the public. This ensured that its very real – albeit, compared to the fighting forces, mundane – accomplishments were not ignored or forgotten. The Prime Minister, the Minister of Aircraft Production, the RAF and the Royal Navy officially recognised the value of the services rendered by the ATA, and nearly fifty individual members of the organisation were also publicly honoured. Finally, when its mission had been accomplished, it departed the scene with dignity, good grace and public acclaim. It left behind an enviable legacy of innovation in training, accident management and equality of opportunity. Few organisations can claim to have achieved so much in so little time.

Far from making itself indispensable to the nation's air force, as the ATA had done, the WASP became an acute embarrassment to the USAAF. It became the focus of negative press and unkind Congressional investigation. Even those officers and commands within the USAAF that appreciated and praised the contribution of the individual women pilots, viewed the organisation as a 'hassle' – a perpetual source of bureaucratic in-fighting and interference in Command prerogatives.

That is the comparative record.

After reviewing the facts and comparing the experiences of the ATA to the WASP, it is clear that the fate of the WASP was anything but inevitable. Despite the admittedly more hostile environment confronting women in the military in the United States, the response to Nancy Love and the WAFS suggests that the USAAF could have adjusted to the notion of women pilots working alongside men on an equal basis. It is particularly notable that there were no instances of sabotage with respect to the WAFS, suggesting that hostility was lowest where their presence was highest.

Furthermore, many of the difficulties encountered by WASP – such as arrests for 'impersonating' officers – might have been avoided if Cochran had not prevented the WAFS from being officially granted the improvised uniform Love had designed. Far more significantly, if Cochran had not vetoed it, the women would have been hired on the same basis as the male civilians of FERD – at the same rates of pay with the same ranks, uniforms, insurance and health benefits. Only Cochran's insistence on creating a bigger and – in her eyes – better organisation prevented an organisational solution that would have enabled American women to enjoy the same successes as the women of the ATA.

Cochran's desire to prove that women pilots could do more than 'just' ferry aircraft (or her desire to hold a commission in the USAAF) was alone responsible for the creation of the expensive but inefficient WASP training apparatus, the WFTD. It was this programme that aroused Congressional disapproval, both because it had not been approved and because it was apparently excessively expensive in view of the results.

Equally, Cochran's obsession with experimenting with women's capabilities created the absurd situation in which even graduated WASP were not left alone to get on with their jobs, but repeatedly sent on temporary duty away from their official units or sent to additional training of one kind or another. As a result, the women were not perceived as pulling their weight in the commands to which they were assigned. Even – or especially – those commanders who valued the services of the individual WASP pilots were irritated by the interference of the WASP command in sending their valued employees on one experiment after another. In short, while resentment towards WASP HQ built-up, the usefulness of the WASP was systematically undermined.

Cochran's insistence on militarisation of the WASP as separate organisation furthermore drew public and press attention at a time when this was far from advantageous. Because the mood in the country had swung against women in the military generally, Cochran's campaign for militarisation was bound to be difficult, but there was nothing inevitable about its defeat. If Cochran had handled the publicity of the WASP more adroitly from the start, the image of the women pilots might have been more positive. At least they might have been perceived as competent, as the women of the ATA were, rather than mere glamour girls. If WASP and their families had been allowed to lobby their own Congressmen, at least some of the seventy-nine abstaining Congressmen might have voted for the WASP, possibly reversing the outcome of the vote. Most important, if Cochran had not already created so many enemies inside the USAAF, there would have been far fewer stories leaked to the press that revealed the weaknesses of the programme. There is no doubt that the press exaggerated those weaknesses, but in almost every case there was just enough truth to make the accusations against the WASP sting.

Without Cochran there would never have been a women pilots' training programme in the USAAF, but it is not correct to claim that women would therefore not have flown for the air force. The WAFS programme had already been approved before Cochran returned to the

United States. While this programme would have been smaller than the WASP because the entry requirements were so much higher, it is only reasonable to assume that it, too, would have grown over time just as the ATA did. FERD needed pilots, and throughout the war private, civilian flying schools continued to operate in the United States. Provided they had the financial means to pay for flying instruction, women interested in working for FERD could and would have obtained the qualifications necessary.

It is also fair to say that most of the problems encountered by the WASP could have been prevented or alleviated by a different leadership and a different leadership style. Had the WASP had a competent and co-operative leadership, intent on serving the interests of the USAAF instead of proving a point, the WFTD might have been better structured to produce more competent pilots. Subsequent training could have been streamlined to meet command requirements rather than researching and recording the physical response of women to high altitude or testing – for the fun of it – whether they could pilot aircraft towing gliders. A co-operative leadership would not have alienated USAAF commanders by interfering in their commands, shifting personnel around without informing their superiors, and demanding payment for expenditures not approved and services not rendered.

If Cochran had not made so many enemies, she might have found the USAAF rallying to her cause in the face of Congressional investigation and the lobbying efforts of civilian males, and no one would have been eager to disband the WASP despite the Congressional defeat of the militarisation bill. If Cochran hadn't been so obsessed with militarisation, maybe it would never have come to the public debacle of the defeated bill in the first place. The historian of the WAFS summarises the situation from the point of view of these successful professionals:

> . . . the women felt betrayed. They had given their all. They knew they were still needed and yet they were dismissed. The Originals were, and still are, understandably bitter over Jacqueline Cochran's interference with Nancy Love's program and her heavy-handed tactics which, ultimately, led to the deactivation of all women pilots flying for the Army in December 1944.[1]

Virtually every weakness in the WASP programme can be traced back to Jacqueline Cochran and her leadership style. That Cochran overestimated her abilities is patent. That she compulsively marketed herself is equally obvious. Both facts are understandable in light of her biography. No doubt she would have subscribed wholeheartedly to a statement recently attributed to Donald Trump that 'subtlety and modesty are appropriate for nuns and therapists, but if you're in business, you'd better learn to speak up and announce your contribution to the world. Nobody else will'.[2]

Yet, while Cochran can be forgiven for being obsessively ambitious, blind to her own inadequacies and for exaggerating her accomplishments, it is harder to understand why the Commander-in-Chief of the USAAF and the President of the United States could fail to see her for what she really was. Perhaps President Roosevelt can be excused on the grounds that he did nothing more than give her a mandate to collect facts about women pilots and present them to the Army Air Force Staff. General Arnold, on the other hand, repeatedly gave in to Cochran's demands and whims, backed her against both Love and senior Air Force commanders such as Tunner, and retained her on his staff after dismissing all the other women pilots. Even if one does not want to sink to the level of the boulevard press that implied Arnold had become sexually involved with Cochran, it is hard to escape the conclusion that he was in some way completely taken in by her.

Sadly, he was not alone. The USAAF/USAF continued to court and promote Cochran as long as she lived, and to this day both official histories and popular literature lavish praise on her in an exaggerated and imbalanced fashion. Paradoxically, with the exception of Arnold himself, the most lavish praise comes from the people who knew Cochran least. Those who had to work with her directly are generally quick to point out her tactless, power-hungry and egotistical nature, but the farther away in space and time, the more she appears to be a glamorous and shining example of success.

The image of Jacqueline Cochran clearly appeals to Americans because she is the incarnation of the 'self-made' woman. The rags-to-riches quality of her biography is the American Dream come true. The degree to which Cochran owed her success to the fortune of Floyd Odlum detracts little from her appeal, because he, too, came from a modest background and made his own fortune. For feminists, Cochran's story has the added appeal of being successful in a man's world – aviation.

What is unsettling is not the admiration for a woman who really did crawl her way up out of the gutter to be a successful aviatrix, but the readiness of Americans to accept and believe Cochran's exaggerated claims without any reference to objective reality. Considering where Cochran had come from, she accomplished a great deal; compared with many contemporaries – male and female – her accomplishments were modest. Despite the patent absurdity of her pretensions to be the 'greatest woman pilot of all time' the phrase is more likely to be quoted than challenged. Likewise, General Arnold did not shy away from putting up a plaque at Avenger Field dedicated to 'the best women pilots in the world'. The best? Many of his subordinate commanders questioned the quality of these women pilots on graduation. In the world? There had never been even an attempt to make an objective comparison between the WASP and the women in the ATA or the Red Army's women combat pilots. The plaque also went up just months before Arnold disbanded the entire programme as superfluous.

It would appear that a general tendency to over-estimate one's self and one's own relative importance in the world enabled a compulsive liar like Cochran to turn herself into a legend. No one who did not know her personally seemed to question the claims Cochran made for herself. She could without fear assert that she had set up the ATA training programme, or had 'years' of experience in military affairs or that she was the 'greatest woman pilot of all time'; the American public docilely accepted her claims. Now and then someone – General Tunner, Gerard d'Erlanger or Nancy Love – might set the record straight, but their voices of reason were lost in the brash hooting of Cochran's own horn-blowing.

The more legendary Cochran became, the more she appealed to the juvenile American craving for 'super heroes'. The country that created Superman, Star Wars and Charlie's Angels appears less interested in the real accomplishments of mere humans than in the super-heroic deeds of fantasy creatures. Jacqueline Cochran is just one small example of the degree to which an American readiness to believe – and even adore – fabricated images of greatness can result in completely unqualified persons being entrusted with very real power.

Notes:
1   Rickman, 332.
2   Trump, Donald, quoted in Reader's Digest, August 2004, p. 133.

Index